UNFAIR GAME

MICHAEL ASHCROFT

UNFAIR
GAME

AN EXPOSÉ OF SOUTH AFRICA'S
CAPTIVE-BRED LION INDUSTRY

Biteback Publishing

First published in Great Britain in 2020 by
Biteback Publishing Ltd, London
Copyright © Michael Ashcroft 2020

ISBN 978-1-78590-611-4

10 9 8 7 6 5 4 3 2 1

A CIP catalogue record for this book is available from the British Library.

Set in Trade Gothic and Minion Pro

Printed and bound in Great Britain by
CPI Group (UK) Ltd, Croydon CR0 4YY

'Until the lion tells the story, the tale of the hunt will always glorify the hunter.'

AFRICAN PROVERB

CONTENTS

ACKNOWLEDGEMENTS

Many people have assisted with this project, but it is a shocking indictment of South Africa's lion industry that some of them must remain nameless for security reasons. The threats and intimidation that are rife in lion farming, canned hunting and the bone trade make it unwise to name every individual linked to this book.

Those who have been notably generous with their time are Dr Andrew Muir, Ian Michler, Dr Don Pinnock, Colin Bell, Linda Park, Amy P. Wilson, Eduardo Goncalves, Kevin Dutton, Stewart Dorrington, Stan Burger, Gareth Patterson, Beth Jennings, Nikki Sutherland, Richard Peirce, Iris Ho, Doug Wolhuter, Dr Peter Caldwell, Dr Pieter Kat, Adrian Gardiner, Christine Macsween and Karen Trendler. None of these individuals was aware of my undercover investigation and, despite their cooperation, some will not share my views as detailed in this book.

Thanks must also go to my corporate communications director, Angela Entwistle, and her team, as well as to those at Biteback Publishing who were involved in the production of this book.

Special thanks to all the undercover operatives who carried out their assignments with courage and professionalism. The Born Free Foundation and South Africa's National Council of Societies for the Prevention of Cruelty to Animals (NSPCA) were also immensely helpful.

And special thanks go to my chief researcher, Miles Goslett, for his outstanding editorial support.

FOREWORD
BY SIR RANULPH FIENNES

Africa holds a special place in my heart. It is where I grew up and learned about the wonder of nature. It is also where the British Empire tragically unleashed the plague of persecuting animals purely for pleasure, which has wrought such devastating damage. Trophy hunters continue to travel to Africa to plunder what remains of the populations of some of the greatest animals ever to walk the planet. This includes lions.

Over the past thirty years, South Africa has become a magnet for people from all over the world who wish to kill a lion in a so-called canned hunt. Through this appalling pastime, the country's captive-bred lion industry has been able to develop, furnishing these alleged 'hunters' with their prey. Yet it is now clear that it is highly destructive in many different ways.

What is truly awful is that its wheels are oiled unwittingly by tourists, most of whom pay to spend time with captive-bred lions without realising their true plight. That it also now feeds the bone markets of Asia once the lions are dead is scandalous.

This is a problem for all of us. Humans everywhere share an extraordinary natural heritage. It is therefore the responsibility of everybody to care for it. Britain may have played a major role in the many crises faced by animals today. We can certainly play a leading role in coming up with some solutions. With this in mind, Lord Ashcroft's investigation of the captive-bred lion industry is timely and I welcome it wholeheartedly.

Sir David Attenborough once said that humans must 'step back and remember we have no greater right to be here than any other animal'. Wildlife is not a resource that we can exploit with no regard for its well-being. We debase ourselves when we consciously ignore the pain and suffering we inflict and then give weasel-worded justifications for what is plainly wrong and immoral. We are the planet's most powerful species. That places upon us a special responsibility to treat all living things with respect.

It is also our responsibility to hand over the baton to the next generation with South Africa's captive-bred lion industry consigned firmly and permanently to the dustbin of history. I hope sincerely that this book will go a long way towards helping to do just that.

AUTHOR'S ROYALTIES

Lord Ashcroft is donating all royalties from *Unfair Game* to wildlife charities in South Africa.

INTRODUCTION

In December 2018, I went to South Africa to report on Footprints of Hope, a unique project arranged by a British charity that aims to combat wildlife crime. Footprints of Hope allows veterans suffering from physical and mental health problems to spend time caring for orphaned baby rhinos. Dozens of these creatures, some only weeks or months old, are found abandoned in Africa every year. In almost all cases their mothers have been brutally shot and dehorned, sometimes while they are still alive, by poachers.

The programme was hosted by a second charity, Care for Wild, whose sanctuary just outside South Africa's famous Kruger National Park has become a home for many rhinos. The aim of Footprints of Hope is for humans and animals, both damaged by traumatic events in their lives, to benefit from the other's existence through animal-assisted therapy (AAT), which brings animals and humans together. AAT is used to complement and enhance the benefits of more conventional therapy. Through my sponsorship of Footprints of Hope, five UK Armed Forces veterans have so far benefited from this project.

While I was planning this trip, I decided I wanted to spend

some of my time in South Africa making enquiries about another imperilled creature: the lion. I was familiar with the ghastly phenomenon of so-called canned lion hunting, in which wealthy tourists pay tens of thousands of dollars to 'hunt' a lion when in reality all they do is pursue a tame creature in an enclosed space and then shoot it. I was also aware that hundreds of lions die in this manner in South Africa each year. As I detest animal maltreatment, I wanted to find out more about this particular form of cruelty so that I might be able to help end it.

As I journeyed around the country, I spoke to many animal experts and conservationists and listened to what they had to say. What I heard shocked me. It soon became clear that, however abhorrent canned lion hunting undoubtedly is, it represents just one element of a far greater problem. It is no exaggeration to say that the abuse of lions in South Africa has become an industry. Thousands are bred on farms every year; they are torn away from their mothers when just days old, used as pawns in the tourist sector, and then either killed in a 'hunt' or simply slaughtered for their bones and other body parts, which are very valuable in the Asian 'medicine' market. In between, they are poorly fed, kept in cramped and unhygienic conditions, beaten if they do not 'perform' for paying customers, and drugged.

This sinister system has sprouted up in plain sight in South Africa, inflicting misery on the 'king of the savannah' on an unimaginable scale. My research suggests it is highly likely that there are now at least 12,000 captive-bred lions in the country, against a wild population of just 3,000. Yet, strikingly, just a small number of people – a few hundred – profit from this abusive set-up. Thanks to South Africa's constitution and laws, they seem to be able to operate as they wish. In a country so vast, it is easy to see how anybody with the means to do so can break into this ugly business. What many will not realise, though, is that the lion trade is inextricably linked with violent international criminal networks. It could hardly be more sinister.

The harrowing details that I picked up during that visit in 2018 forced me to see just how desperate the situation has become. As I have learned more about the grim life cycle faced by any captive lion in South Africa, I have become determined to do whatever I can to bring to an end the abysmal industry in which these animals are caught. Quite apart from the harm inflicted upon the creatures themselves, their rampant exploitation is a stain on a country that I love. Indeed, it is a stain on all of us.

It is clear to me that the overwhelming majority of South Africans and, I would happily bet, citizens everywhere feel just as strongly as I do about this disgraceful situation. For all of these reasons, I decided to launch two undercover investigations into the lion trade. Their results, contained in this book, show clearly why governments all over the world must do everything they can to stamp out this appalling business. By necessity, this book is divided into two sections. First, I explain how South Africa finds itself in the unenviable position of being at the centre of the world's lion trade. The second part covers the covert operations.

It is important to acknowledge at the outset of this exposé that the trade in exotic wildlife which is so popular in Asia is believed to have triggered the outbreak in December 2019 of Covid-19, also known as coronavirus. This disease has killed hundreds of thousands of people around the world and, at the time of writing, the full extent of its effects on public health and on the global economy remains unknown. Lion bones from animals which are bred in captivity in South Africa and are then slaughtered there represent a significant part of this trade because of their value to the so-called traditional medicine market. As this book explains, lions and their bones can carry tuberculosis, among other potentially serious infectious diseases. According to the World Health Organization, TB was responsible for 1.5 million deaths in 2018. Several experts have told me of their belief that by continuing to trade in lion bones, those involved in South Africa's captive-lion industry are increasing the likelihood of sparking another major public health crisis. It could be a surge in TB, or it might be a rise in another infectious disease which spreads from animals to humans, such as brucellosis. Indeed, like Covid-19, it could be a new disease altogether. As a result of this alarming theory, it must be hoped that if anything positive is to emerge from the Covid-19 pandemic, it will be a severe crackdown on the lion bone trade. Certainly, it is the case that everybody who reads this book will understand that this warning has been made loudly and clearly. As it is, the South African government must be held to account for enabling this set of circumstances to develop as it has done. Should a health crisis ensue, South Africa would be lambasted internationally – something it and its people can ill afford.

Nobody should be in any doubt about the fact that South Africa now stands at a crossroads. There are many difficult decisions ahead, but it is imperative that everybody – especially tourists and hunters – does their bit to ensure that the rank abuse of lions is stopped immediately.

PART I

CHAPTER 1

DEAD CERT

Animals have always been exploited in South Africa. Hundreds of thousands of years ago, primitive man responded to his survival instincts by roaming the Highveld in search of meat. Later, the hunter-gatherer San, who have inhabited the country for at least 20,000 years, developed a formidable reputation for tracking and then killing large mammals including giraffes with bows and arrows. Later still, the Nguni, who settled in the Transvaal region from about 1500, became adept at dispatching lions and elephants for a range of purposes using spears and dogs.

The Portuguese were the earliest Europeans to reach South Africa, in 1488. Although they would shoot and eat smaller prey such as antelopes, it was not until after 1652, when the first Dutch settlement was recorded at Table Bay in Cape Town, that the immigrant population began to disturb the relative harmony in which man and beast had lived up until that point. Majestic predators like the Cape lion, a slightly less bulky subspecies of lion whose natural habitat was concentrated in the mountainous Cape Town area, faced a new threat for reasons which had nothing to do with being turned into food or clothing. They were culled in order to protect the Dutch incomers and their farmers' livestock.

As Dutch power in South Africa receded during the late eighteenth century, the British filled the void, settling in the Eastern Cape from 1820. Their arrival marked a radical turning point in man's relationship with nature in South Africa. For while excited explorers and zoologists were treated to a seemingly endless supply of unusual creatures to discover and chart for educational purposes, some of their countrymen introduced to the vast new colony the concept of killing animals for pleasure, rather than for ritual or survival. Just as hunting parties were a regular fixture in the social calendars of the ruling classes in Victorian and Edwardian Britain and Europe, so they became in South Africa's interior. The recreational pursuits of adventurers and professional hunters including Henry Hartley, Sir William Cornwallis Harris, Frederick Selous, Petrus Jacobs and the elephant stalker known intriguingly as 'Cigar' ensured the grassy veld came to be regarded as the best game-hunting territory on the continent. Then, as now, male lions were considered more desirable than lionesses. Their manes, a sign of strength and overall health, have always been eminently valuable.

As well as quenching a bloodthirst, there was also a romanticism attached to the idea of the heroic white man taming this sometimes hostile environment by slaying feral brutes. The numerous photographs taken in the nineteenth century in which early modern hunters can be seen posing with their trophies bear witness to this sense of swagger. South African environmental author and academic Dr Don Pinnock says:

Originally, the colonial process was to explore wild and wonderful countries and to bring the word of God. The original explorers were biologists. They were very good environmentalists. They were very good artists. They brought back to Britain and Germany and France these beautiful pictures of these wonderful, exotic creatures. If you were living in Europe and you wanted to be a hunter, you would probably hunt grouse. But in South Africa, you could take down ten elephants and be the hero of your own mirror. The local people were aghast. They couldn't believe so many animals were being killed at once. There were so many, they were left rotting. They'd cut the face off an elephant and leave the carcass. So in those early colonial days there was a mixture of bravado and exploration when it came to man's relationship with animals.[1]

Sport was not the only reason that animals were killed in massive numbers throughout the 1800s in South Africa. Armed with increasingly reliable rifles, professional hunters were also able to furnish merchants with the skins, hides, horns and feathers that they would in turn sell to fashionable Europeans who wished to display them in their houses or on their clothes. One hunter, M. J. Koekemoer, apparently boasted of shooting 108 lions in a year in South Africa in the 1870s. If Koekemoer really was capable of such a feat, it should not come as a surprise to learn that more than a decade earlier, in 1858, the aforementioned Cape lion was declared extinct. An entire subspecies of this carnivore was simply shot out of existence.

---

1   Interview with Dr Don Pinnock, 2 August 2019

Trophy hunting in South Africa continued after the country had gained full independence from the British in 1931, remaining popular among tourists. As time wore on, however, hunting lions undoubtedly became more cumbersome. For one thing, their numbers across the African continent fell markedly thanks to increased poaching. Furthermore, human population growth resulted in the destruction of their habitat. In 1980, there are thought to have been about 80,000 wild lions in Africa. Today, there are an estimated 20,000 wild lions, 3,000 of which are in South Africa. The majority of the others are to be found in Zimbabwe, Botswana, Tanzania and Kenya. Indeed, lions are now extinct in twenty-six countries across Africa and are listed as 'vulnerable' on the International Union for the Conservation of Nature Red List of Threatened Species. Towards the end of the twentieth century, this sharp decrease had a profound effect on hunting, according to Stewart Dorrington, the president of Custodians of Professional Hunting and Conservation South Africa. He believes that the expense of undertaking a traditional hunt from this point on 'started going through the roof'.[2] Those involved in the hunting industry in South Africa found themselves open to the idea of adapting.

It was under these conditions that the disturbing phenomenon known as 'canned' lion hunting began to take root. The origins of this term are still debated, but what this undesirable extension of trophy hunting entails is simple enough to explain. A lion – usually, but not exclusively, one which has been raised in captivity – is released into a fenced enclosure ranging

---

2   Interview with Stewart Dorrington, 6 December 2018

in size from an acre to several hundred acres. This means it is unfairly prevented from escaping its hunter, who is often positioned advantageously on the back of an open-top vehicle. It is then killed, probably at close range. Unlike in traditional or 'fair chase' hunting, in which animals might be pursued cross-country for up to three weeks with no guaranteed outcome, the canned hunted lion faces certain death perhaps within hours, seemingly for nothing more than the amusement of the hunter. Sometimes, the animal is drugged before the hunt takes place in order to move it more easily to the contained area where it will meet its end. As it is likely to suffer the physical effects of any such tranquilliser for many hours, its wooziness cements further the pathetic inevitability of its plight. In canned hunting, the balance of power is tilted so heavily away from the quarry and in favour of the stalker that it is absurd for it to be considered in any way an honest contest. Indeed, it seems most appropriate to use the phrase 'shooting fish in a barrel'. Tenacity and skill come a distant second to securing the instant gratification of a quick hit.

The history of canned hunting in South Africa is not definitively known, almost certainly as a result of it initially being kept underground through being such a squalid activity, but the country is now considered to be its global centre. Gareth Patterson is a South Africa-based environmentalist who in 1989 rehabilitated three young lions which had previously been in the care of his murdered friend George Adamson, the naturalist whose wife Joy wrote the book *Born Free* about raising a lion cub. Having investigated canned lion hunting himself, Patterson believes it was imported to South Africa. 'Its origins are

North American and it was brought over here,' he says. 'One of my contacts told me she witnessed a canned hunt involving a lion on one of the private reserves adjoining the Kruger National Park way back in 1976, but it is not clear how common it was at that time.' He believes it was probably not until the late 1980s that it became more firmly embedded in South Africa.[3]

A report published in the *Dallas Morning News* on 1 May 1988 under the headline 'Tame Lions Shot for Sport' details a canned hunt which took place on a Texas ranch owned by a Mr Larry Wilburn. If this was not the first time that this phrase had been used in the media, it is certainly one of the earliest known examples, and the tone of this article suggests the term only entered the mainstream in America around then. '"Canned" lion hunts have become quietly popular in recent months,' the report states, with Wilburn revealing that he had been involved in this burgeoning venture for about two years and was paid $3,500 (equivalent to $7,700 in 2020) by each client to shoot a lion. 'We threw rocks in to spook [the lion] out and he charged us at that point,' Wilburn was quoted as saying. 'We killed him at 10 feet away.' He added that he had a waiting list of eager trophy seekers who were happy to take part in a staged lion hunt because they 'don't want the trouble of going to Africa'.

According to Patterson, the first documented evidence in South Africa of domestic canned hunting came in the summer of 1990, when a report was published in *The Star*, a Johannesburg-based newspaper. Under the headline 'R20,000 for a "Canned" Lion – Wrangle as Old Circus Animals Let Loose for Trophy

---

3   Interview with Gareth Patterson, 11 September 2019

Hunters', this news story revealed that retired circus and zoo animals were being released onto farmland in the Eastern Cape for the explicit purpose of being shot by trophy hunters, explaining, 'but before they pay up to what is believed to be about R20,000 for what some hunters refer to as "canned lions", they have to sign a form stating they are fully aware that the lions come from a circus, zoo or lion park'. It continued: 'They [the hunters] know it will not be a wild animal [they are hunting] but a lion that was once hand reared as a cuddly cub, destined to die for the gratification of man.'[4]

Public outrage at this new craze followed, with a petition signed by hundreds sent to the Department of Nature Conservation (now the Department of Environment, Forestry and Fisheries). It was only through this lobbying exercise that it came to be understood firstly that hunting a lion which has been born and bred in captivity was not illegal in South Africa, and second that no legal definition for canned hunting existed. Astonishingly, this remains the case today.

Throughout the 1990s, the number of lions held in captivity in South Africa for the purpose of being subjected to a canned hunt was comparatively low, being in the hundreds. By 2005, its popularity had soared, and there were an estimated 2,500 non-wild lions in South Africa.[5] As a result, attempts were made under the administration of President Thabo Mbeki to both define and regulate canned hunting. This included

4   Quoted in Gareth Patterson, *Dying to be Free: The Canned Lion Scandal* (Peach Publishing, 2012)
5   Vivienne Williams, David Newton, Andrew Loveridge, David Macdonald, 'Bones of Contention: An assessment of the South African trade in African Lion *Panthera leo* bones and other body parts' (TRAFFIC International and WildCRU, July 2015)

introducing regulations in the relevant environmental legislation, the National Environmental Management: Biodiversity
Act of 2004 (NEMBA), and the Threatened or Protected Species Regulations of 2007 (TOPS). These moves were challenged
in the courts by powerful pro-hunting groups, however, notably
the organisation now known as the South African Predator Association (SAPA). SAPA's influence on successive South African
governments has never been in doubt. Among its arguments
were suggestions that the regulations had not been properly
researched. It also raised as a concern the potential economic
impact of the proposed regulations on those involved in the
lion industry. The case made its way to South Africa's highest
court of appeal, which in 2010 essentially found in favour of the
hunting industry. Insofar as some of the NEMBA and TOPS
regulations related to lions, they were set aside, allowing the
status quo to continue. And so, while there are certain restrictions in law as to the manner in which lions may be hunted,
there is no strict legal definition of canned hunting in South
Africa. Neither is there any direct prohibition of it.

Two primary legal circumstances have allowed canned hunting to continue. Firstly, South African law classes all wildlife
generally speaking as the property of the person on whose land
the animals live, meaning that landowners are effectively free
to do as they wish with those animals, subject to certain excep-
tions. Second, the 'right to environment' provision enshrined in
South Africa's supreme constitution allows for the 'sustainable
development and use of natural resources while promoting
justifiable economic and social development'. In other words,
using animals for commercial gain is deemed acceptable, as

long as over-exploitation is avoided. Disastrously, though, this privilege has been interpreted in such a way that has to all intents and purposes ensured, and even promoted, lions' ill treatment. So bastardised has the well-meaning concept become that many in South Africa now joke about 'sustainable abuse' rather than sustainable use.

Currently, canned hunters are willing to pay anything from $3,000 to more than $40,000 to shoot a male lion in South Africa, depending on its size and the quality of its mane and skin. According to Four Paws, the international animal rights organisation, between 600 and 1,000 lions are killed in canned hunts in South Africa annually. Exactly thirty years after this inhumane 'sport' became known about more widely, the digital age offers hunters an even simpler way to take part in it. Wealthy clients, many of whom have little hunting experience and may be a poor shot, are emailed brochures by hunting companies with photographs of available game. Rather like a customer at a drive-through hamburger restaurant, they place their order before, eventually, pulling the trigger or firing their crossbow.

In 2016, safari cameraman Derek Gobbett made public some deeply unpleasant canned hunting footage taken on a property owned by a firm called De Klerk Safaris in Wilzenau in North West Province. It remains unclear to what extent the owners of this property were involved in organising, as opposed to merely hosting, this 'hunt'. Gobbett had filmed it at the request of a group of American hunters four years previously who wished to keep it as a souvenir. Yet he remained so appalled by what he witnessed that he leaked the film to draw attention to this debased form of hunting. Through this, the names of the nine hunters involved then became known. It is worth describing the footage briefly in order to illustrate what a lion might face when it is subjected to a canned hunt.

In Gobbett's recording, one large lion with an impressive dark mane which has been released into an enclosure is seen padding slowly past the hunting party without a care in the world. It pauses after being whistled at by one of the hunt's organisers. This makes it an even easier target than it might otherwise be and confirms that, far from being a wild animal, it was in fact used to interacting with humans. The impact of the first bullet, fired into its front leg at close range from a jeep despite it being illegal in South Africa to shoot an animal from a vehicle, makes it leap into the air. It then rolls forward, gets up awkwardly, and reels for a few seconds in confused agony as though on hot bricks. As it scampers off on three legs to hide in the bush, the guide shouts to his client, 'Shoot him again! Shoot him again!' The hunter obeys, multiple times. Having killed the animal, he is seen standing over it and saying in a mock-feeble voice, 'Hey you, I'm sorry, but I wanted you.' Then, nauseatingly, he kisses the carcass. Another canned kill in the video is a lioness. Terrified after being pursued, she is seen taking refuge in a warthog hole. Eventually, she is shot while underground, also at close range. Once dead, she is dragged into the sunlight by euphoric group members, who are evidently proud. In separate scenes, a second lioness is seen hiding in a tree, showing no sign of wanting to attack the canned hunters, before also being dispatched. Having been shot once, she falls from the tree but becomes stuck on a branch. She is shot again before collapsing onto the ground.

The way the men in Gobbett's film indulged in excited commentary and analysis as mortally wounded animals lay suffering in front of them is striking. It is very hard to understand why they and their guides were unwilling to put dying creatures which had no chance of escape in the first place out of their misery. Once each lion *had* expired, the kill was marked with sustained laughter, celebratory high-fives, gleeful handshakes or slaps on the back – acts of jubilation that simply were not warranted given the relative simplicity of each target.

If anything positive is to be learned from the canned hunting recorded by Gobbett, it is that the tourists were tricked. Gobbett made clear that the hunt organisers drove their clients around the compound for hours pretending to track what they claimed were dangerous wild animals when in reality they knew that this contained space had been filled with a known number of relatively tame specimens that could be found without much struggle. They elongated the exercise because they were fearful that an activity they had promised would last for days would be over in a matter of hours because it was just too easy. The hunters were named as Peter Campisi, Antonio Tantillo, Jack Dellorusso, Victor Como, Armond Mkhitarian, Pete Louloudis, Carmine Marranzine, Bob Vitro and Frank Gagliardo. It is hard to know who is the more pathetic: these men who were duped out of thousands of dollars and who naively believed they were taken on a proper hunting trip, or the lions whose fates they sealed.

In fact, the first principal alarm to be sounded alerting people outside South Africa to the fact that its lions were being maltreated came almost twenty years before Gobbett's footage surfaced, in May 1997, when a documentary made by the British investigative journalist Roger Cook titled *Making a Killing* was broadcast in the UK. It was considered so shocking that a South African current affairs TV programme, *Carte Blanche*, also broadcast it shortly afterwards in order to inform the country's own people of this sick pastime. Quite apart from telling millions about canned hunting, *Making a Killing* also hinted at the scale of the abuse of lions in South Africa and showed that those involved in this twisted business were willing to threaten human lives in order to protect their commercial interests.

In the undercover film, part of the long-running ITV series *The Cook Report*, the redoubtable Cook posed as a business-man who was willing to pay $18,000 to take part in a canned trophy hunt on the remote Mokwalo Game Farm in Limpopo Province, the furthest north in South Africa, run by husband-and-wife team Sandy and Tracy McDonald. Sandy McDonald bragged to Cook that his company, then called McDonald Pro Hunting, had killed more than 1,000 lions in 1996 alone. He advised his 'client' that his 'kill shot' should be fired into the lion's leg or under its chin in order to keep its head unblemished so that it would make a decent trophy. This tactic, of course, makes the animal's death slower and more painful.

Regrettably, the master copy of this film was lost in a fire and no known recordings survive, but Cook later recalled in print his experience of canned lion hunting. He wrote:

I soon realised we were driving around in circles, but they wanted to make it look good, as if it was a real hunt. We eventually came across our lion, apparently asleep under a tree. I had a professional cameraman with me, ostensibly making a vanity video. The jeep was bristling with weapons – including the one I was supposed to use, a heavy-calibre Remington hunting rifle. When McDonald told me it was time to use it, I refused, telling him the canned hunting of such a helpless animal was at best immoral, and that I was not a rich businessman but a television reporter. We were then driven at speed back to camp where a very angry McDonald and friends demanded that we hand over our tapes. However, in the interim, we had taken the precaution of concealing our evidence in the upholstery of our minibus. We then palmed them off with blank tapes. Had we not given up what they thought was our evidence, said one of McDonald's men, we would have been involved in an unfortunate fatal shooting accident.[6]

It is worth observing that the McDonald family is still in business, the company website proudly advertising that three generations of McDonalds have provided hunting opportunities to paying customers since 1953.

Cook's film certainly made an impact, winning the Brigitte Bardot International Award for best wildlife investigation of 1997 at the annual Ark Awards. It also inspired the South African environmental journalist and safari operator Ian Michler, whose eyes were at that time beginning to be opened to the many unpleasant consequences of this activity. He had first heard about canned hunting earlier in the 1990s. Since then, he

---

6   Roger Cook, 'Shooting a lion for fun… What sort of person does that?', *Daily Mirror*, 12 August 2019

has devoted more than twenty-five years to investigating and exposing the ruthless exploitation of lions in his country, and his work has rightly earned him a reputation in conservation circles as a pioneer. His 2015 documentary *Blood Lions* shone a powerful light on this uncomfortable subject. Michler says he first stumbled upon canned hunting by chance. 'I used to live in Botswana,' he says.

I ended up as a co-owner of a lodge and also assisted great friends at their horseback operation in the Okavango, and out of the hunting season we would hear gunshots going off and sometimes light aircraft taking off or landing on this little air strip which wasn't far from where our horse riding camp was. Very soon I found a link between professional hunters – fair chase hunters operating in the Okavango – and one of our provinces here in South Africa, the Free State, which at the time I discovered was a centre for canned hunting. That was the first time I was exposed to this link. Clients who came to the Okavango to hunt lions but who couldn't bag one were sometimes flown to South Africa afterwards to take part in a canned hunt. And this information was given to me by pilots who were flying these charter aeroplanes. That was when I started piecing together the notion that you could go from a two-week fair chase hunt to a one- or two-day canned hunt. When the *Cook Report* came out, I would dare to say it was the first time most people in South Africa and in the world gained an understanding that animals were being shot in these very confined spaces. But people in general didn't really have an understanding of how the whole industry was going to turn out. After that, I intensified my research. I started writing about it.[7]

What soon became clear to Michler was that canned hunting operations were able to flourish in South Africa thanks to the country's private property laws and were bolstered by the Game Theft Act 1991, a piece of legislation introduced during the apartheid era which regulates the ownership of game. Michler says:

In South Africa, unlike in most of Africa, we have private land laws, so you have title deeds. The law is simple: you can do on your land what you want to do. If you have a wild animal on your land, you have ownership of that wild animal in the same way farmers own livestock. The leap in canned hunting came when someone said: 'This is commercially possible as a revenue stream.' That was probably in the late '90s.

Indeed, he adds, it is frighteningly easy to become a canned hunt operator if you have access to private land. 'You have to have a two-metre-tall fence that's double stranded and electrified. That's it. You're supposed to submit an Environmental Impact Assessment to the authorities. Some people do, some don't.'

There is one further aspect of this barbaric transformation of traditional hunting that makes it quite distinct from what went before: breeding. After a time, the animals that were being

---

7   Interview with Ian Michler, 31 July 2019

offered up to canned hunters were not just those that had been sold to farmers by circuses and zoos. As shall become clear, they were born and reared in captivity for the ultimate purpose of being killed – literally, bred for the bullet. Michler says:

> With hindsight, when I look back to some of the farmers I spent time with in the late '90s and early 2000s, one individual particularly used to take me around his property and tell me what his plan was. He would say, 'I can make a fortune.' He wanted to use elephants. He wanted to put hunters on the backs of elephants to go and shoot lions that he'd bred in cages. He showed me the whole layout. Commercially, the mid- to late 1990s was when canned hunting started taking hold.

In his capacity as a professional hunter who is anti-canned lion hunting, Stewart Dorrington agrees with Michler's analysis. He says:

> I had been a professional hunter since 1988 and the first time [canned hunting] came to my notice was the exposé of the *Cook Report*. The industry grew because there were limited wild lions to hunt and those were, and still are, very expensive. As the number of wild lions available to hunters declined, mostly due to bad management by governments and also because of habitat loss, so the demand to shoot a captive-bred lion increased. In the early days, most hunters hunting a captive-bred lion had no idea it was captive-bred, as many were sold as 'problem' lions or wild lions. However, that has changed as far as I know, and hunters know they are shooting

a captive-bred lion and there is still a demand for it, much like there is a demand for shooting bred pheasants in the UK.[8]

Having established that canned hunting is an especially cruel way of killing a lion, the important question arises of what kind of person would facilitate this form of so-called entertainment. Michler is in no doubt about the answer. He believes that canned hunting, together with every other element of the lion farming industry in South Africa that has grown up around it, is dominated by the country's white population. Some of them, he thinks, have not moved on mentally from the days of apartheid despite its legal apparatus having been abolished thirty years ago. 'Nearly all of the lion breeders and farmers come out of the apartheid era and they have no respect for human rights,' Michler says. 'They supported a doctrine that discriminated against humans. Now you're asking these same people to have some sort of respect for animal welfare, but it's not in their lexicon. I challenge you to find a black farmer who's involved in the lion farming industry.'

Surprisingly, Michler says that religion, particularly the Calvinist beliefs traditionally held by Afrikaans-speaking farmers, may play an important role in the breeders' and farmers' outlook as well. 'There is this conservative, God-fearing sense that man has power over all other species and that "we're entitled to do this". It's strong, and it's been told to me on these farms.' He adds that canned hunting itself is also, in his view, an almost exclusively white pastime.

---

8   Interview with Stewart Dorrington, 30 September 2019

I challenge you to find a black trophy hunter who wants to shoot these animals. I've run safari operations across sixteen countries. I've been writing as a journalist about issues across the continent for thirty years. I don't know a single ethnic African group that kills animals for fun. They kill for food, for ritual, for ceremonial purposes. But they never kill animals for fun. They don't go out and shoot five lions. It's a colonial construct, brought in by the colonials.

His opinion is backed up by research. One academic study published in 2018 examined the attitudes of African people towards trophy hunting, of which canned hunting is now considered an integral part. By sifting the social media posts of 1,070 indigenous citizens, it was concluded that there was overwhelming 'resentment towards what was viewed as the neo-colonial character of trophy hunting in the way it privileges Western elites in accessing Africa's wildlife resources'. Most revealingly, the study stated that trophy hunting per se was not considered unacceptable from an animal rights perspective by Africans, but instead 'as a consequence of its complex historical and postcolonial associations'.[9]

Due to its opaque status, it is difficult for anybody to be certain how much land in South Africa is used by the predator breeding industry. It is, however, easier to reflect upon the likely consequences of so much land being owned by South Africa's white population. According to a report produced by the Institute for Poverty, Land and Agrarian Studies at the University of the Western Cape and co-authored by Professor Johann Kirsten

---

9   Mucha Mkono, 'Neo-colonialism and greed: Africans' views on trophy hunting in social media', *Journal of Sustainable Tourism*, Volume 27 (2019)

of the University of Stellenbosch, 64.8 million hectares (160 million acres) of farmland in South Africa is owned by white people. The report, which relies on data from 2018 published by the Department of Rural Development and Land Reform, states that this amounts to 53 per cent of total land in the country. To put this in context, the latest census, carried out in 2011, found there were 4,586,838 white people living in South Africa. They made up 8.9 per cent of the population. With roughly half of the country's land therefore being in the hands of less than a tenth of its people, it seems reasonable to conclude that canned hunting and lion farming, both of which rely on the availability of open spaces, almost certainly are businesses controlled by a small portion of South Africa's white minority.

The desire to derive the maximum return has prompted an increasing number of white farmers and landowners, many of whom have inherited acres from their ancestors, to turn their businesses from livestock or crop farming into the more lucrative trade of exploiting lions for a living. According to Stephen Palos, chief executive of the Confederation of Hunting Associations of South Africa, 'South Africa has seen some 20 million hectares (50 million acres) of land convert from agriculture to wildlife over about four decades.'[10] This phenomenon may even have intensified in recent years given that South Africa's economy is regarded as one which is underperforming badly.[11] Its gross domestic product has declined every year since 2011, when it hit a

---

10   Letter from Stephen Palos to the Dallas Safari Club, dated 13 January 2018
11   Peet van der Merwe, Melville Saayman, Jauntelle Els and Andrea Saayman, 'The economic significance of lion breeding operations in the South African Wildlife Industry', *International Journal of Biodiversity and Conservation* (2017)

high of $416 billion, and in the spring of 2019, the Daily Maverick online newspaper carried a well-sourced article estimating that one third of the country's GDP over the previous decade was lost to corruption. With unemployment hovering at 30 per cent and fraud of one kind or another having infected almost every state-run industry, the overall economic picture is frighteningly fragile. Lion farming is considered easier than cattle farming, particularly in the arid areas of North West Province, where most canned hunting takes place and where the terrain is almost like desert. All of these factors help to explain why, over the past decade, hundreds of lion farms have sprung up in the country and the private sector is responsible for managing the largest portion of the lion population in South Africa. It has been estimated that lion breeders contribute the equivalent of $42 million annually to the South African economy by employing farm workers, hunting operators, taxidermists and even slaughterhouse workers.[12] With much of the business conducted in cash, however, it would be hard to verify this statistic.

If it is the case that white farmers and landowners have always been the profiteers of what is demonstrably an insidious trade, they cannot have known in the 1990s exactly how that trade was going to develop. Yet, as we shall see, it is undeniable that canned hunting is directly responsible for the growth of even greater evil when it comes to the abuse of lions in South Africa.

---

12   Ibid.

CHAPTER 2

EXOTIC PLAYTHINGS

South Africa is the only country in the world to classify lions under three categories: wild, managed wild and captive-bred. Wild lions are truly free, living as apex predators in vast national parks and game reserves such as Kruger National Park in the north-east and Kgalagadi Transfrontier Park in the Kalahari desert region. Their close cousins, managed wild lions, are kept in private or government-run fenced reserves typically less than 100,000 hectares (250,000 acres) in size and are organised in such a way that their population growth is limited and their genetic integrity preserved. Together, these two groups represent the lions in South Africa that conservationists consider to be of value. The third group, captive-bred lions, is altogether different. It consists of two sub-categories: 'tourism-bred' and 'ranch-bred'. The former are accustomed to humans. The latter are also used to humans, though the South African Predator Association claims they are raised with as little human contact as possible. Not only are captive-bred lions the most populous variety of lion to be found in South Africa but, from the point of view of nature, they are also the most tragic. Ecologists believe they have no conservation merit whatsoever because they are highly likely to be genetically tarnished through inbreeding. Furthermore, scientists consider that, having been reared by or around humans, they have in effect been corrupted and for all practical purposes could never survive in the wild.

Professional hunters and adventurers in Victorian and Edwardian-era South Africa might have earned the retrospective outrage of many people for shooting certain species such as the Cape lion to extinction. As is clear, however, having introduced canned lion hunting into the country in the late twentieth century, their modern-day counterparts are responsible for sustaining what is undoubtedly a far more sinister killing system, given its one-sided nature. This dark enterprise is now reliant solely upon the captive-bred lion population.

In order for canned lion hunting to have thrived in South Africa as it has done over the past three decades or more, a sufficient amount of stock has had to exist to meet demand. This has necessitated the commercial breeding of lions in captivity for the explicit purpose of their exploitation. The king of the savannah, revered internationally for generations in heraldry and still to be found on South African banknotes, has been reduced to little more than an organism that rolls off a production line. So rampant has this unregulated business become in recent years, no precise figure exists indicating how many captive-bred lions there are currently in South Africa. Educated estimates, including from the National Council of Societies for the Prevention of Cruelty to Animals (NSPCA), range from 6,000 to 14,000.[13] The South African government claims there are 'more than 6,000 lions in captive breeding facilities across the country'.[14] Without question, this means that many thousands of captive lions will have been slaughtered in South Africa since the early 1990s. It also means the number of captive lions dwarfs the existing wild lion population. Indeed, South Africa has the biggest captive cat industry in the world. As shall become clear, although some of these lions are destined to be shot in canned hunts, many more will be killed simply for their bones.

Lion breeding has ushered in some appalling spin-off sectors which only add to the sense that the abuse of these extraordinary predators has reached a critical point. It is worth emphasising from the outset that one of the most nefarious aspects of the captive-born lion industry is that its practitioners lure tourists into their web to perform an unwitting role in the ghastly cruelty to which these animals are subjected from the very earliest stages of their lives. In what has come to be known as 'consumptive tourism' or 'encounter tourism', lions become the exotic playthings of the general public solely for the financial advantage of their owners. The South African Institute of International Affairs estimates this business is worth $180 million a year.[15]

---

13 Ross Harvey, 'The Economics of Captive Predator Breeding in South Africa' (South African Institute of International Affairs, 2018), p. 8

14 Department of Environmental Affairs press release, 'Minister Mokonyane moves to address concerns on captive lion breeding and associated trade activities', 19 March 2019

15 Ross Harvey, 'The Economics of Captive Predator Breeding in South Africa' (South African Institute of International Affairs, 2018), p. 63

If the manner of a canned hunted lion's death is vicious, the existence awaiting any lion unfortunate enough to come into the world as the possession of a professional lion dealer or lion farmer in South Africa is wretched. In the wild, a cub will spend about two years under a watchful maternal eye as it learns the art of survival. Yet within a few days – or sometimes just hours – of being born in a cage, a captive cub will be taken from its mother, still unable to see, to be bottle-fed synthetic milk or cows' milk. Invariably, this ruthless separation is achieved by tempting the lioness away from her cubs with bait such as fresh meat. As soon as she has left the cage to collect the welcome snack, the cage door slams shut. She will never see the cubs again.

Breeders subject lion cubs to this harsh treatment for two reasons. Firstly, it allows a young animal to become used to human contact from an early age, making it less of a threat to its handlers and the crowds of people to which it will likely be exposed as it matures. Second, it means that the lioness which gave birth to the cub can return to a state of reproductive pre-paredness as soon as possible. Some know this phenomenon as 'speed breeding'.

In the wild, lionesses, which can mate from the age of three or four years, give birth every eighteen to twenty-four months. An average litter consists of between one and four cubs. Yet because they have a gestation period of 110 days, and can therefore potentially procreate two or even three times per year, captive females are turned into breeding machines, each capable, in theory, of producing between six and nine cubs annually. As

Karen Trendler, who managed the Wildlife Trade and Trafficking portfolio for South Africa's National Council of Societies for the Prevention of Cruelty to Animals until October 2019, says:

> Lions in captivity breed like flies. It's the one carnivore that breeds easily in captivity. They remove these cubs from the mother anywhere between two days and fourteen days after birth. She's 'designed' to only produce a certain number of litters during her natural life. So she might lose some cubs in one litter and breed fairly soon afterwards, but generally she only has a certain number of cubs during her life. When you're taking the cubs away from her every single time, she doesn't have time to recover between litters. Removing cubs stimulates oestrus and then she breeds again. And then they take those cubs away. So every litter she has, she gets weaker and weaker. Her physical state deteriorates with each litter. Her mental state is affected, too. The hormones prepare her to be a mother. Take the cubs away and she's depressed.[16]

The physical strain on a lioness of this repeated pregnancy and birth cycle, to say nothing of the emotional toll of having to surrender her offspring when they are most helpless, is of little or no concern to those seeking to make money from the lion trade.

At this point, a cub's fate is obviously dependent to a degree on its environment, but one fact is inescapable: because it has

---

16   Interview with Karen Trendler, 8 August 2019

begun to be weaned on a foreign milk product, its immune system is weaker than it would be had it been allowed to consume its mother's milk. In the wild, cubs take natural milk for about six months. In captivity, cubs which are reared on a milk substitute are much more susceptible to infection, disease and perhaps death – particularly if, as is so often the case, they are housed in filthy conditions which are never subject to third-party checks. Trendler says she first encountered the effects on lionesses and their offspring of denying cubs their mother's milk about fifteen years ago. She says, 'I was in rescue and response at the time and two cubs were dumped on us that had the most horrific nutritional deficiencies. They'd been taken from the mother, nobody knew how to rear them, so that was my first introduction to it.' Trendler and her colleagues kept them alive for three weeks, but the cubs were too ill to recover and had to be put down. Ironically, the cubs that do die very early on, and therefore fail to make it to the next stage of the depressing existence that lies in store, may be considered the lucky ones.

Once it has been taken from its mother, a captive-born lion cub faces two potential onward routes, each of which is equally undesirable. If it has been born within a breeding facility that is open to the public, it will probably remain there. If it has been born to a private breeder, it will be rented or sold to a tourist venture such as a safari park or petting zoo. (Conceivably, it might even be sold to a private collector. Stories abound of criminals keeping lions on their properties to deter rivals and trespassers.) Whichever commercial route it is set on, those in charge of the cub will seek to extract as much money from it as possible at every stage of its growth before it is big enough to be killed. These money-making schemes require the participation of unsuspecting tourists.

Over the past ten to fifteen years, thousands of mainly young people from all over the world, particularly Europe, have been hoodwinked into parting with significant sums of money by those involved in South Africa's lion trade. This has happened – and continues to happen – in one of two ways. Either these international animal lovers sign up to so-called voluntourism programmes, in which they spend several weeks paying to live in a facility which is home to lion cubs, or they might visit facilities that encourage the public to interact with the animals by playing with them, cuddling them or going on a walking excursion with them.

In the first case, voluntourists look after these appealing young creatures in the early weeks of their lives, including the exhausting responsibility of round-the-clock feeds and cleaning up after them. Often, they are told falsely that the cubs on the site are orphans which have been rescued from a certain death in the wild. Another tall story they might hear is that the cubs' mother rejected them and the site offered sanctuary. Those who run this type of facility may also claim bogusly that the cubs will be released back into their natural, wild environment as soon as they are old enough to fend for themselves. They pretend that these lions have a conservation value when, by virtue of their captive-born status, the opposite is the case. This is how young women such as Beth Jennings from Britain are persuaded into paying to do the breeders' work for them.

Jennings explains:

In February 2015, when I was twenty-one, I paid about £1,500 [$2,250 at the time] to volunteer for two weeks at Ukutula Lodge in North West Province. This was money I had been given for my 21st birthday. I spent another £1,000 [$1,500 at the time] on flights and jabs. It represented all of my savings, but I was passionate about working with animals, so I was delighted when I booked the trip. We would work from nine until five each day. We weren't given any training. Instead, we were given an induction and then a tour of the park and shown what to do. We would either do cub duties or ranger duties. Cub duties would involve us supervising young cubs up to the age of three or four months until the tourists arrived each morning and wanted their photos taken with them, which we would have to oversee. Ranger duties involved us preparing the chickens or collecting a horse carcass from a nearby farmer, which would be fed to the older lions.[17]

Jennings says she is haunted by the mewing noise made by the tiny cubs. Many tourists assume this sound is 'cute' or 'sweet'. Yet Jennings says she soon worked out that it is indicative of nothing but distress, as the animals call through sheer desperation for their mothers.

She goes on:

Within the first couple of days I had some questions about

---

17   Interview with Beth Jennings, 17 September 2019

how the lions were treated after we volunteers were told to bash them on the nose if they were misbehaving. We once had to lock five lions in a cage overnight, with no access to food or water, because they were considered too big for their enclosure. It was so cruel. There were probably twenty or twenty-five voluntourists there at one time, so there wasn't even enough work for us to do! Places like Ukutula are making a lot of money out of voluntourism. We were told the cubs were orphaned or had been rejected by their mother because they were too unruly. But when we were once told to remove a twelve-day-old cub from an enclosure because it was too unruly – a cub whose eyes hadn't even opened fully yet and who howled in anguish – I knew this was nonsense. This cub was removed by us just so that it could be hand-reared and used as a tourist magnet. It was even allowed to sleep in a volunteer's room. After it was removed, a male lion was put into the enclosure with its mother so that he could mate with her.

Jennings adds that parties of schoolchildren visited the site during her stay there in order to have a supposedly educational experience, and she remains scathing about this. 'I just don't understand what is remotely educational about fifty children passing around a couple of captive-bred lion cubs,' she says. 'Humans are not meant to be anywhere near lions, which are supposed to be wild creatures. Teaching children from such a young age that it's OK to handle a lion cub is indefensible. Any parent who is considering letting their child go near a lion cub should never allow it.'

No doubt preying upon the tourists' own parenting instincts, the men and women who run voluntourism programmes of this type are surely no better than thieves, leaching money from innocent people by lying about how the lions came to be in their possession and what their future is. Assuming Jennings's figures are correct, and the nineteen individuals who volunteered with her at Ukutula Lodge also paid the equivalent of about $1,125 per week, this facility could have made a net sum of about $22,500 every seven days through voluntourism alone. Even if this represented an exceptional week, it is apparent that voluntourism is big business in South Africa, with dozens of sites offering this type of experience. Those who run these ventures have devised a hugely cynical system which encourages an utterly perverse form of reliable middle-class labour. Those young people who can afford to pay for the privilege of spending time with lion cubs toil gladly in their cages in the naive belief that they are doing some good. Yet, as Karen Trendler says, they may actually be doing harm. 'Volunteers don't necessarily know how to feed and monitor the welfare of these cubs,' she says. 'Plus, the feeding formulas are expensive, so the owners cut down on supplying it or use a cheaper unsuitable product. So there's also cruelty at that level.' She adds, 'Large numbers of international volunteers paying massive amounts to rear a cub they believe is going back to the wild and has been abandoned by the mother? It's nonsense. They really think they're saving lion. And they're taking away jobs from South Africans.'

As these paying volunteers do not spend more than a few weeks at a time in this environment, meaning the teams change regularly, it is easy for the owners and breeders to conceal from them the lions' true fate. Yet by doing some of the owners' and breeders' hardest work on their behalf, the voluntourists are in effect helping to prepare these animals for death. Their blameless participation gives an air of respectability to these companies as the lions are moved closer towards the impossibly cruel situations into which they will be thrown at a later stage before they die unnaturally.

Animal lovers who choose to become involved in voluntourism are, quite simply, funding animal haters who have no serious interest in lion welfare. It seems astonishing that in the digital age, when news spreads so quickly, such an atrocious scam has been allowed to thrive. It would be entirely understandable if those who *have* handed over money felt foolish for having done so. But, having been made aware of the reality, it is surely their duty to tell as many others as possible never to repeat their mistake. To that end, Beth Jennings must be congratulated. Since her own voluntourism experience, she has launched Claws Out, which campaigns to end this practice.

Ian Michler believes that enormous damage is being done by voluntourism in many different areas surrounding lion welfare. He says:

The insidious part of the lion trade is the tourism industry. At least it's pretty clear what the guy who's selling lions and breeding them and shooting them in a canned hunt is doing. The tourism industry is a lot more dangerous because there are a lot of facilities in this country that have lions on their properties. And they are making a hell of a lot of money selling a false message that they're involved in conservation, that this is for educational purposes, or that these lions are going to be released. The revenue streams are significant. A lot of people choose not to see the link between these facilities and canned hunting. Who are they kidding that this is a conservation facility or an educational facility? What kind of education do you get about lions when you've only got ten minutes to cuddle a cub? I've heard some of the stories [told at these places]. It's complete hogwash. These are kids, moving you through this facility. They don't know the first thing about lion ecology and conservation. So what you are learning is that it's OK to breed lions in captivity and enslave them in this cycle of brutality. That's what you're learning. Lions don't live like that. We shouldn't be treating lions like that. But what they're doing is subtly reinforcing a message that it's OK to do that, and that is how these animals live, and that it's OK to cuddle them. But it's brutal. This is the same species that we're trying to market as the king of Africa, the savannahs, the apex predator. And this is how we're treating them. Many of these facilities win awards for responsible tourism because they've spun the story that this is a conservation initiative and an education facility. You can do the maths. There's maybe space for one or two proper sanctuaries in the country based on our lion population. But we know there are over 200 facilities.[18]

Michler adds that the fact that white lions, which are extremely rare in the wild, are so abundant now within the captive-bred

---

18   Interview with Ian Michler, 31 July 2019

population is proof of a breeding programme which has spiralled out of control, catering for visitors who like to see these unusual creatures because they look even more attractive than 'normal' lions. 'Do you know how many white lions there are in the wild?' he asks. 'In a decade, you might see three or four. And they're only found in one very specific area of South Africa. I can tell you there are probably 500 to 1,000 white lions in facilities across South Africa now.'

Surely it should become the urgent priority of South Africa's Department of Tourism to review, regulate and, if necessary, to outlaw voluntourism. When all else fails, it is the government's responsibility to stop people who mistakenly believe they are helping animals from aiding and abetting the sad lives which come before a captive-bred lion's death. Those who support breeding and exploiting lions claim it has positive economic benefits, including employment and tourism, although there are no official government statistics or indeed any rigorous independent research showing how many jobs the lion industry actually supports.[19] Yet even if businesses connected to lion exploitation *are* considered for some skewed reason to be acceptable to the South African state, legitimate questions persist. For one thing, is it not immoral to allow wealthy foreign tourists to visit South Africa in order to pay to do this work, in the process denying local labour the chance to earn a living by doing it themselves?

As well as voluntourism, lion cub petting has also become commonplace in South Africa. Karen Trendler says:

---

19   'Cash Before Conservation: An Overview of the Breeding of Lions for Hunting and Bone Trade' (Born Free Foundation, 2018), p. 13

As of August 2019, there were an estimated 333 facilities that we are aware of that are breeding lions in South Africa. Of those, only eighty-one as far as we've been informed are open to the public. We are seeing horrific issues with the ones that are open to the public. You can just imagine what is going on at the facilities that are *not* open to the public. It is industrialised, legalised cruelty. Cubs are petted, they're played with, but their bones are soft. A developing cub needs to sleep and rest to grow, not be cuddled and played with.

In order to get a sense of the places Trendler has referred to, it seems appropriate to describe visits that some members of my team made to three of them, including the Lion and Safari Park near Johannesburg. Based in an area called Cradle of Humankind, about 55 km (35 miles) north of the city, it is the type of sophisticated wildlife park that might be found in Europe or North America, with modern premises, a gift shop and restaurants. It is also considered the top tourist attraction in Gauteng Province. It first opened in the 1970s, but in recent years it has weathered a series of highly negative media stories. These include an exposé by the American television network CBS, whose programme *60 Minutes* revealed in 2014 that the park had sold lions into the canned hunting industry.[20] The following year, an American tourist and wildlife enthusiast, Katherine Chappell, was mauled to death by a lioness at the park while on a safari tour. The guide driving Ms Chappell stopped his car in order to get a better view of a group of the animals. At that

---

20   *60 Minutes*, 'The Lion Whisperer', CBS, 30 November 2014

point, Ms Chappell, a 29-year-old visual effects editor on the television programme *Game of Thrones*, is said to have rolled down the passenger window to take photographs. She did so without realising that a lioness was approaching from the side of the vehicle. It lunged at her through the open window, biting her neck and causing profuse bleeding. Tragically, she died at the scene.

Weeks later, the business declared that it would cease offering cub petting at its facility partly as a result of the release of Ian Michler's film *Blood Lions*, which had shown very successfully why it was an unacceptable form of entertainment. Within a year, in July 2016, it had also relocated to its present premises following a $6.4 million upgrade. Less than a month after re-opening, however, it came to light that the park's management had gone back on their word. The park was offering cub petting once again. Its chief executive, Rodney Fuhr, was open about the reason for this about-turn, saying that stopping cub petting had resulted in fewer visitors, who simply took their business to those rival attractions which continued to offer this activity. In a written statement, Fuhr said:

> We are not competing on a level playing field and unless our competitors also stop the cub interaction, the massive R100-million investment in the new facility and the survival of our business will be at stake. Reluctantly, we have no choice but to temporarily reintroduce cub interaction. In light of our commitment and determination to eradicate this activity we are willing to join with, and help, other organisations and the government to ban cub petting altogether. We

will give our full support to this cause and help to lobby the authorities to introduce legislation as soon as possible.[21]

This evidence proves that lion cubs represent a key part of the financial health of Mr Fuhr's business – and, presumably, of his rivals' businesses – and to that end it speaks for itself. No matter how many schoolchildren visit this facility, fulfilling some dubious notion that it is a centre of education as well as of leisure, the fact remains that these captive-born animals are on the site primarily to make its owners and backers as much money as possible.

There is another aspect of Mr Fuhr's statement that warrants attention. In it, he said that his business had agreed to reintroduce cub interaction 'temporarily'. It is unarguable that his idea of what this word means is very different to most other people's understanding of it, for three years later it was still possible to interact with cubs at the Lion and Safari Park. For about $5, visitors are invited to enter a dusty lion cub enclosure roughly the size of a small football pitch, where they may remain for between five and ten minutes. During a visit on a randomly chosen day in August 2019, three cubs, including two rare white lion cubs, were to be found dozing there in the midday sun. Lion cubs which are less than six months old, as these were, need plenty of rest. Animal experts say they require between sixteen and twenty hours' sleep every day. But these ones were not left in peace for long. Upon entering the pen, their keeper, who warned that they can bite and scratch, prodded them

---

21   Written statement from Rodney Fuhr, published 16 August 2016

awake so that they could be stroked, picked up and played with by their human visitors. They were also disturbed in order that they would pose for the all-important selfie opportunity.

Young lions have surprisingly soft fur and are undeniably endearing when they are merely months old. With their long legs and large paws, they bound around like overgrown puppies, brimful of curiosity and mischief. Indeed, they are so sweet that it is easy to forget that by paying to be in their presence one is in a sense helping to prolong their agony and that of other lions who are similarly exploited. The cubs occupying the pen on this occasion appeared to be in acceptable health, with few blemishes on their fur. They were also docile, so much so that the stories one hears about cubs in similar environments being sedated to guarantee their good behaviour are eminently believable. The harsh reality, however, is that these animals should not exist. Having been bred for the specific purpose of attracting tourists to the park before they are considered old enough to be slaughtered, they serve no purpose in the animal kingdom. Their only point in life is to enrich those who own them or who have rented them from a breeder.

Since thousands of animals like these ones *are* bred in South Africa, however, and since the country *is* full of creatures like them, it is important to recognise another unpalatable truth: namely, that by existing in captivity they are denied the quieter life they would almost certainly enjoy in the wild. Using the Lion and Safari Park as an example of what a tourist attraction lion can expect out of life, this facility is open every day of the year. From Monday to Friday it welcomes visitors between 8.30 a.m. and 6 p.m. At weekends and on public holidays, its hours are extended from 8 a.m. to 8 p.m. It is therefore operational for a minimum of seventy-one and a half hours each week. Much of this is precious time when young cubs should be sleeping and developing. Instead, these captive-bred animals are expected to amuse tourists all day long simply in order to swell a company bank balance.

At this point, it is worth reflecting on whether those members of the public who choose to touch and stroke lion cubs, or to interact with older lions, are aware of some of the health and safety risks they face by doing so. In May 2019, four-year-old Dina-Marie de Beer sustained horrific injuries when a lioness went for her during a visit to the Weltevrede Lion Farm in Heilbron in North West Province. It was reported that the little girl asked her parents if they could go to the lion park on their way home from a holiday so that she could pet a cub. Dina-Marie was in her father's arms when they were attacked through the fence of a bordering camp. The juvenile lioness reportedly got hold of her father, Pieter, who suffered minor injuries, but Dina-Marie's scalp was ripped off and her skull was penetrated by the lion's claw. Dina-Marie was taken to hospital, where part of her skull was reportedly removed to relieve pressure on her brain and she was placed in an induced coma.[22] Brutal incidents such as this are by no means isolated.

Linda Park has been involved in campaigning against cruelty to lions since the 1990s and in 2018 co-founded the non-profit organisation Voice4Lions. Having researched the strange world of captive-bred lions intensively, she believes that there are

---

22   'Lion rips off toddler's scalp at Heilbron lion park', News24, 14 May 2019

some potentially serious consequences for both humans and cubs as a result of all petting activities. Park says:

> Some of the infections you could pick up from handling cubs include sarcoptic mange, ringworm, toxoplasmosis, babesiosis, giardiasis, cysticercosis and E. coli. I've been in facilities and diarrhoea has been pouring out of the cubs as they've walked. So what infection are they harbouring? Especially if you're picking them up and cuddling them but you don't wash your hands and you then go and eat a hamburger afterwards. There are various worms you can pick up and the segments are really small. Think about children who pet these animals. They might put a finger in their mouth afterwards. Some of these hazards lie dormant for a while and if someone gets sick and goes to a doctor in their home country, a doctor might not know what they're dealing with. You don't know what's on the fur. The cubs might bite. You don't know what they might transfer. They scratch a lot. Their claws are extremely sharp. If they've been walking in faeces or diarrhoea and they scratch you, you might get an infection. There's a long list of things they could potentially carry. What is wrong with people that they don't think about safety and sanitation? Why don't these places point out the health risks more carefully?[23]

Perhaps the best-known recent illustration of Park's point about the risk of disease comes in the form of the unfortunate Welsh professional rugby player Scott Baldwin. In September 2017, he

---

23   Interview with Linda Park, 9 August 2019

visited the Weltevrede Game Lodge on the outskirts of Bloemfontein with some other members of his team, the Ospreys. There, his left hand was badly bitten by a lion which he stroked through a fence. The incident was captured on camera and the panicked screams of this front-row forward as he was caught in the grip of a lion's jaw make for unpleasant listening. Apart from the wound itself, worse was to follow for Baldwin. He quickly developed an infection and is considered lucky not to have had his hand amputated. He has said publicly how grateful he is to his surgeon, Faf Weyers. 'The infection was the major issue,' Baldwin said after the incident. 'The next day it started tracking up my arm. The surgeon said there was a chance I could lose my hand. The surgeon said [after the operation] it was the best possible outcome considering I had been bitten by a lion.'[24] Baldwin's case probably only became known about because of his status as a famous sportsman. And, presumably, he was lucky in that the manager of his tour party would have ensured he had access to the best available medical attention as quickly as possible. But one is bound to ask: how many similar incidents have gone unreported by the media? And how many tourists have not been so fortunate in getting the right medical treatment straight away?

While Linda Park is the first to admit that she has no professional medical background or training, her careful studies of various academic papers relating to lions' health have convinced her that anybody who touches a big cat is taking a risk. She is not alone. In 2007, Dr Vito Martella, associate professor at the

---

24 'Lion bite victim thanks surgeon who saved his hand', BBC Sport website, 7 April 2019

Faculty of Veterinary Medicine of Bari, Italy, published findings confirming the presence of the highly contagious norovirus in captive-bred lions. Park also cites the example of John Varty, a South African wildlife filmmaker. In 2000, he set up a private reserve, Tiger Canyons, in the Free State. Its aim was to create a self-sustaining tiger population outside Asia. In 2016, Varty underwent major surgery to have two large echinococcus hydatid cysts removed from his liver, potentially fatal worms which some believe might have been passed to him through his interaction with the tigers.

Although visitors to the Lion and Safari Park in August 2019 were advised to wash their hands before and after entering the cubs' petting pen, it would be an exaggeration to say that this rule was imposed vigilantly, despite it being one of South Africa's premier wildlife attractions. Certainly, no staff enforced it. Why, after all, would such a business want to scare its customers with warnings about the harmful side effects of cub cuddling? But it is not just human beings who need to worry about these interactions. Park points out that animals' health is also put at risk by coming into contact with so many people. She says:

We should wash before we touch them. As much as we can get something from them, they can get something from us. These are little cubs that did not get immunity from their mothers because they were taken away from them when they were a couple of days old. Their immune systems are not strong. The mortality rate among cubs is quite high because they have a weak immune system. They are bottle fed. It's not the same as mother's milk. The stress on them is huge because they are meant to sleep most of the day and eat in between. These animals in the petting set-up don't sleep because they aren't allowed to. It's a constant cycle of pick up, pet, get a hiding if you misbehave. In some places they drug them to keep them more pliable. You think of the stress on the whole system because they have been removed from their natural environment and you've got all of these people touching them, so what is that doing to its immune system? People should certainly wash before touching a cub and sure as hell scrub themselves having touched one.

Others have focused their attention on the mental health of large animals which are kept in pens and cages. In 2003, re-search conducted by University of Oxford zoologists Ros Clubb and Georgia Mason was published which stated that 'among the carnivores, naturally wide-ranging species show the most evi-dence of stress and/or psychological dysfunction in captivity'.[25] While this study focused on zoo animals, it suggested that all captive animals unable to meet their instinctual needs are more likely to display neurotic behaviour, which can include pacing, tail-chewing, toe-sucking or excessive grooming. This, surely, includes some captive-bred lions, which are effectively held hostage in an unnatural environment like a tourist attraction.

On the same trip to the Lion and Safari Park in August 2019, it was possible to go on a short safari around the impressive

[25]   Ros Clubb and Georgia Mason, 'Animal Welfare: Captivity effects on wide-ranging carnivores, *Nature*, Volume 425 (2 October 2003), p. 473

600-hectare (1,500-acre) property. Tickets cost approximately $15 each. As well as giraffes, zebras, antelopes and ostriches, there were several large enclosures containing lions of varying ages from six months to six years. Strikingly, the guide told the dozen or so tourists who were on the tour bus that the park has a total of 'about seventy-five' lions on the property. Oddly, only twenty-five were available to see. When asked where the other fifty were located, the guide provided no concrete answer, saying something about them being in what he jokingly referred to as the 'retirement village' area of the compound. This fuelled suspicions about the conditions in which these other fifty lions were being kept and, moreover, their ultimate fate. Some subsequent detective work has allowed a little light to be shed on this situation. In November 2019, operatives working for me managed to enter the so-called retirement enclosure unobserved. They counted no more than fifteen old-looking lions, some wild dogs and three cheetahs. Pens containing the lions were cramped and the enclosures were covered in a foul carpet of faeces and chicken feathers. The big cats looked hungry, pacing the fences and following my agents' pick-up truck, no doubt thinking they were about to be fed. Their final destination remains unclear. For a business which is so determined to make money that it is prepared to breach a self-imposed ethical guideline in relation to petting lion cubs less than a year after enacting it, however, it does not seem unreasonable to query the animals' prospects – not least because of the expense of keeping and feeding carnivores which are not even on display to the general public. (An adult lion needs to eat 6–8 lbs (2.75–3.5 kg) of meat per day.) In the wild, a male lion can expect to live for ten or twelve years, while a lioness can live up to the age of fourteen or fifteen. In captivity, nature's guidelines do not apply.

Finally, it was possible to embark on a 'lion walk' at the Lion and Safari Park. Lion walks have become a very popular way of enhancing tourists' interaction with these predators while adding an element of risk which undoubtedly makes the blood pump faster. Anybody taking part in a lion walk must sign a release form beforehand, acknowledging that they accept full responsibility for the dangerous situation into which they place themselves by coming into close contact with these carnivorous animals, and recognising that serious injury or even death could occur. In light of the fate of a 22-year-old woman who was mauled to death in February 2018 by a lioness at a wildlife reserve made famous by the world-renowned 'lion whisperer' Kevin Richardson, this is no surprise.

The woman, who is believed to have been South African, was at Richardson's Dinokeng Game Reserve in Gauteng, near Pretoria, when she was attacked. Ironically, she was not on a lion walk at the time but had instead been accompanying a friend for an interview with the manager of the camp. They were taking photos as they prepared to leave the site when the lioness, which *had* been on a walking excursion, appeared in front of them unexpectedly. At the time, Richardson said:

Myself and an experienced colleague took three lions walking in the reserve, as we do on a weekly basis, as part of their exercise and stimulation regiment [*sic*]. We assessed the landscape for other Big Five animals and as per procedure sent out a notification that we were walking in the reserve. One of the lionesses charged off after an impala and must have run 2 to 2.5 km, where she encountered the 22-year-old outside the car.[26]

Richardson has found fame via his relationship with the big cats, many of which are rented out so that they can feature in advertisements for global luxury brands or in television documentaries. Indeed, shortly before the tragedy at Richardson's reserve, the model Cara Delevingne had taken part in a promotional shoot there for a Swiss watch brand. If this ghastly event proves anything, it is surely that it is desperately ill-advised to encourage or allow the general public to be exposed to any captive-bred lion that is in the habit of roaming freely, whatever its owner thinks he or she understands of its nature.

There are different kinds of lion-walking activities across South Africa, some of which can last several hours, but it is most common to be locked in a compound roughly the size of a full-size football pitch with two lions so that you can stand within a few feet of them and, if you wish, touch and stroke them. During my team's visit, two male lions – one of them a rare white breed called Nigel, the other named George – were driven up to the enclosure on a trailer. These creatures were far larger than the cubs that had been made available for petting and cuddling earlier in the day. Aged eighteen months, they were not fully grown, but they were certainly very powerfully built, the equivalent in size of an adult Great Dane. The two

26 Brian Clark Howard, 'Fatal Lion Mauling Highlights Controversy of Private Reserves', *National Geographic*, 2 March 2018

guides described them as being like 'teenagers' as they explained the ground rules of the walk, the most important of which was that nobody in the enclosure should turn their back on the lions or try to run away if they appeared to be giving chase. It was obvious that either of these 'teenagers' could savage a man or woman with ease given the chance.

When the two animals were released, they were very curious and rather energetic, but the guides, who were not armed, were able to keep them occupied by throwing chunks of pungent-smelling raw meat in their direction. This was apparently horsemeat, which, surprisingly, given the huge financial turnover of this park, had been 'donated' by a local farmer on whom they have come to rely for handouts. Each of the five tourists in the pen was invited to stroke the animals as they were guided around by the keepers, the promise of more horsemeat never far away. In many ways, these lions were little more than circus animals, trained to obey and to allow foreign hands to touch them. Yet at the same time their size and behaviour made it impossible to lose sight of the fact that they were beasts with a killer instinct. Being in such close proximity to them was faintly surreal. It was certainly not natural. After twenty minutes or so, they were rounded up and put back onto their trailer. As the guides prepared to drive the lions to their compound for the evening, they mentioned that the animals had grown too big for walking excursions and from now on were going to be hired out to television and film production companies involved in making advertisements, programmes and films, with a particular focus on the lucrative Chinese market.

If the Lion and Safari Park is considered slick, Moreson Ranch in the Vrede district of the Free State sits at the other end of the captive-lion market. Co-owned by two professional hunters, Awie Marais and Tielman de Villiers, it is located about 200 km (125 miles) south of Johannesburg in an isolated rural setting near a cattle farm and is reached by driving along a mile-long dirt track surrounded by fabulous, if desolate, views. It is a much smaller operation, catering to a significantly lower number of tourists than the Lion and Safari Park, but it offers some guest accommodation and hunting opportunities for those interested in shooting zebras, wildebeest, bucks, impalas and ostrich. It also touts itself as a wedding venue, even having its own chapel on site. On the day of my team's visit, the entire area was empty save a handful of staff. As the wind whistled through the trees, this made it seem rather eerie. Outside the ranch's main building, which contains a bar, three lions including an older male lay in a small grassy fenced area. Their coats appeared to be in beautiful condition and they looked relaxed and happy. Yet a miserable scene awaited just yards away. In exchange for about $4 per person, it was possible to pet and cuddle some of the ranch's lion cubs. When my team had paid the fee, a barmaid pointed to a thin metal door in the yard just beyond the small pub garden. Behind it were ten cubs aged between two weeks and two months. The products of at least two different litters, they were housed in a squalid concrete pound estimated to be barely 12 feet wide by 20 feet long which was covered in lion excrement and chicken feathers. With no obvious sign of sufficient shade or clean drinking water, it was a surprise to find the cubs so playful and responsive, yet they made for a truly depressing sight. A young guide said they would remain there until they were nine months old or until they could be sold on, whichever came first. Some might be hunted, he admitted, adding that each cub would cost the equivalent of about $640 to buy. Looking into the eyes of these innocent animals, their destiny unknown, the only obvious consolation for them was that they had each other for company.

After ten minutes, an older guide arrived and began the game tour, driving the team several miles away over windswept ground high above the farm. Seemingly more experienced, he showed off three large adjoining fenced compounds which housed a total of about twenty-five well-fed and very vocal lions, the oldest of which was seven. The guide said there were fifty-eight lions on the property in total, though, as with the Lion and Safari Park, because so many of them were not in evidence it is impossible to know where they were or what was going to happen to them. It was as though the oldest generation, those aged eight and over, was simply missing. A fourth compound housed three Bengal tigers: two females aged four and one male aged five. No formal explanation was provided as to what they were doing there, far away from their native Asia. The guide's silence on this when questioned was deafening.

My team left Moreson Ranch harbouring various suspicions. Something was not right about the place. Each of them spoke of a sense of creepiness hanging over it. As will become clear in Part II of this book, their instincts were spot-on. Keeping petting cubs cooped up in a filthy pen is appalling enough. Behind the scenes, though, some extremely dark things have gone on at this ranch involving shocking cruelty to lions which is impossible to justify and shows exactly why the mass breeding of these creatures is entirely unacceptable. Its owners should be deeply ashamed of their conduct.

Ukutula Lodge, where, by coincidence, Beth Jennings was a voluntourist several years ago, is about 110 km (70 miles) from Johannesburg near the town of Brits, in North West Province. With a hotel, two swimming pools, a bar and a restaurant, it is considered one of the smartest wildlife operations in South Africa. Situated on a 260-hectare (650-acre) reserve and owned by Willi Jacobs, it is home to a large variety of animals including three tigers and about fifty lions, many of which were born there. During my team's visit, twenty-five lions were available to view. Their ages ranged from a few weeks to thirteen years old. The petting and cuddling opportunities that have become de rigueur at such places were, of course, on offer. Despite it being the low season, there were plenty of tourists from all over the world, including South Africa, Britain, France and Portugal. And Monique, the guide on duty, said that six voluntourists from France, Belgium, Britain and Norway had left that morning.

For about $38, it was possible to go on a tour of the park, including its small but very modern-looking scientific research centre, where genetic testing and veterinary study is carried out in conjunction with members of the University of Pretoria. Monique claimed that Ukutula's staff and their scientific partners plan to artificially inseminate lions in the wild for conservation purposes, though it is not clear how this could ever work and she was unable to throw further light on this impressive-sounding scheme. What is certain is that Ukutula is, at root, the same as any other commercial wildlife business in South Africa: it makes money from tourists who want to see lions at close quarters. It pitches itself as a centre of learning and conservation, and it certainly holds seminars for veterinarians and scientists, but behind this veneer it is hard to accept that its aims are markedly different from, say, those of the Lion and Safari Park. Furthermore, there was no plausible explanation from its staff of where the many older lions that have passed through Ukutula since it opened in 2007 have been sent before they die. The same question should be asked in relation to the many younger lions there, some of which, according to Monique, are swapped with other facilities to widen their respective lion gene pools. In a video on Ukutula's website, the company's owner, Willi Jacobs, states: 'We are the first to admit keeping animals in captivity is not ideal. That is not the way it was meant to be from the very beginning. But we do not live in normal circumstances. We do not live in normal times.' He then goes on to justify keeping lions in captivity and charging people to see them by saying that the object of his business is 'connecting people to the beautiful, natural heritage that they have'. Ukutula may be a place which strives to score various noble goals, but it surely exists primarily for financial gain. Indeed, it is worth adding that business at Ukutula must be booming because the driver who took my team there was given free tickets to activities which were worth more than $40.

Ukutula's focus on genetic research does, however, introduce an important point about animal conservation which must be addressed in this context. Many – perhaps most – of those involved in captive-lion farming maintain that it is a vital tool in the conservation of animals in South Africa, but the truth is that the reverse is the case. Its proponents say it protects the wild lion population by easing the pressure that previously existed from the hunting fraternity to shoot lions in the wild. There is no evidence to back up this assertion, however. Indeed, as shall become clear, my team has obtained evidence showing that wild lions are being kidnapped in order to improve the bloodlines of captive populations by increasing the gene pools. Furthermore, defenders of the lion farming trade say it is an example of the aforementioned 'sustainable utilisation of natural resources', as set out in South Africa's constitution, which also forms an important part of the green economy. Yet those who advocate for the protection of wildlife and the environment disagree entirely with this analysis.

Dr Andrew Muir is one of Africa's premier conservationists. As the chief executive of Wilderness Foundation Africa, he campaigns to protect and sustain all wildlife on earth – apart from captive lions, on the basis that they have absolutely no conservation worth. Dr Muir says:

> The problem is that captive animals have no true natural value to an ecosystem. You can't reintroduce a captive animal to its ecosystem. You can't re-wild a manipulated lion, in particular. So the problem with the lion trade is that these animals exist outside of the natural system. We also have a duty to protect wild lions from genetic contamination from farmed lions.[27]

He adds that, however brutal it might seem, there is only one solution to settling the question of what to do with South

---

27   Interview with Dr Andrew Muir, 1 August 2019

Africa's captive-lion population. 'The toughest call we as a society would have to make would be to euthanise however many thousands of animals there are,' Dr Muir says. 'But that would be the right call. They would all need to be euthanised.' Dr Muir is at pains to explain why this radical solution is, in his opinion, the only realistic course of action to be taken. He says:

> The vast majority of captive wild lions are kept and bred in the most deplorable conditions. Those that are destined for the lion bone trade are literally starved to death. Under such circumstances, and if the captive-lion industry were to be closed down, most of these lions would need to be put down humanely and by wildlife vets and animal welfare support structures. Whilst I would like to see as many of the remaining and more healthy captive lions living out the rest of their lives in large enclosures in the wild, as the Born Free Foundation facilitates, the sheer number and scale of captive lions will sadly mean that a lot of these would also need to be put down. All of us in conservation and wildlife management bear some responsibility for allowing this terrible situation to have developed to where it is now. But it's time to do the right thing as conditions continue to deteriorate and the numbers of captive lions are increasing.

Having visited these three tourist attractions – the Lion and Safari Park, Moreson Ranch and Ukutula Lodge – it is impossible to view them and other businesses like them as anything other than operations which enable the captive-bred lion industry in South Africa to prosper. And it is a poisonous trade which is mired in secrecy. Nobody knows how many thousands of captive-bred lions there are in South Africa at any one time; the trade is entirely unregulated; and it generates millions of dollars annually from a largely unsuspecting global client base. Much of this money finds its way into the bank accounts of those who seem to have no conscience.

In November 2019, the Southern African Tourism Services Association (SATSA), a non-profit body representing the region's private sector tourism companies, did produce a guide for tour operators and tourists to help them evaluate captive wildlife interactions and make informed decisions about which facilities to avoid. It certainly represents a step in the right direction from an ethical point of view, though as the Campaign Against Canned Hunting has pointed out, lion farmers are astute enough to be able to present their businesses as genuine sanctuaries even when they are not. Unsuspecting tourists cannot always know who or what to believe. SATSA's guide also raises the question of how conservationists and animal lovers are going to move from being better informed to having this key decision made for them via a certification process. Surely professional inspectors should decide whether a facility should be promoted by SATSA.

The campaigning organisation Blood Lions said of SATSA's statement:

> We appreciate that SATSA does not have the directive to regulate or legislate this industry, but they have now 'set the

stage' to position Brand South Africa positively, and clearly expect the authorities (such as SA Tourism and Tourism
Business Council of South Africa as well as environmental
and agricultural departments) to rise to the challenge and
stand united in taking these guidelines forward.[28]

To what degree the South African government can be steered to
protect Brand South Africa in the way that Blood Lions advocates remains an open question.

Aside from these points, though, there remain major concerns about that most basic matter: what captive-bred lions eat.
In the wild, lions enjoy a wide selection of food. Yet in captivity,
it is common for animal carcasses to be tossed over lions' fences
with little thought given to the source or condition of that meat.
Those who keep lions seem content to feed them mainly on the
cheapest foods, such as raw chicken or, if it is available, horse or
donkey flesh. Good-quality beef and venison is more expensive.

Wildlife veterinarian Dr Peter Caldwell, owner of the Old
Chapel Veterinary Clinic in Pretoria, carries out work for a
range of animal welfare organisations in South Africa. He
warns that the largely chicken-based diet on which so many
captive lions appear to exist is entirely insufficient. 'If you keep
an animal in captivity you've got to know that species and understand how that species reacts in the wild. You've got to know
what they eat,' he says.

---

28   Blood Lions press release, 1 November 2019

In the wild, they don't only eat muscle meat. In the wild, when a pride of lions goes hunting, and they hunt an antelope, some lions will eat the rump meat, some will eat some of the organ meat – that's the heart, liver and lungs – and some will eat some of the intestinal content, which contains a lot of the vitamins and minerals in micro and macro elements.[29]

Dr Caldwell is particularly concerned by the source of much of the food that is fed to lions in captivity. He adds:

Most people who keep lions don't have access to fresh antelope or fresh wild meat carcasses. So they feed them offcuts or animals from abattoirs that are not fit for human consumption. That's 80 to 90 per cent of what people feed these lions in captivity. With that comes a lot of risk. Firstly, if they feed them organ meat – for example, only livers – they would suffer and eventually die from heavy metal toxicity or hormone toxicity because the liver of any animal is like a sponge and toxins, heavy metals and hormones would accumulate in this one organ and concentrate and be toxic for the lion to eat. Second, those who keep lions in captivity don't realise these animals need extra vitamins and minerals and these need to be specially formulated to balance the diet. If, let's say, they feed them mostly horsemeat, that's high in phosphate and low in calcium, in which case you've got to add extra calcium, increase the Vitamin A and also balance the

---

29   Interview with Dr Peter Caldwell, 10 December 2019

amino acids. It's a work in progress. You've got to evaluate those animals regularly to assess whether they're getting sufficient nutrients.

He also believes that while the risk of bacterial infection from rotting meat is high, frozen meat also threatens lions' welfare.

If a piece of meat has been frozen and is given to a lion without being defrosted to room temperature, cold-loving bacteria which are not part of the normal gut bacteria can overgrow and cause infections and cause severe gastrointestinal imbalances and diarrhoea. If they get sick, they don't grow, so their diet is so important.

The supplement of vitamins and minerals – fat soluble and water soluble – is highly essential in these animals. Most people want to make a quick buck and don't want to spend money on nutrition. They get free dead chickens from the local chicken breeding farms, where chickens have died through heat stress or something and they aren't fit for human consumption. But it is critical to feed these animals the correct food. And even if they do feed them venison, if those antelope have been shot, the bullet that goes through the meat can cause lead toxicity in lions as well, so there are so many elements involved in feeding these animals. It's not just about giving them chicken. One must consider bacteria, heavy metal toxicity, calcium–phosphate ratio balance. You can't just give them calcium supplement because you've got to get a special calcium–phosphate balance together with Vitamin D, because a lion cannot convert UV like sun into Vitamin D, as humans can. Cats need it in their diet. And if they don't have the optimal amount of bio-available calcium with the appropriate calcium–phosphate ratios in their diet then they get metabolic bone diseases like rickets and so on. In my opinion, keeping a lion in captivity and not giving it supplements is cruel and it is a welfare issue.

The next questions to address are what happens when a captive-bred lion is considered old enough to be killed in a canned hunt, and what kind of person would want to kill one?

CHAPTER 3

CANNED CAPTIVES

Lions reach maturity at three to four years of age. Depending on their sex, by then they will have grown to a shoulder height of approximately 3 feet, a length of 6 or 7 feet, and a weight of 350–500 lbs (160–225 kg). It hardly needs to be pointed out that, if they live in captivity, at this stage of their lives their size and strength makes them extremely difficult to control. In the wild, lionesses, which are smaller than lions, are the more active members of the species. Generally, they hunt and provide for the pride, while lions tend to protect the pride. For this reason, captive-bred lionesses can be busier and therefore more troublesome for their handlers than males. Having been raised within a tourist attraction of some description, the experience of both lions and lionesses of being hand-reared, cuddled and stroked by the general public in South Africa means they will have little or no fear of humans. Therefore, they pose a threat to safety. Whatever time they have left alive will almost certainly be spent in a carefully controlled environment effectively as inmates, living either behind bars or in a fenced compound.

If they are already living in a sightseeing attraction, lions will likely be moved to an enclosure upon reaching maturity. They will remain there for an indeterminate period so that they can be seen, but not touched, by tourists. Usually, they are considered to be surplus to requirements between the ages of four and seven. This is also the time at which the manes of the males will begin to look truly majestic and, consequently, when they will become most desirable to trophy hunters. Although their handlers may claim to inquisitive visitors that they will be shipped to a country such as the Democratic Republic of Congo to live out their remaining years in peace and comfort, the reality is invariably very different. The odds are that they will be transported elsewhere in South Africa, either to enter a breeding programme or to die. Whenever it is decided that they are to be sent to their death, they will either be shot in a canned hunt or killed at a slaughterhouse.

It is essential to point out that the danger to the public of moving captive predators like lions between locations is not to be underestimated. This most recently became apparent in October 2019 when, it was reported, the driver of a Toyota Landcruiser pick-up truck which was taking three males and one female on a trailer from a breeding facility in Hertzogville in the Free State to a hunting farm at Leniesdeel in North West Province crashed on the R34 highway. As a result of the accident, one lion escaped but, mercifully, it did not get far because it had been sedated before the journey. It was quickly darted and then loaded back into a crate to continue the trip together with the remaining three creatures. A case of reckless and negligent driving was opened against the driver of the Toyota. A passenger, believed to be a farm worker, sustained a broken leg and was later transferred to Klerksdorp Hospital.[30] Luck certainly played its part in ensuring that no innocent passers-by were attacked.

As is now clear, during its life a captive lion in a tourist facility can potentially generate significant sums of money for those in charge of it simply through its natural beauty. The fascination a lion holds among paying customers is almost boundless, as confirmed by the vast number of people who like to pose for photographs and videos alongside them. Perversely, that same level of enthusiasm among some members of the public applies when it comes to killing lions and then cannibalising them. Many will wonder how these magnificent beasts, whose mere existence is one of the chief reasons that thousands of animal-loving tourists want to visit South Africa each year, can be exploited in a civilised country in the twenty-first century. Yet the reprehensible fact is that the law constitutes just as much of a threat to lions as do lion owners, farmers, breeders and hunters. It is important to explain briefly how this is so.

'There's a long and very complicated history relating to the legalities of the captive-bred lion industry in South Africa,' says Amy P. Wilson, a lawyer and director of Animal Law Reform South Africa.

> While there is a plethora of issues with the current regulation of wildlife, including its enforcement, in my view there are two fundamental underlying legal circumstances which form

---

30   Voice4Lions, Facebook, 9 October 2019

the basis as to why the captive-lion business has flourished. Firstly, while animals are generally considered as property in most jurisdictions in the world, laws passed during apartheid in South Africa effectively enshrined the property status of wildlife, too. This status gives owners a large amount of discretion as to what they can do with their 'property' or on their land and has largely promoted the commodification of wild animals, including lions. Secondly, Section 24 of the constitution guarantees the right to the 'sustainable utilisation … of natural resources'. The interpretation of this provision by government has effectively enshrined the wide-scale use and abuse of wild animals – so-called resources – for commercial purposes, the limitations of which are unclear. As there is also no legal definition of 'sustainable utilisation', there exists no consensus of what it means in practice, so true conservation and environmental rights have been flouted for the economic benefit of a few. This interpretation means that wild lions, once the pride of South Africa, have essentially been reduced to agricultural animals.[31]

Wilson is right. Shockingly, in May 2019, the South African government quietly approved an amendment to the Animal Improvement Act which covers livestock breeding. Captive lions are among thirty-three animals, including rhinos and zebras, which are now considered to be farm animals as a result of this change. As Don Pinnock, the author of an article revealing this, concluded, 'By the stroke of a legislative pen, a list of iconic and

---

31   Interview with Amy P. Wilson, 11 November 2019

in some cases endangered wild animals can now be manipulated as farming stock. What happens next is anyone's guess.'[32] The amendment was made without any public consultation in response to a request from breeding societies and has prompted fears of an increase in experiments to create cross-breeds and genetically 'superior' animals. It gives breeders the ability to operate on a par with livestock farmers by carrying out artificial insemination, the collection of semen and embryos and the transfer of embryos and genetic material. Even the hunting lobby has voiced misgivings about the change. On hearing the news, the South African Hunters and Game Conservation Association claimed that species on the list would be 'at risk of genetic manipulation and genetic pollution.'[33] What this boils down to is that human selection has been given a licence to trump natural selection. After all, this is what lies behind the domestication of any species. It is therefore true to say that in the twenty-first century, the South African government will have sanctioned lions becoming a domestic species. Politicians and bureaucrats tampering with nature in this way without thinking through the outcome ought to give everybody in the world pause for thought.

Wilson believes an important failure in the regulations is that wild animals form part of the environment and nature conservation. These areas are managed by the department in charge of the environment, which largely concentrates on biodiversity and species conservation. This department is not concerned

---

32 Don Pinnock, 'SA reclassifies 33 wild species as farm animals', Daily Maverick, 16 October 2019

33 'Lions and rhinos are farm animals, says South Africa', The Times, 18 October 2019

with the welfare of animals and operates on the basis that their well-being is outside its jurisdiction. Domestic and agricultural animals, however, fall under the department in charge of agriculture, which *is* tasked with welfare. Captive lions straddle the divide between these two areas and, therefore, between these two departments and their mandates. This has led to loopholes that have been exploited over the years, with a considerable amount of buck-passing to boot.

Alongside this undeniably confused and confusing national departmental structure, South Africa's constitution grants simultaneous jurisdiction to the national and provincial governments for environmental and nature conservation matters. This means that hunting is set out in both national and provincial laws, which differ depending on which of South Africa's nine provinces you are in. Legally, 'canned hunting' is not a defined term. Rather, hunting per se is restricted or limited in certain ways.

The lion breeding and hunting industries are based mainly in three provinces – North West, Limpopo and the Free State. Eighty per cent of lion hunting takes place in the Free State and North West Province.[34] This is unsurprising given that these two provinces have the most lenient rules when it comes to killing lions for fun on private land. In the Free State, a lion must by law be able to roam free for thirty days before it can be hunted in an area that has to be (barring exemptions) a minimum of

---

34   Peet van der Merwe Peet, Melville Saayman, Jauntelle Els and Andrea Saayman, 'The economic significance of lion breeding operations in the South African Wildlife Industry, *International Journal of Biodiversity and Conservation* (2017)

100 hectares (just under 250 acres) in size.[35] In North West Province, it only has to be set free ninety-six hours before a hunt, but the minimum area size requirement is 1,000 hectares. This more relaxed time allowance means that the vast majority of lion hunting takes place in North West, and as a result it is often referred to colloquially as 'The Wild West'.[36]

'The concurrent jurisdiction between national and provincial governments and between the provinces themselves has led to a huge amount of legal uncertainty and enforcement issues,' says Wilson. 'Laws are generally old and outdated, they differ significantly from one province to the next and, frankly, trying to navigate the legal landscape leads one on a wild goose chase. In many instances, this uncertainty is actively relied on so that there is an excuse for lack of accountability.'

On top of this, there are other problems. The lion hunting industry is regulated through permits and licensing, but the process of issuing these permits is not standardised or transparent and it is also riddled with complications. For example, permitting conditions differ between provinces; there is no sharing of information between provinces; and different provinces do not know what their counterparts are doing. Furthermore, the businesses which breed lions also rely on permits to operate and similar difficulties arise. In 2019, the national government stated that nearly 40 per cent of the 227 registered breeding facilities inspected in four of the provinces did not comply with

---

35 *Free State Provincial Gazette*, 1 February 2013, p. 7
36 Free State High Court, Bloemfontein Case No. 1900/2007 between the South African Predator Breeders Association, Matthys Christiaan Mostert, Deon Cilliers and the Minister of Environmental Affairs and Tourism, heard on 1 and 2 December 2008

regulations or were operating with expired permits – yet they were renewed anyway. Permits were issued retrospectively to what had previously been classed as illegal breeding operations.[37] Wilson says, 'There is no specific formal regulation of these operations by government, and these failures mean that critical issues like welfare provisions, knowledge required to start a business, worker safety requirements, the transfer of diseases and slaughter among others are not properly controlled.'

As a result of this legal vacuum, hunting industry bodies such as the South African Predator Association have set their own standards for captive lions, but adhering to these guidelines is voluntary. In any case, Wilson says that they are insufficient in terms of both their content and their enforcement and do little more than ensure the continuation of the industry and the abuse of animals. Furthermore, as they are not legally binding, they do not need to comply with the legal requirements to which other law is subject. 'Enforcement of these laws is a whole other can of worms,' says Wilson. 'The police usually don't enforce the law, so it's up to the NSPCA to monitor the situation, but they, of course, have limited funds and resources. Overall, as you can see, it's a perfect storm that has allowed this industry to flourish.'

Stewart Dorrington, the president of Custodians of Professional Hunting and Conservation South Africa, an anti-canned hunting group which aims to promote ethical hunting, claims that the hunting industry is properly regulated, but he acknowledges that regulations around it have become tangled. He says:

---

37   Source: Conservation Action Trust, Captive Lion Breeding coalition submission to DEFF, June 2019

There is very strict legislation guiding all hunting in South Africa, with inspections of property and facilities and scrutiny of all hunting permits and permissions. As the vast majority of hunting takes place on private land, the owners generally will not conduct themselves in a way that is detrimental to the game numbers on which they depend. The biggest problem we have is that there are nine provinces in South Africa and each province has its own laws pertaining to hunting and conservation. In most provinces, the breeding of captive-bred lions for hunting is not allowed under any circumstances. However, the Free State and North West Province do allow for hunting of captive-bred lions but have different rules regarding size of area and release periods for lions. Matters would certainly be simplified and streamlined and made easier to monitor and control if the country had just one department instead. The provinces do not want this scenario; they want their own autonomy. It's a frustration to many of us.

As well as examining the legality of canned hunting, it is equally illuminating to explore an aspect of this vicious pastime which relates to the psychological motivations of those who take part in it. Specifically, what kind of individual would choose to spend their time and money shooting a relatively tame animal in a confined area from which it cannot escape? Why would anybody wish to indulge in what is, ultimately, a ridiculously contrived experience?

These questions encompass territory which those who study the science of the mind believe is little understood because of a lack of proper research. Dr Xanthé Mallett, a forensic anthropologist and criminologist attached to the University of Newcastle in Australia, has noted that a history of cruelty to animals in childhood is a potential indicator of serious violent crime as an adult. However, she continues:

> The need to hurt animals that some children feel doesn't explain why some adults hunt and kill large, and often dangerous, animals that they have no intention of eating. I have searched the psychology literature and, while there's a lot of conjecture about what it means, the fact that very little research exists to support any assumptions makes reaching an understanding of this behaviour very difficult. Perhaps hunting large animals is an example of some people's need to show dominance over others. Research shows increased levels of hostility and a need for power and control are associated with poor attitudes towards animals, among men in particular.[38]

It is important to say from the outset that not every person who participates in a canned hunt does so knowingly. As referred to earlier, some hunting companies will trick their clients into believing that they are paying to go on a 'fair chase' hunt when, in fact, this is a lie. Furthermore, it would be irresponsible to suggest that every trophy hunter fits a specific psychological profile and quite wrong to think that every canned hunter is a psychopath or a potential murderer of human beings. With all

---

38 Xanthé Mallett, 'Why we may never understand the reason people hunt animals as "trophies"', The Conversation, 7 August 2015

of that said, however, there can be little doubt that many people who kill lions and other animals in their capacity as trophy hunters do so in order to inflate their own status and to burnish their credentials as an alpha male or, more rarely, an alpha female. Their principal aim is to flex their muscles, so to speak, just as some colonial adventurers in the nineteenth century sought to quench their bloodthirst. An uncomfortable reality of this behaviour, as observed by some clinicians who analyse serious mental disorders, is the high number of common traits identified in those who take part in canned hunts and trophy hunts and those who kill innocent people for self-gratification.

In their book *The Serial Killers: A Study in the Psychology of Violence*, Colin Wilson and Donald Seaman examine the mindset of murderers and note that some killers retain victims' body parts 'for much the same reason as the big-game hunter mounts the head and antlers from his prey'.[39] Wilson and Seaman also discuss the case of the American serial killer Robert Hansen, a baker and big-game enthusiast who 'hunted his naked prostitute victims through the snow before shooting them dead' in the 1970s and 1980s. Hansen apparently 'stalked his victims gun in hand as though they were wild animals'.[40] He, at least, might arguably be an example of a man who saw little difference between the hunting of animals and the hunting of women.

Dr Kevin Dutton is a research psychologist at the University of Oxford. One of his specialist areas is the psychopathic personality. He has reflected on the similarities between serial

---

39 Colin Wilson and Donald Seaman, *The Serial Killers: A Study in the Psychology of Violence*, (Virgin Books, 2007), p. 68
40 Ibid., p. 170

killers and canned hunters and found several characteristics shared by them. 'A lot of serial killers are psychotic and live in a world of their own because of things that happened in their childhood and their dysfunctional backgrounds,' Dutton says.

The same cannot necessarily be said of everybody who takes part in a canned hunt, but my observations do suggest that there are some striking parallels that have to be considered. In canned lion hunting, as opposed to traditional lion hunting, there's a lack of remorse at the lion having no possible exit from the enclosure where it's killed. This signifies a distinct lack of empathy. It is a fact that people who are high on the psychopathic spectrum will not be bothered by seeing an animal that is injured or in pain. I would also say that serial killers and canned hunters both plan their kills carefully and, you could argue, stalk their victims. They are also both turned on by goal-related literature. For serial killers, this could, for instance, be violent pornography, while trophy hunters often subscribe to specialist hunting magazines which are full of pictures of prey being slaughtered. Then we must consider that serial killers, like trophy hunters and canned hunters, sometimes retain trophies or souvenirs from their victims like a lock of hair, an item of clothing or a body part. This reminds them of their power over life and death. Both canned hunters and serial killers are also selective in their kills. For example, a serial killer might only go for a certain physical type of woman or man, and a hunter might only shoot a certain type of game. I would add that both canned hunters and serial killers allude to the thrill of killing. In some cases, this is a physical thrill. In others, it is more spiritual and tran-scendental. There is also a variety of serial killer who doesn't kill straight away, and the same can be said of some canned hunters. Instead, the victim or animal might have to endure a slow death. And finally, canned hunters often film or pho-tograph their kill. This seems to be an important part of the activity for them, perhaps for self-gratification purposes or to show off to others. As is well known from cases going back to the Moors murders in the 1960s, there are many examples of serial killers recording, in one way or another, their vic-tims being tortured, harmed or killed.[41]

To Dutton's observations it seems timely to add that interact-ing with lions in any context is a risky business, whether they have been raised in a captive environment or not. Take the example of Swane van Wyke, a game ranger aged twenty-one. In February 2020, she was mauled to death by two lions after entering their enclosure unaccompanied. The attack occurred at the Zwartkloof Private Game Reserve near the town of Bela-Bela in Limpopo Province. The facility specialises in hosting school groups, functions and team-building exercises.[42] Leon van Biljon, a seventy-year-old owner of the Mahala View Lion Game Lodge, a tourist outfit 50 km (30 miles) north of Pretoria, is another recent victim. In August 2019, this self-styled 'lion man' was savaged by one of his own animals. He was mend-ing a broken fence in the lions' enclosure when it seized his

---

41 Interview with Dr Kevin Dutton, 1 October 2019
42 Jane Flanagan, 'Ranger, 21, mauled to death by her lions', *The Times*, 11 February 2020

neck with its claws, locking it between its jaws. All three of his lions, which were billed as a star attraction at the game reserve, were shot by a ranger, but, sadly, Mr Biljon could not be saved.[43] And in May 2018, another lion was shot dead after attacking Michael Hodge, the owner of the privately run Marakele Predator Centre in Limpopo Province. This mauling was recorded in a graphic video which shows Hodge walking in an enclosure behind the lion and then running for an exit when the animal turns and chases him. Having caught Hodge, it quickly drags him towards some bushes before a member of staff destroys the animal. Hodge suffered neck and jaw injuries and had to be treated at a Johannesburg hospital.[44] These are pertinent examples of why keeping lions in captivity is not only cruel and without any conservation value at all, but also why confining these predators to a small piece of ground abuses their nature and therefore risks human life.

Of course, it isn't just lions that are dangerous when hunting. The activity of killing them in a canned hunt itself is just as hazardous. The best recent example of a canned hunt gone wrong that I know of came in January 2018 when a 75-year-old Croatian blood sport enthusiast called Pero Jelenić was killed by a stray bullet during one of these impossibly unfair attacks on the captive-bred population. The bullet struck Mr Jelenić's head as he took aim at a lion at Leeubosch Lodge, a hunting facility about 65 km (40 miles) from the border with Botswana.

43　Jane Flanagan, '"Lion Man" Leon van Biljon killed by his own cats at safari lodge in South Africa', *The Times*, 21 August 2019

44　Christopher Torchia, 'Lion that mauled man in enclosure in South Africa is killed', Associated Press Newswires, 2 May 2018

According to reports at the time, Mr Jelenić had shot one lion that day shortly before his own sudden and unnatural death.[45]

Many successful canned hunters like to brag about their kills, but they do so in such a way that attracts high-voltage negative attention online. In July 2019, canned hunters Darren and Carolyn Carter, who own a taxidermy business in Edmonton, Canada, incurred the wrath of thousands through one particularly provocative show of triumph. They posed for a photograph while enjoying a celebratory kiss as they stood over the carcass of a beautifully maned lion which one of them had killed. The image, which was posted on the Facebook page of Legelela Safaris, the tour company which organised the Carters' trip, was captioned: 'Hard work in the hot Kalahari sun... well done. A monster lion.' Under a second photo of them with another lion which one of them had killed, the tour company wrote: 'There is nothing like hunting the king of the jungle in the sands of the Kalahari. Well done to the happy huntress and the team.' With some justification, the picture of the Carters kissing was considered so disturbing that it was shared online by people around the world, many of whom branded it 'disgusting'.[46] But as the storm around their foul deed gathered pace, British-born hunter Carl Knight, who runs the Johannesburg-based company Take Aim Safaris, backed the couple and the hunting profession. 'This lion was bred for hunting and for lion bone export to the Far East,' he told the *Daily Express*'s website. He added, 'This

45   Nicola Stow, 'Big game hunter Pero Jelenic killed by stray bullet while taking aim at lion in freak hunting accident', *The Sun*, 31 January 2018

46   Dianne Apen-Sadler, 'Canadian couple happily kiss for a photo as they kneel behind magnificent lion they have just killed on a hunt in South Africa', *Daily Mail*, 15 July 2019

is not Mufasa or Cecil, this is an animal that was farmed like a cow, a sheep or a crocodile that is farmed for meat and skin.' Mr Knight also claimed that as the lion in the incriminating photograph was not wild, its death would not have any impact upon population numbers for the species. He continued, 'The money these clients paid for this lion is much needed in poverty-stricken southern Africa. Why do we have to answer to your armchair conservationist readers that know nothing about Africa?'[47]

Mr Knight's candour cannot be faulted. His reported attempt at justifying the breeding of an animal solely for the purpose of gunning it down in appalling circumstances in exchange for money is abhorrent, however.

---

47   Luke Chillingsworth, 'British hunter defends slaying of lions for sport', *Daily Express*, 16 July 2019

CHAPTER 4

ROGUE ELEMENTS

Given the innumerable unpleasant aspects of canned hunting and the trade in captive-bred lions, it is not surprising that many people in South Africa – including some within the professional hunting fraternity – have come out against it over the past two decades. Since 1997, at least two senior politicians, Environment Minister Pallo Jordan and one of his eventual successors, Marthinus van Schalkwyk, have attempted to tackle it head-on. In April 2005, Van Schalkwyk even convened a committee of experts which spent six months examining the issue. It recommended that canned hunting and all captive breeding should be banned, except for the purposes of science and conservation. Chaired by the former director-general of the Department of Environmental Affairs and Tourism Dr Crispian Olver, the panel included Khungeka Njobe from the Council for Scientific and Industrial Research; Tony Frost from the World Wide Fund for Nature; Nick King from the Endangered Wildlife Trust; Stewart Dorrington, then of the Professional Hunters' Association of South Africa; Marcelle Meredith from the National Society for the Prevention of Cruelty to Animals;

Professor Koos Bothma from the Centre for Wildlife Management at the University of Pretoria; and Dr Holly Dublin of the Species Survival Commission of the International Union for the Conservation of Nature. Van Schalkwyk himself concluded that canned hunting was a 'cancer' in South African society.[48] Yet despite his proposed legislation that captive-bred lions should be set free on large areas of land for at least twenty-four months before they could be hunted, the hunting lobby argued successfully against any clampdown in subsequent court cases, as outlined in Chapter 1.

There is no question that Van Schalkwyk was motivated partly by what he believed to be the routine abuse of the regulations around hunting. The difficulty in enforcing them was illustrated brilliantly in December 2007 by Carla van der Vyver of the organisation now known as the South African Predator Association, which represents members of the breeding and hunting industry. Ms van der Vyver's perhaps unintentionally honest interview with the online newspaper News24 laid bare the near-impossibility of controlling the situation. Given her status as an employee of the Environment and Conservation divisions of North West Province between 1993 and 2007, she presumably spoke from experience. 'Even with the issuing of the necessary conservation hunting permits, irregularities still take place,' Ms van der Vyver said.

It is impossible to catch the illegal lion breeders because their area of operation is so large and isolated. There are only

---

48 'South African Panel Recommends Canned Hunting Ban', Environment News Service, 25 October 2005

four nature conservation officials and four managers for the whole province. The lion breeding and hunting industry has been developed by operators to get rich quickly and has been growing steadily since 1994. Unethical hunting methods like the drugging of the lions before they are shot or the using of bait to lure others is the order of the day.[49]

This description shows as well as any other the scale of the problem facing captive-bred lions that persists in South Africa today.

Regrettably, there is also clear evidence that the spirit in which Van Schalkwyk's crusade was fought does not appear to have been imbibed by those with political influence who operate at a provincial level. A press release circulated by the Agriculture, Conservation, Environment and Rural Development department of the North West provincial government dated 17 June 2009 and headlined 'Tshwene Assures Predator Breeders of His Support' is a shining example of the intransigence they faced. It details a meeting addressed by Boitumelo Tshwene, a member of North West Province's Executive Council, whose mandate covered environmental matters, during which he told more than seventy lion breeders who were in attendance that under him their business was safe. Considering North West's pivotal status within the captive breeding and canned hunting industry in South Africa, the importance of Tshwene's view at the time was obvious. The memo stated, 'The North West MEC for Department of Agriculture, Conservation, Environment

---

49 Quoted in 'Cash Before Conservation: An Overview of the Breeding of Lions for Hunting and Bone Trade' (Born Free Foundation, 2018), p. 13

and Rural Development, Boitumelo Tshwene, has extended his unwavering support to the predator breeders and urged them to work together with the department towards making the industry a success.' It continued:

> Predator breeders are one of the important stakeholders within the department who are continuing to contribute greatly towards addressing the fundamental challenges of unemployment and poverty, by having their fair shares in improving the economic situation of the province and the country at large ... MEC Tshwene made his intentions clear by assuring these breeders of his cooperation, respect and trust in making the industry grow.

Unsurprisingly, it added, 'Farmers applauded the MEC for his initiative to meet with them.'

Those farmers with a vested interest in maintaining the status quo could not have wished for a better ally. Indeed, Born Free estimates that between 2010 (the year after this press release was published) and 2018, the number of lions held in captive-bred conditions in South Africa trebled.[50] From this distance, it looks very much like lion farming's alleged ability to combat 'unemployment and poverty' was used by Tshwene to justify the breeding of lions in North West Province. The lack of any independent statistics demonstrating how many people were employed in lion farming at that time, together with the

---

50   'Cash Before Conservation: An Overview of the Breeding of Lions for Hunting and Bone Trade' (Born Free Foundation, 2018), p. 11

large amount of anecdotal evidence suggesting that this is in any case a cash business reliant upon casual low-wage labour, mean others must judge for themselves whether Tshwene was guilty of hyperbole as part of a tactic to shut down debate.

It is worth adding that the politician who succeeded Marthinus van Schalkwyk as South Africa's next-but-one Environment Minister in 2010, Edna Molewa, had a long background in North West Province politics. According to the Born Free Foundation, Ms Molewa 'played a prominent role in setting environmental policy in North West', having been the Member of the Executive Council of the province in charge of wildlife policy and regulation from 1996 to 2004. That year, she became the premier of the province, a post she held until 2009.[51] Ms Molewa died suddenly in 2018 after contracting a virus on an official trip to China. By then, she had served for eight years as South Africa's Environment Minister. She was regarded as a 'good comrade' within her party, the African National Congress, but, as Chris Mercer of the Campaign Against Canned Hunting has said, 'she never attempted to … put animal welfare on the agenda and to assume a broader responsibility for preserving the natural environment'.[52] And, as we shall see, when it came to stamping out the appalling trade in the parts of dead lions, serious questions surrounding her effectiveness remain.

It is not only South Africa's politicians who have taken

---

51   'Cash Before Conservation: An Overview of the Breeding of Lions for Hunting and Bone Trade' (Born Free Foundation, 2018), p. 9
52   Chris Mercer, 'Sustainable use has put conservation in a straitjacket', *The Mercury*, 9 October 2018

conflicting positions on lion farming and canned hunting in recent years, however. Within breeding and professional hunting circles, the question of whether these practices should continue has also caused a significant amount of turbulence. There are several organisations in the country representing the hunting and breeding industries, of which two are notably prominent. The Professional Hunters' Association of South Africa (PHASA) is the biggest and was founded in 1978. It acts and lobbies for approximately 1,200 members who are involved in the professional hunting industry and has historically been concerned with speaking up for businesses which rely on international hunters who visit South Africa to take part in blood sports. The other body is the aforementioned South African Predator Association. This smaller organisation succeeded the South African Breeders and Predators Association in 2008 and represents professional hunters as well as those who breed lions. (Incidentally, SAPA's president is Kirsten Nematandani, who was president of the South African Football Association between 2009 and 2013. In 2016, he was banned for five years from professional football by FIFA's ethics committee in connection with a match-fixing scandal which took place in 2010. He was found to have violated articles on general conduct, loyalty and disclosure.[53])

The year 2015 was a watershed moment in changing attitudes to lion hunting, among both politicians and hunting groups. Firstly, Ian Michler's acclaimed film *Blood Lions* was

---

53   'Former Safa boss Nematandani banned over match fixing', *Mail and Guardian*, 8 December 2016

released, providing much-needed coverage of how the gruesome industry operated. Shortly afterwards, the government
of Australia announced it was banning the importation of lion
trophies. That July, global attention turned to Cecil, Zimbabwe's
most famous lion, who was shot in Hwange National Park by
Walter Palmer, a middle-aged dentist from Minnesota. Using
a crossbow, Palmer wounded this wild animal severely, but he
only put it out of its misery by killing it with a second arrow
between ten and twelve hours later. Cecil's skinned carcass
was found subsequently by investigators, who were then able
to trace Palmer. He paid a reported $50,000 for this 'experi-
ence'. Cecil's head was removed as a trophy. When his actions
became known publicly, they sparked a firestorm of protests
around the world, drawing further attention to the matter of
lion hunting.

The sense of anger surrounding Cecil's death prompted conservationists to call for an EU-wide ban on the import of lion
trophies, a measure that the French government implemented in
November 2015. That month saw another crucial development
in South Africa's growing lion scandal when the then president
of PHASA, Stan Burger, asked his association's members at their
AGM to amend PHASA's stance on captive-bred lion hunting –
which they did. Burger had argued for at least two years that
the reputation of all types of hunting was at risk if PHASA continued to condone killing captive-bred lions. His view was that
it went against the principles of 'fair chase' hunting. In fact, to
this day, he refuses to talk about captive-bred 'hunting'. Instead,
he speaks of captive-bred 'shooting' because he feels that killing

captive-bred lions has nothing to do with traditional hunting and is both 'ethically and morally indefensible'.

Burger explains:

The preamble to the 2015 decision to urge PHASA members to vote against captive-bred lion shooting started as early as 2013 when I attended the SAPA annual general meeting as the then vice-president of PHASA. My message was clear: captive-bred lion shooting was no longer deemed to be an acceptable practice by other conservation agencies, for example the International Union for Conservation of Nature or, indeed, fellow hunters and hunting associations in Africa and the world at large. There had been a steadily growing outrage against it amongst the general public. The breeders of these lions had to prove the conservation value of captive-bred shooting and re-evaluate their entire business model or face the wrath of public opinion worldwide. I warned them that they would be closed down as an unethical and morally unsustainable industry and a blot on the great South African conservation model, which was damaging Brand South Africa. I told them that the reforms they needed to make should have been made years ago and that they needed to act with extreme urgency. You can imagine that I was not given a standing ovation, and PHASA was severely criticised for this standpoint by the lion breeders. SAPA continued to claim that what their members were doing had a conservation value, and the industry went ahead with what they were doing with no intention to make any reforms. They were killing upwards of 800 lions per annum at between $25,000 and $30,000 per lion. The revenues were huge and the government therefore refused to support PHASA despite appeals to close down the industry.[54]

The motion was passed at the 2015 AGM by 147 to 103 votes. Having been won, PHASA published a resolution underscoring its intentions:

PHASA distances itself from all captive-bred lion breeding and hunting until such time as the South African Predator Association can convince PHASA and the International Union for Conservation of Nature that captive-bred lion hunting is beneficial to lion conservation. The above decision is effective immediately and is binding on all PHASA members. If any evidence arises implicating a PHASA member as having participated in the hunting or marketing of a captive-bred lion, such member will be subjected to PHASA's internal disciplinary process, which will include expulsion if found guilty.

The organisation made good on its promise, even defending the resolution in court (albeit unsuccessfully) after some PHASA members were suspended by the executive committee because of their involvement in the hunting of captive-bred lions.

Cecil's death, together with PHASA's vote, also influenced

---

54   Interview with Stan Burger, 31 October 2019

the American government's decision in December 2015 to list as 'threatened' all lions in South Africa. This automatically banned the importation into America of trophies from captive-bred lions as of October 2016 unless it could be proved that the hunting activity helped the conservation of wild lions. Announcing this decision, the US government said:

> In response to the dramatic decline of lion populations in the wild, the U.S. Fish and Wildlife Service today announced it will list two lion subspecies under the Endangered Species Act (ESA). *Panthera leo leo*, located in India and western and central Africa, will be listed as endangered, and *Panthera leo melanochaita*, located in eastern and southern Africa, will be listed as threatened.[55]

This move was also made in response to intense lobbying by various groups, including the Humane Society of the United States, which trumpeted the fact that most lions hunted in South Africa are slain by people from America.[56]

Expecting all of PHASA's members to fall into line with its principled new policy was always going to be a tall order, however, since many of them had a financial interest to protect. At PHASA's AGM in November 2017, by which point Burger had stood down, another resolution was passed which effectively crushed the measure. The new decree stated, 'PHASA accepts the responsible hunting of ranched lions on SA Predator

---

55   US Fish and Wildlife Service press release, 21 December 2015
56   Humane Society of the United States press release, 21 October 2016

Association-accredited hunting ranches within the relevant legal framework and/or according to recommendations of the applicable hunting association.'

Burger's admirable attempt to restore some credibility to his organisation's stance on lion farming and captive-bred lion hunting was dismantled by this decision to promote the hunting of 'ranched lions'. Allegedly, ranched lions have a chance of evading their hunters whereas a canned hunted lion has no such luck. As mentioned in a previous chapter, ranch-bred lions are also captive-bred, but it is claimed they have been raised with minimal human imprinting compared with lions which have been raised in tourist facilities. Supposedly, this makes them, in effect, semi-wild. Those who sanction ranch hunting also say that while canned hunting does nothing to protect species or habitats, ranch hunting does both. They argue that the biggest threat to wildlife is habitat loss and that if a ranch can make enough revenue from hunting or tourism or sustainable wild products, that habitat will be preserved. If not, usually some other land use will take its place. But this does not alter the fact that PHASA reversed its position to one in which it condoned the idea of killing non-wild lions as long as it was in a 'legal framework'. Some might cite this as an example of PHASA dissembling. After all, something that is considered 'legal' is not always ethical.

For the avoidance of doubt, I believe that killing in a confined area any lion which has been raised in any sort of captive environment should be classed as canned hunting. I have no truck with nuanced arguments about perceived differences between tourism-bred and ranch-bred animals. I believe that trying to compare a 48-hour ranch or canned hunt, which takes place in a confined space (no matter how large), with a truly free-range hunt which takes place in the wilderness over a period of two to three weeks, is like trying to compare apples and oranges.

There was an immediate outcry at PHASA's volte-face among many different hunting groups in South Africa. Stewart Dorrington, who had previously served for three years as PHASA's president, spoke for many when he said, 'We, as a concerned group of professional hunters, distance ourselves completely from such acceptance and no longer view PHASA as the legitimate mouthpiece for professional hunting in South Africa.'[57] Dorrington quit the group and went on to help found Custodians of Professional Hunting and Conservation South Africa along with six other past presidents of PHASA. The African Professional Hunters Association in Tanzania also cut ties with PHASA over its decision to endorse canned hunting, as did the Operators and Professional Hunting Associations of Africa (OPHAA), the Boone and Crockett Club in America, and the Nordic Hunting Club. OPHAA, which has members in nine African countries, released a statement saying, 'PHASA's actions completely disregard one of the fundamental concepts of hunting, namely fair chase, and will, without doubt, jeopardise not only conservation efforts but the livelihoods of those who rely on well-managed and ethical hunting practices far beyond the borders of South Africa.' The motion agreeing to allow the concept of hunting captive lions was defended by SAPA and

---

57 Simon Bloch, 'Canned Lion Hunting Splits Hunters', *The Mercury*, 24 November 2017

the amateur National Confederation of Hunting Associations of South Africa (CHASA), which represents about thirty organisations. As Ian Michler claimed at the time, it seems that these two groups were motivated by little more than pure greed.[58]

Two years after that event, Dorrington says, 'The reversal of the 2015 decision was all about money, and the fight became personal, too, especially for Stan Burger.' Dorrington explains why he, as a long-standing professional hunter, had to divorce himself from any notion that canned hunting and lion breeding is acceptable. He says:

> The expression 'canned' needs to be defined. There is the lasting impression that canned hunting is shooting a tame or drugged animal in a small enclosure, which of course should be condemned and banned. The problem we have with captive-bred lion hunting is that it does not contribute to the conservation of the species in the wild. We believe hunting must have a conservation value and must never be detrimental to a species or a given population. Trophy hunting has a very low environmental impact when done responsibly – much lower than many tourism activities which consume and pollute substantially. PHASA was started to maintain a high level of sportsmanship, ethics and respect for wildlife. The shooting of captive-bred lions does none of that and is the reason why we split away from the old association, which changed its constitution and replaced the word 'ethics' with 'legal'. [They claimed] if it was legal it was OK, despite

---

58   Ibid.

the enormous negative effect it was having on the entire industry. I don't think you will find a single respected hunting association anywhere in the world that accepts [shooting] captive-bred lions as a legitimate form of hunting.[59]

Dorrington remains a doughty defender of hunting per se, however, and for the sake of balance it is important to acknowledge his reasons for this. He says:

All hunting needs to be controlled and done on a sustainable basis, whether it is traditional hunting or trophy hunting. Why is it that the majority of rural folk are fine with hunting and those in the cities, who are far removed from the realities on the ground, are opposed to it? Through history, man has hunted. It's wired into our DNA. But if you have never been brought up in that environment, how will you know? Yet the city folk are consuming the environment and habitats and doing far more damage than controlled hunting has ever done. Just think of the environmental cost of every plate of food you eat. Every aspect of your day has a negative environmental impact. And can you possibly quote me one species that has gone extinct or become endangered because of legal controlled hunting? I can name you many that have been saved by hunters!

It is clear that the hunting profession in South Africa is split into two distinct groups. There are those, like Stewart Dorrington and Stan Burger, who continue to condone the stalking of animals in a 'fair chase' context in the belief that they do so responsibly, and there are others who throw their weight behind the intensive breeding of animals for the sake of profiting from them at every stage of their life and death. This latter group is the rogue element which has infected the hunting industry to such a significant degree that the rest of the profession has felt compelled to challenge it publicly. In January 2018, the US-based hunting group the Dallas Safari Club also rejected canned hunting or indeed any hunting of captive-bred lions. In a statement, it said that 'there is no evidence or scientific research to suggest that captive bred lion hunting contributes to the conservation of wild lion[s]'. It added that it 'is not a practice that is in keeping with [the club's] values of ethical and fair chase hunting'.[60]

This opinion was dismissed by Stephen Palos, chief executive of CHASA, who responded by claiming that captive-bred hunting 'is capitalism at its finest in a society mostly run on socialist values, and is the only way that wildlife is to be encouraged and expanded in our country'.[61] On the surface, Palos's somewhat flippant reaction did the pro-canned hunting lobby little good. In February 2018, Safari Club International (SCI), the highly influential American organisation which is considered the world's largest hunting club, also entered the debate, stating that it, too, opposed canned hunting. 'Considering that the practice of the

---

60   'Dallas Safari Club Position on Captive Bred Hunting', Dallas Safari Club, 11 January 2018

61   'Response to Dallas Safari Club Position on Captive Bred Lion by Stephen Palos', National Confederation of Hunting Associations of South Africa, 13 January 2018

captive breeding of lions for the purpose of hunting has doubtful value to the conservation of lions in the wild ... SCI opposes the hunting of African lions bred in captivity,' it revealed. 'SCI will not accept advertising from any operator for any such hunts, nor will SCI allow operators to sell hunts for lions bred in captivity at the SCI Annual Hunters' Convention.'[62]

Sadly, the SCI's laudable declaration appears to have been hollow. When undercover reporters working for the animal rights group Humane Society International (HSI) attended the following year's annual convention, in 2019, they approached the stall occupied by De Klerk Safaris, the company mentioned in Chapter 1 that hosted the appalling canned hunts filmed by Derek Gobbett in which lions and lionesses were slaughtered in the cruellest way. HSI representatives recorded an individual manning the De Klerk Safaris stall who admitted that the firm buys lions for hunting purposes from breeders and can even 'order' big lions if required. Another stallholder offering hunts at the 2019 SCI convention was Mabula Pro Safaris, one of whose staff told HSI's observer that it is 'the biggest breeder of lions in South Africa' and that some lions are kept for continued breeding rather than shot. Madubula Safaris was also present in 2019. Their staff apparently told the HSI team that they buy lions from a breeder who moves them, after they have been weaned, to a hunting area. And another firm, Serapa Safaris, allegedly showed the HSI observer pictures of what 'top lions' look like versus cheaper lions, said that they could 'definitely get

---

62   'SCI Adopts Policy On Captive Bred Lions', Safari Club International, 2 February 2018

one', and volunteered that lions are bought from a 'sanctuary' and can be pre-baited before being shot if required.

All of this flies in the face of the SCI's 2018 statement suggesting that it wishes to protect lions which have been bred for the purpose of being killed in a canned hunt in South Africa. In February 2020, a member of my team attended the 48th annual SCI convention, held, as usual, in Reno, Nevada, over a period of four days, to see what – if anything – had changed. This event, which generates millions of dollars, is a spectacle in its own right. Almost 900 exhibitors and some 15,000 hunting enthusiasts (nearly as many women as men, it seems) gathered in an exhibition centre in this casino town in the desert to immerse themselves in their passion for hunting bears, birds, fish, antelope and big game – including lions – around the world from North America to South America and from mainland Europe to Africa. Videos of animals, among them elephants, being shot could be seen at stands around the conference hall, which was filled with the work of taxidermists. Attendees could buy guns, knives, field equipment, clothes, jewellery and artwork; they could organise hunting trips; or they could attend seminars with titles such as 'Designing and Building Your Trophy Room' and 'Managing Hunting Stress'. Auctions and awards ceremonies were held each night, honouring some of the most prolific hunters in the world. The 2020 convention was briefly overshadowed by a row over an appearance by the Beach Boys, whose former lead singer Brian Wilson urged fans to boycott their gig at the convention due to his opposition to trophy hunting. The band performed anyway.

Among the hundreds of stallholders present in 2020 were a significant number of representatives from South African hunting businesses offering lion hunts, including the four companies mentioned above which had been exposed by HSI. And once again it appears that SCI's anti-canned hunting message of 2018 had been quietly and conveniently forgotten. De Klerk Safari's 2020 brochure was dotted with pictures of men (and one woman) proudly showing off dead lions they had slain and contained a price list offering blood sport enthusiasts the opportunity to shoot a lioness for $3,000. Shooting a male lion aged two or three was available for $6,000. For each subsequent year of a male lion's life, the price of shooting it on a De Klerk safari increased by $2,000. These relatively low sums are a reflection of the fact that the hunts are short, being held over a period of days rather than weeks, and are almost certainly indicative of the lions being the product of a captive breeding programme as opposed to being wild. Logic dictates as much, given there are only 3,000 wild lions left in South Africa and the cost of shooting a wild lion would be far greater than $3,000 or even $6,000. As such, these captive-bred specimens will be released into contained areas on the De Klerks' fenced property before being shot, which surely counts as a canned hunt. When my representative spoke to one of the De Klerk family in Reno, he even said it would be possible to kill a lion from the back of a 4x4 vehicle if a client was very old. Strictly speaking, this is legal, but it is ethically questionable. Incidentally, another South African firm at the SCI convention, Kwalata Safaris, had a sign on its stand openly offering 'free roaming as well as ranch safaris'. As established above, a ranch safari is just another term for a canned hunt. HSI again sent an undercover team to Reno in 2020 and named in its subsequent report three more South African companies – Bush Africa Safaris, Shaun Keeny Safaris and Quagga Safaris – as vendors which 'offered to sell or broker trophy hunts of captive-bred lions or hunting of lions'.[63] In light of all this, it is extremely difficult not to conclude that SCI's stated aim in 2018 of excluding from its convention those operators which sell hunts for lions bred in captivity was just a public relations exercise. Certainly, it fell far short of what most people expected.

Figures published by South Africa's Environment Department suggest that the US government's ban on the importation into America of trophies from captive-bred lions as of October 2016 has not resulted in a significant decline in the number of American hunters visiting South Africa to take part in blood sports. Indeed, at the 2020 SCI convention in Reno, Dries van Coller, the president of PHASA, gave a lecture titled 'What makes South Africa different?', which my representative also attended. In it, Van Coller revealed that Americans still represent 45 per cent of all foreign hunters in his country, making the USA the principal overseas market which those involved in the hunting industry in South Africa must tap. The number of lions which individual provinces have reported as having been shot in trophy hunts *has* fallen dramatically since 2015, however. Like many statistics of this nature, these should probably be viewed as a trend rather than an exact account of what has

---

63   Humane Society International: https://www.hsi.org/news-media/investigation-safari-club-international-convention-2020/

taken place. For one thing, it seems eminently possible that for public relations reasons there may have been some deliberate under-reporting about the number of lions which have been shot in trophy hunts. Just because an event is not recorded in a logbook does not mean it did not happen.

The data claims that in 2013, 608 lions were killed. A year later, that number rose to 793. In 2015, it dropped to 638. In 2016, it virtually halved to 355. And in 2017, the year for which the most recent statistics are available, 363 lions were supposedly shot. The South African government has also published the average unit price per lion killed. It was reported as having been $22,260 in 2015, $21,200 in 2016 and $10,000 in 2017. These figures take no account of the many unofficial, illegal canned hunts that still occur today. But if they are even close to the truth, the marked drop in the number of lions killed and the lowering in the perceived financial value of those lions certainly points to disruption in the lion hunting market. This can be attributed to the so-called Cecil effect which led to so many hunting organisations turning their backs on canned hunting and the US government imposing its ban on trophy imports. As will become clear, the massive growth in the lion bone trade is almost certainly a factor as well.

According to the South African government, between 2013 and 2017 there were eleven countries from which hunters who pursue game in South Africa were most likely to come. American hunters have consistently topped this league table, although, based on what the statistics say, it is important to point out that most of these hunters were not in South Africa to shoot lions. Equally noteworthy is that Denmark and Norway – two famously liberal countries with populations well below 6 million people – feature so prominently in this table.[64] It is doubly ironic given the popularity among so many Danes and Norwegians of visiting South Africa to take part in lion 'voluntourism' holidays.

	USA	DEN	GER	SPA	CAN	FRA	MEX	SWE	NOR	AUS	UK
2013	4,233	513	211	246	326	201	197	161	193	109	138
2014	3,894	460	300	335	345	177	177	84	155	141	92
2015	4,478	550	250	225	207	160	160	178	131	132	135
2016	3,790	408	263	283	213	140	52	140	107	N/A	124
2017	4,774	427	296	280	249	180	165	163	132	129	124

Attempts are now being made to promote South Africa as a hunting destination in markets not traditionally associated with this activity, such as Pakistan and China. The wealthy citizens of these countries are thought to hold the keys to the continuation of South Africa's canned hunting industry. Indeed, in June 2019, the first ever international hunting show was held over four days in Shanghai. 'The rise of China will be a boon to the hunting industry,' its organisers promised. 'Of the 1.4bn China population, fully 400 million are part of the burgeoning middle class. In 2017, about 130 million Chinese tourists travelled abroad. A growing pastime for many of this voracious travelling class is hunting.'

With such sustained condemnation coming from the hunting lobby, it is a certainty that canned hunting, which began as

---

64   Source: South African Department of the Environment, Forestry and Fisheries statistics

an underground activity in the 1970s and 1980s, is now widely regarded as a pursuit that has morphed into a many-headed monster that should itself be culled. This pastime has spawned industrial-scale lion breeding – a venture in which organisms are robbed of their true identity as wildlife and are instead treated as products created solely in order to be exploited and then killed relatively cheaply and easily. Its negative impact on the image of South Africa is plain to see.

Advocates of canned or captive-bred lion hunting often argue that it aids conservation and has a positive effect on wild lions. The thinking is that the revenue generated by this kind of hunting can help the state to protect the wild population and maintain land. Proponents also maintain that breeding lions in captivity takes the pressure off wild lion populations, while profits are reinvested in conservation efforts. Yet any sense that canned lion hunting acts as a safeguard against the killing of wild lions is dismissed by those who have watched as the breeding and killing of captive lions in South Africa has mushroomed this century. Indeed, the irony is that lion poaching is undoubtedly still prevalent. Just consider the story of a poacher like David Baloyi, a fifty-year-old from Mozambique who crossed the border into South Africa in February 2018 to illegally hunt wild game and was eaten by the pride of lions he was stalking in an attack so vicious that the animals left only his head as evidence.[65]

There are scores of others like Baloyi who take their chances and survive. In October 2019, a pride of lions at the Rietvlei

---

65 Jamie Pyatt, 'Poacher eaten by lions identified', *Daily Mail*, 14 February 2018

Nature Reserve near Pretoria was butchered by poachers in a black magic 'muthi' killing. The four animals were fed poisoned meat and died in agony. Their jaws and paws were then hacked off with machetes to be sold to witch doctors for use in black magic potions. The tragic irony of this case is that these animals had been rescued from a canned lion reserve and a private owner who had kept them illegally. They were not allowed to have any interaction with the public but were instead used by the rangers at the reserve to educate tourists and children about the scandalous exploitation of lions who are subjected to lion petting and 'walking with lions' excursions.[66] 'Muthi' killings are far from rare, incidentally. Linda Park of the non-profit organisation Voice4Lions estimates that about seventy such incidents have been reported in South Africa since 2017. Another recent attack came in January 2020, when sixteen lions were slaughtered by poachers who hacked their faces and paws off to sell for black magic potions. Gert Blom, the owner of the Predators Rock Bush Lodge in Rustenburg, North West Province, found the scene of devastation and realised that the animals – some of which were twenty-four hours from giving birth to cubs – had also been fed poisoned chicken. Witch doctors sell lion-based potions to South Africans who believe the product gives them powers to ward off evil spirits or to bring luck.[67]

The widespread view is that canned hunting is considered responsible for the surge in poaching that has been observed. As is evident, the increase in demand for lion parts like bones has led to an increase in supply. And, as we shall see, wild lions are

---

66   Jamie Pyatt, 'Pride of lions butchered by poachers', MailOnline, 29 October 2019
67   Jamie Pyatt, 'Pure Evil: Vile poachers slaughter 16 lions', *The Sun*, 4 January 2020

also being kidnapped and taken to lion breeding farms in order to rejuvenate bloodlines as a way of tackling the conditions and diseases brought on by rampant inbreeding.

Perhaps surprisingly, there are others who have argued that banning trophy hunting imports, as has happened in America and Australia, undermines efforts to protect lions and other endangered animals. In August 2019, more than 100 conservation scientists and academics from British and South African universities published a letter in the American journal *Science* saying that income from trophy hunting helps to protect the species targeted and that without it land could be developed, which would lead to much greater loss of wildlife. The letter was organised primarily by the Wildlife Conservation Research Unit at the University of Oxford and the International Union for Conservation of Nature. It stated, 'There is compelling evidence that banning trophy hunting would negatively affect conservation. In African trophy hunting countries, more land has been conserved under trophy hunting than under national parks and ending trophy hunting risks land conversion and biodiversity loss.'[68] The signatories also argued that trophy hunting provides income for poor communities that are often based in remote areas and claimed that focusing on trophy hunting distracts attention from the greatest threats to wildlife, such as poaching and habitat loss. It should be mentioned that one of the organisers of the letter, Amy Dickman, a conservation biologist at the University of Oxford, has made clear she finds images of hunters posing beside their kills 'repugnant'. It is also worth

---

68 'Trophy hunting bans imperil biodiversity', *Science*, Volume 365, Issue 6456 (30 August 2019), p. 874

saying that in October 2019, Jeremy Berg, the editor-in-chief of *Science*, admitted that four of the signatories had financial links with hunting bodies including the Russian Mountain Hunters' Club and the Dallas Safari Club. Berg said it was wrong not to have disclosed this potential conflict of interest.

Needless to say, those who oppose trophy hunting responded forcefully to the letter. Ross Harvey, an economist who works with the Conservation Action Trust, made the point in an article in *The Ecologist* magazine that while it may be true to claim, as Ms Dickman and her colleagues did, that trophy hunting can provide income for marginalised and impoverished people, 'the question is whether it *should* provide that income'.[69] This, surely, goes to the heart of the matter. For how long can conservationists rely on economic arguments to support the idea of lions being shot for trophies?

In July 2019, the *Financial Times* delved into this question by asking, 'Which is worth more: trophy hunting or wildlife tourism?' The newspaper noted that 'tourism groups and trophy hunters both claim to encourage conservation by giving animals a financial value', but, it wondered, which activity is worth most? It estimated that $40,000 is about as much as any trophy hunter would realistically pay to kill a wild alpha male. Using figures obtained from the charity LionAid, which calculated that a male in the Serengeti brings Tanzania $890,000 in tourism revenues during five years of pride dominance, the *FT* concluded that the financial value of hunting is overrated. 'We conservatively assumed the country's rising wildlife tourism

---

69   Ross Harvey, 'Trophy hunting is not sustainable', *The Ecologist*, 19 September 2019

revenues plateaued and lions attracted only one-third of these,' it stated. 'Discounted over a twelve-year life, any lion would have a net present value of $179,000. That is still more than four times higher than the price for shooting a pride master. Wildlife tourism and trophy hunting are not always mutually exclusive. When conflicts arise, Africans should kick out the hunters.'[70]

In its 2018 report 'The Economics of Captive Predator Breeding in South Africa', the South African Institute of International Affairs concluded that the continuation of predator breeding using lions and other species could cost South Africa over 54 billion rand (approximately $4.25 billion) over the ensuing decade through loss of tourism. It stated that canned lion hunting, cub petting and 'voluntourism' damage the image of South Africa as a desirable destination. The report's author, Ross Harvey, was damning in his outlook.[71]

Stan Burger agrees with Harvey:

The captive-bred lion and canned industry in South Africa has taken a big knock due to hunters lobbying hunting organisations like Safari Club International, the Dallas Safari Club, the Boone and Crockett Club, the United States Fish and Wildlife Service and many others, all of which have taken a stand against captive-bred lion shooting and canned hunting. The US Fish and Wildlife Service has banned the import of captive-bred lion trophies into the USA, as has Australia and France. This has led to an 80 per cent reduction in the demand

---

70   'Trophy assets: lion prices, dead or alive', *Financial Times*, 6 July 2019
71   Ross Harvey, 'The Economics of Captive Predator Breeding in South Africa' (South African Institute of International Affairs, August 2018)

for captive-bred lion shooting. But ironically these developments have not had the devastating effect on the captive-bred lion industry that we hoped for. The breeders just found new markets in the east and Russia, and a roaring and lucrative trade in lion bones with China and Vietnam perpetuates this nefarious industry. The captive-bred lions are worse off now than ever. There are welfare and cruelty issues and they are being bred and then slaughtered in lion abattoirs for their bones alone. This allows the captive-bred lion industry to continue unabated even though very few are still being shot. This will continue until the government passes legislation to outlaw captive-bred lions or removes the export quota for lion bones altogether. The world must put pressure on the South African government to act against this damaging industry.[72]

As we shall see, the exploitation of captive-bred lions in South Africa does not end when a lion is killed. Even in death they must endure yet more atrocious abuse.

---

72 Interview with Stan Burger, 31 October 2019

CHAPTER 5

THE BONE TRADE

Many people will wonder why the quantity of lion breeding facilities and tourism venues in South Africa is increasing when the number of canned lion hunts taking place in the country does not appear to be growing exponentially. The reason is ultimately attributable to tiger bones.

The skeletons of these beautiful creatures are highly prized in parts of Asia among those who favour so-called traditional medicines. Showing an astonishing level of naivety, some gullible citizens of these states are prepared to pay handsome sums of money for products which purport to contain tiger bone. They do so in the belief that it has properties which are capable of curing conditions including joint pain, arthritis and osteoporosis. Others buy tiger bone products because they think they will give them greater physical strength. And an absurdly high number remain convinced that tiger bone can boost their virility or is suitable to use as an aphrodisiac. This is pure quackery, of course, but its impact has been devastating for the world's dwindling wild tiger population.

As a result of decades of consistent demand, it has become harder to source sufficient supplies of tiger bone. Those involved in South Africa's lion breeding industry have stepped in to plug this gap, supplementing the tiger bone trade over the past decade by cannibalising their own stocks and thereby creating a steady market for lion bones. It is generally accepted that these lion bones are being passed off as tiger bones to unsuspecting buyers rather than holding an intrinsic value in their own right. Nonetheless, research suggests that sales have expanded particularly quickly since late 2016, when the American government harmed the lion industry's cash flow via its suspension of imports of captive-bred lion trophies. One study published in May 2018 surveyed 117 captive-lion facilities registered in South Africa, most of which had previously dealt in live lions. Eighty-two per cent of these businesses reported that the American ban had affected them to some degree, with 30 per cent of the facilities surveyed turning to the lion bone trade to make up the shortfall.[73]

Tiger bones have been used as a 'medicine' in China, the largest animal bone market, for 1,500 years. Despite modern science being able to prove that they are of no physical benefit to humans, their popularity has seemingly never been greater. One of the biggest-selling substances within this mythical health arena is tiger wine. It is produced after a bone is steeped in alcohol – sometimes for a period of years – and then blended with herbs and spices such as sage and ginger. Tiger cake is another popular 'health' substance. It is made with the glutinous residue that rises to the top of a saucepan in which bones

---

73   Vivienne L. Williams and Michael J. 't Sas-Rolfes, 'Born Captive: a survey of the lion breeding, keeping and hunting industries in South Africa', PLoS ONE, Volume 14, Issue (2019)5

have been boiled at a high temperature. As with tiger wine, it is also mixed with herbs, and perhaps other animal bones, before being turned into a bar. Crushed tiger bone powder, which can be converted into pills, is also prevalent. Alongside these bone-based potions and mixtures, tiger body parts including claws, whiskers and teeth are regarded as status symbols in south-east Asia and may be used in jewellery or for other decorative purposes. So many tigers have been butchered since the start of the twentieth century in order to profit from these products that the species is now classed by wildlife groups such as the World Wide Fund for Nature (WWF) as endangered. WWF estimates that over the past century the number of wild tigers has plunged from approximately 100,000 to fewer than 4,000.

In 1993, the Chinese government prohibited all domestic trade in tiger bones when it became obvious that tigers were being pushed to the brink of extinction. Predictably, the country continued to harbour dozens of breeding farms housing thousands of tigers, but in 2007 the Convention on International Trade in Endangered Species of Wild Fauna and Flora (CITES) – an international agreement between 183 governments to set worldwide rules on the sale of wild animals and animal products – imposed a further ban on all tiger farming for commercial purposes. Despite this decree, however, the number of tigers in captivity across Asia has risen to more than 12,500, creating an industry that is strikingly similar in size to South Africa's lion farming business.[74] Through this trade, people who wish to buy tiger bone merchandise continue to do

---

74   Terrence McCoy, 'The harrowing truth about tiger farming in southeast Asia', *The Independent*, 24 May 2019

so on the black market in the border towns of Burma, Laos and Thailand. Yet it is so sought-after that dealers are happy to use lion bones, which masquerade as tiger bones, as well. The two are barely distinguishable to the naked eye.

The wildlife campaigner Karl Ammann estimates that the bones that make up an adult tiger skeleton usually weigh between 15 and 18 kilograms (33–40 lbs) and tend to sell for about $1,000 per kilogram, or approximately $20,000 in total. Ammann's research, carried out over more than two decades, leads him to believe that one skeleton can produce about sixty bars of tiger cake, with each bar being sold for up to $1,000. He says a tiger skeleton is therefore worth up to $60,000 to whoever is prepared to exploit it fully. A lion skeleton sells for considerably less – between $3,000 and $4,000 – so the appeal to both sides is obvious: for the Asian dealers, the initial cash outlay of buying lion bone is markedly lower; for those in South Africa's lion industry, they are selling into a ready-made business.

Not everybody who campaigns on behalf of animals agrees with Ammann's valuations, but even if his figures are on the generous side, it is undeniable that tiger – and, ultimately, lion – products can command very steep prices. Tiger wine, which is sometimes drunk by businessmen who are keen to display their wealth, is as costly as champagne. By way of example, Ammann told me in October 2019:

I have just surveyed a store which is part of the biggest tiger farm in Harbin, China, and there were about a dozen different bottle sizes in elaborate casings and packaging, going from about $80 for a small bottle to about $600 for the bigger ones. There were also more speciality wines, one a penis wine and one a blood wine, which actually seems to have a different consistency liquid at the bottom with the alcohol on top. It kind of depends how fancy and upmarket the packaging is, but maybe they sell from $60 to $200 for a small bottle. This store has a shipping facility attached to it which involves the biggest Chinese courier company. We have also been shown tiger skulls for $16,000 and a very large canine for $6,000.[75]

Until 2007, when the CITES embargo on tiger farming for commercial purposes came into force, lion bones were not considered to be of any particular value to South African breeders. Indeed, they were often disposed of after a canned hunt as a mere by-product. Nowadays, anybody who goes on a lion hunt is likely to have to sign a contract before it begins in which they agree to keep only the animal's head and, perhaps, skin as trophies. The bones belong to the hunting facility, whose owner will be aware of their worth as fake tiger bones. Ammann believes that Asian consumers have no idea they are being doubly duped, firstly because animal bone is of no benefit to human health, and also because buyers are not even obtaining the product they think they are buying. 'They all seem to believe it is tiger bone material, since tiger products are more valuable than lion ones,' he says.

That extends to jewellery, which should not be ignored. Overall, the claws, the teeth and some special bones like the

---

kneecaps can go for thousands of dollars, and the rest of the skeleton can still be used for the wine production. South Africa is today the lead nation when it comes to commodifying wildlife. The policy of 'if it pays it stays' is more pronounced there than anywhere else. A major call for a tourism boycott might be the kind of wake-up call necessary to get to the policymakers.

Incidentally, Ammann has also identified a particularly sick new trend within the bone market known as 'pink bone'. As its name suggests, this bone is distinct through being light red in colour, an effect achieved by deboning the tiger or lion while it is still alive. This technique leaves blood in the bone and the resulting products are therefore held in even higher regard by some of those in Asia who use traditional 'medicine'.

The idea of anybody truly expecting to improve their health or love life by consuming an animal bone is almost laughable until one reflects on the fact that there is nothing remotely amusing about the lion bone trade. Buying bone is as bad as purchasing any Class A substance from a drug dealer. The whole sordid business around lion bones is, seemingly, immersed in corruption at an official level and is intricately entwined with organised crime at street level. Those involved in the production and export of lion bones also smuggle rhino horn, elephant ivory and pangolin scales. The global trade in wildlife parts is worth billions of dollars a year. Indeed, it is considered to be the third most profitable trade on the black market after narcotics and weapons, meaning there is likely to be substantial crossover between all three of these areas. The business even has a

LEFT This drawing of the British explorer and hunter Frederick Selous appeared in 1894. The British were the first to kill animals for pleasure in South Africa, and Selous was one of the most prolific hunters of the Victorian and Edwardian eras. He used a ten-bore muzzleloader to shoot lions.

© Sir Leslie Ward / Royal Geographical Society via Getty Images

BELOW Prince Arthur of Connaught, a British military officer and a grandson of Queen Victoria, served as Governor-General of the Union of South Africa from 1920 to 1924. Like Selous and many of his countrymen, he also enjoyed hunting lions.

© Bettmann / Getty Images

ABOVE British investigative journalist Roger Cook is widely credited with exposing canned lion hunting in South Africa to a mass audience via his 1997 ITV documentary *Making a Killing*. Cook received death threats after it was shown.
Private collection

LEFT Environmental journalist and safari operator Ian Michler was inspired by Roger Cook's film to investigate the lion industry himself. He went on to help make the acclaimed 2015 documentary *Blood Lions*.
Private collection

Cecil the Lion was wounded with an arrow by American dentist Walter Palmer in Zimbabwe in 2015. Between ten and twelve hours later he was tracked and killed. His death sparked international outrage and helped draw attention to the plight of Africa's lions. In 1980, there were about 80,000 wild lions in Africa. Today, there are an estimated 20,000 wild lions, 3,000 of which are in South Africa. There are thought to be 12,000 captive-bred lions in South Africa. © Shutterstock

The petting of lion cubs by tourists is a major plank of South Africa's captive-bred lion industry. They look sweet, but these animals can harbour serious infections and often bite and scratch. Cubs need up to eighteen hours' sleep a day, but their status as tourist magnets means they rarely rest. Badly behaved cubs can be beaten or drugged.

© schusterbauer.com / Shutterstock

So-called 'walking with lions' experiences are also popular and lucrative in many South African tourist facilities despite the obvious risk to human life posed by these predators.

© Stephen Murdoch / Shutterstock

ABOVE In 2015, 29-year-old US citizen Katherine Chappell was mauled to death by a lioness at the Lion and Safari Park near Johannesburg. The business subsequently said it would cease all cub petting activities, but my research suggests they are still on offer there.

LEFT In 2017, professional rugby player Scott Baldwin was bitten by a lion he tried to stroke at the Weltevrede Game Lodge near Bloemfontein. He quickly developed an infection and is considered lucky not to have had his hand amputated.

© Scott Baldwin

American big game enthusiast and serial killer Robert Hansen is said to have stalked and hunted his human victims as though they were wild animals. Some psychologists believe there are close parallels between murderers and canned hunters.

© Anchorage Daily News / Tribune News Service via Getty Images

I have a profound dislike of so-called kill shots, in which people pose for a photo alongside an animal they have recently slaughtered. In 2019, canned hunters Darren and Carolyn Carter from Canada incurred the wrath of thousands worldwide with this provocative – and disturbing – show of triumph.

These distressing images were captured at the Wag-'n-Bietjie farm near Bloemfontein in April 2018. Owned by lion breeder André Steyn, the facility styles itself as an 'eco-farm' that puts 'nature first'. Behind the scenes, fifty-four lions were killed there in two days, and their bodies were stripped for parts.

Private collection

Tourists are lured to Moreson Ranch in the Free State with the promise of cub petting. This was one of ten young animals my team found living in a squalid concrete pound there. Note the chicken feathers on the floor. Most captive-bred lions exist on a very limited diet. Wildlife veterinarian Dr Peter Caldwell says the risk of bacterial infection from the rotting meat they are fed is high.

Private collection

kingpin, dubbed by investigators 'the Pablo Escobar of wildlife trafficking'.[76] He is Vixay Keosavang, originally from Laos, and a figure so notorious that in 2013 the US government placed a bounty of up to $1 million on his head for information leading to the dismantling of the Xaysavang Network, an international wildlife trafficking syndicate with extensive roots in Africa and south-east Asia which he is believed to run. On the strength of all this, it is no exaggeration to say that the contemptible lion bone trade touches violence and evil, and yet some of it is perfectly legal. Moreover, it is actively encouraged.

Since 2008, the South African government has issued thousands of CITES export permits for the body parts of lions, most of which have been sent to China, Laos and Vietnam. Between 2008 and 2011, the average number of annual lion skeleton exports was 314. Between 2013 and 2015, it jumped to 1,312 per year.[77] This surge contributed to fears of over-exploitation and in October 2016, at the 17th CITES conference, held in Johannesburg, it was proposed by conservationist groups that lions should join tigers in being listed in Appendix I of the CITES classification system. This category is reserved for those species considered most endangered among CITES-listed animals and plants, prohibiting any international commercial trade in their parts. Yet, in common with most countries which voted on this measure, South Africa did not support it. A zero annual export quota *was* agreed for the bones, claws and teeth removed from

---

76 Thomas Fuller, 'In Trafficking of Wildlife, Out of Reach of the Law', *New York Times*, 3 March 2013

77 'Guidelines for the Conservation of Lions in Africa', compiled by the IUCN Species Survival Commission Cat Specialist Group for CITES/CMS, p. 56

the carcasses of wild lions to be traded for commercial purposes. But it was decided that all lions – wild and captive-bred – should remain in Appendix II of the CITES ranking, where the lion has been since 1977. Appendix II is for species 'that are not necessarily now threatened with extinction but that may become so unless trade is closely controlled'.

As the country which deals in most of the world's lion parts, it was further agreed that South Africa would establish annual export limits for trade in these parts from its captive breeding operations and report to CITES each year. This diluted decision resulted in the government setting an allowance of 800 lion skeletons leaving the country in 2017, a figure many believe to be arbitrary but which was apparently 'based on an assessment done by the South African National Biodiversity Institute of previous years' trade data (10 years' trade data) (including trade in bones and hunting trophies)'.[78] In 2018, then Environment Minister Edna Molewa raised this number to 1,500 skeletons, claiming that it chimed with the government's policy of sustainable utilisation of natural resources and was supposedly supported by solid scientific evidence. After a public outcry, however, Molewa's highly questionable decision was reversed and the limit of 800 skeletons was restored.

In August 2018, South Africa's lion breeding industry was reviewed by the parliamentary portfolio committee on environmental affairs in a two-day colloquium which was open to the public. This meeting was so well attended that extra seating had to be provided, strongly suggesting that the public's interest in the

---

78   Quoted in Richard Peirce, *Cuddle Me, Kill Me: From Bottle to Bullet – A True Account of South Africa's Captive Lion Industry* (Struik Nature, 2018), p. 196

lion trade is greater than ever. According to the committee chairman, Mohlopi Mapulane, the principal aim of the event – titled 'Captive Lion Breeding for Hunting in South Africa: Harming or Promoting the Conservation Image of the Country' – was to have a constructive debate. To that end, representatives from local and international charities and non-governmental organisations as well as pro-hunting groups were present. They included members of the EMS Foundation, Ban Animal Trading, the Born Free Foundation (UK), Professional Hunters' Association of South Africa, South African Hunters and Game Conservation Association, Custodians of Professional Hunting and Conservation, and the International Council for Game and Wildlife Conservation.

The committee's final report was damning:

Captive breeding of lions for hunting has long been a blemish on South Africa's wildlife and tourism landscape. This tragic story needs to be arrested forthwith to avoid inflicting further and irreparable damage to South Africa's conservation image and the responsible hunting industry that the country has succeeded to build over the years.

It also asserted that captive-lion breeding holds no conservation value, noting:

The revenues which this industry generates, while highly lucrative for the owners, constitute only a tiny proportion of South Africa's tourist revenue that the captive lion breeding industry threatens to undermine. There are public sentiments that that captive bred lion industry is unethical and the lion bone trade is damaging to SA's conservation record, damaging the socio-economic welfare of South Africans, damaging to South African tourism and hence must be stopped immediately by enacting relevant legislation.

The committee called on the Environment Department 'as a matter of urgency to initiate a policy and legislative review of captive breeding of lions for hunting and lion bone trade with a view to putting an end to this practice'.

This sense of outrage was soon reflected by the courts. In August 2019 at the High Court in Pretoria, Judge Jody Kollapen ruled in favour of the NSPCA, which had launched an action against the government regarding the welfare of lions in captivity and how that should affect the setting of an export quota for lion bones.

Judge Kollapen decided it was simply not credible that the Environment Department and its then minister, Edna Molewa, could have ignored the animals' well-being. 'My view is that [Molewa] erred in concluding that since she was not seized with the welfare mandate for lions in captivity, she was not obliged to give consideration to welfare issues relating to lions in captivity when determining the quota,' the judge opined. 'Simply put, if as a country we have decided to engage in trade in lion bone, which appears to be the case for now, then at the very least, our constitutional and legal obligations ... require the consideration of animal welfare issues.'[79]

Kollapen's finding could not reverse the quota process; the court's task was merely to establish the legality of the action. The

---

79   Don Pinnock, 'Court victory for NSPCA over welfare of captive lions', News24, 8 August 2019

court therefore did not halt the export in lion bones. Following this judgment, however, the incumbent Environment Minister, Barbara Creecy, was supposed to introduce a new export quota for 2019. Until she did so, all official bone exports were put on hold. Yet, absurdly, no announcement for the 2019 quota was made during that calendar year. The likely upshot of this indecision about legal exports is that South Africa's illegal bone trade was able to flourish.

Some people believe that those Asians who have bought lion bone legitimately through the official quota system can hardly be vilified for their actions given that South Africa's leaders actively promote this market. Campaigners remain unconvinced, however. After all, the mere existence of a legal lion bone trade offers an opportunity for an illegal market to thrive. Lion breeders and dealers often mount the argument that their industry protects wild lions, but the trade in bone has done the opposite, establishing a market and a demand that has almost certainly already harmed the wild population through poaching and which could in future have major conservation implications. Put another way, a monster has been created and it must be fed at whatever cost, even if that means plundering some of nature's most precious species. The routes are well established: once smuggled out of the country, poached lions end up in the hands of organised crime networks in Vietnam and Laos and then make their way through south-east Asia and into China.

An example of this came in November 2018, when six Vietnamese nationals and two South Africans were arrested in North West Province, about 240 km (150 miles) from the capital, Pretoria, after more than forty lions were slaughtered at a nearby lion farm. A team from South Africa's Directorate for Priority

Crime Investigation also found knives, a saw, gas cylinders and burners – equipment that it is believed the suspected poachers intended to use to process the lion carcasses into a paste which would likely have been sold as a tiger cake. In July 2019, the Vietnamese citizens in the group were ordered to leave South Africa having paid fines ranging from R8,000 to R50,000 ($440 to $2,750). This punishment was described by Fiona Miles of the animal charity Four Paws as a 'mere slap on the wrist'.[80] It is impossible not to agree with her. If the South African justice system fails to mete out proper penalties to gangs of men who visit South Africa in order to slaughter lions and then profit from their carcasses, getting involved in this barbaric trade will only ever be regarded by criminals as a low-risk enterprise and therefore one which they are happy to enter.

Having demonstrated that South Africa has become the centre of the world's captive cat industry, and can lay claim to the shameful boast of being the global chief exporter of lion bones as well, it is worth learning more from those who have had to try to police these squalid, poorly regulated businesses. Just as the mass breeding of lions has encouraged some lamentable spin-off industries to which they are subjected while alive, so the element of the trade concerned with their death has fostered a truly startling environment which should appal everybody who reads about it. If the miserable life cycle of a captive lion begins with the poor creature being torn away from its mother and used as an exotic plaything for tourists and voluntourists, then moves on to walking tours, before it is finally

---

80   'Vietnamese "lion slaughterers" kicked out of SA', News24, 10 July 2019

shot in a canned hunt, the lion bone trade can be regarded as the fourth spoke in this hopeless wheel.

Reinet Meyer has worked for the SPCA in Bloemfontein, in the Free State, for thirty years and has been a senior inspector for twenty years. In April 2018, she received a tip-off that lions were being left in cages for long periods of time at the Wag-'n-Bietjie farm, 32 km (20 miles) outside the city. Owned by lion breeder André Steyn, it calls itself an 'eco-farm' that puts 'nature first'. This description now appears to be closer to a twisted joke than to reality. Ms Meyer's visit to the farm turned out to be the start of a grotesque and macabre chapter in her career that continues to haunt her.

Ms Meyer recalls:

We got a complaint from a member of the public saying there are two lions in very small transport crates which had been there the previous two or three days without food and water. The lions weren't taken out of the crate. We went to investigate. I thought they were dead. They were just lying there and showed no reaction. As we got nearer, they seemed alive but I thought they were sedated. Then we saw they were alive and we asked the owner if we could take them out of the crates because they couldn't move. The moment they got out of the crates they began urinating. Their bladders would have burst if we hadn't got them out. We took a video of it. It was very sad. A lion is clean, like a cat, and it was sad to see immediately they urinated. For me, that was suffering.[81]

---

81 Interview with Reinet Meyer, 5 August 2019

Despite her long experience in the field, even she was not prepared for the scene she encountered shortly afterwards inside an anonymous-looking shed on the property. The building was being used as a lion slaughterhouse. A foreman, Johan van Dyke, was overseeing eight workers who were stripping the skin and flesh from the fresh carcasses of a group of animals. More dead lions, some already skinned and others waiting to be skinned, littered the bloodstained floor. A pile of innards and skeletons lay elsewhere inside, while discarded internal body parts were piled high in overflowing black plastic bags on a trailer outside, creating an overpowering stench that Ms Meyer has found hard to forget.

Ms Meyer goes on:

We walked around on the farm and we saw this guy [van Dyke] and his team of eight people actually slaughter other lions. This was the first time we came across something like that. We didn't know what to do or to expect. They were professionals. They told us they skin the lions and they pack the coat, the bone and the meat of the lions separately. There was a big heap of rotting meat. That day they'd skinned twenty-six lions. We were there for about eight hours. During the day, other farmers came with dead lions, so the farm was actually a point where people can come with their lions to be skinned. Later in the afternoon there came a big lorry with twenty-eight more lions which were alive. I said, 'What is going on now?' and he said, 'They will be skinned tomorrow.' So they wanted them to stay in the transport crates until the next day. I said, 'No, that is unacceptable, you can't do that.' So they were unloaded and the next morning the vet came and darted them and then they were shot and they were skinned.

It is now known that a total of fifty-four lions were killed at Steyn's farm in just two days. Some of them are believed to have been trucked hundreds of miles from a safari park near Johannesburg. After being sedated with tranquilliser darts, they were shot dead with a .22-calibre rifle. It is thought the bullets were fired through the ear and directly into the brain because overseas buyers will not pay for damaged skulls, but this method guarantees a horribly slow and painful death. While this picture of organised slaughter shatters further the myth that lions in South Africa are revered and protected, what is more remarkable is that the workers at Wag-'n-Bietjie are allowed to kill lions. It is one of a series of South Africa's licensed lion slaughterhouses, each of which feeds the demand for lion bones from Asia. Steyn, who is a former council member of the South African Predator Association, gave Ms Meyer unfettered access to Wag-'n-Bietjie. Although the farm appears to have been issued the relevant permits by the Free State, his foreman, Johan van Dyke, now faces animal welfare charges related to the two lions kept in small cages and may face further charges related to the way lions were being killed and the abysmal condition of the abattoir. The farm's permits have now been revoked, and the fate of its remaining 246 lions will be decided when the court case is over.

Ms Meyer adds that she and her staff subsequently faced threats and intimidation for the action they took, but with impressive resolve she refuses to bow to this danger of her job. 'People did threaten us, but it's fine,' she says coolly.

We have all the evidence and I'm not the only witness that saw it, so if they want to do something to me, there are others who know about it also, so it's not going to disappear. It's not nice, but that is life. We will always be on the lookout.

Karen Trendler managed the Wildlife Trade and Trafficking portfolio for the NSPCA until October 2019 and was interviewed for this book while still in post. She has faced some equally unsettling experiences during her career, encountering corruption and serious welfare issues when conducting farm inspections. She says that many lions killed for their bones die in pop-up abattoirs whose operators pack up and move on before anybody even knows they were there. 'There's no doubt this problem is worse than it was five years ago,' she says.

The illegal wildlife trade has grown exponentially since 2015. What for us has been a huge challenge is that South Africa has a very strong policy of sustainable utilisation, which is a brilliant conservation principle. I mean, water and soil and air – you have to use them sustainably and there may be an element of consumptive use. But it's gone from being a conservation function to being 'If you make money from wildlife it's OK, it's sustainable.'

She goes on:

Having been trained both on the legal side and on welfare, our inspectors are authorised in terms of the Animal Protection Act, a national act, and it's a criminal offence to contravene it. Once you are an authorised inspector you have the same powers as a police officer in terms of the Animal Protection Act. So we can't enforce other acts, but we have the right to go onto property, the right to investigate with a warrant, the right to get a warrant. We used to just be able to go onto a property.[82]

Trendler says there are 'definite incidents' of collusion between law enforcement and breeders. She adds, 'The lion breeding industry is one of the most powerful. They have a huge amount of money. When we say corruption, it's not just a theory. It's there.'

She describes a typical visit to a property where NSPCA employees carry out an inspection.

The NSPCA will go onto a farm and one of the first questions asked on an inspection is: 'Do you have permits?' The NSPCA can't enforce whether they have permits or not. But if the NSPCA becomes aware of illegal issues, including no permits, it is passed on to the authorities. There is a mixed response, from good cooperation to outright opposition and obstruction. National government sets policy, but permits are issued at a provincial level, with massive variation on permit conditions and requirements from province to province and little to no concern for welfare.

Ms Trendler says she first became aware of the bone trade about ten years ago.

---

82   Interview with Karen Trendler, 8 August 2019

At this point, the bones were a by-product of the hunting industry. With global opposition to trophy hunting and the hunting of captive-bred lions, the hunting of 'farmed' lions decreased and there was a swing from lion bone as a by-product to bone as the primary product. Lions were being bred purely for bone or cycled through the petting process and then passed on for bone and product. For a trophy, the hunter wants a lion that is in reasonably good condition, requiring better levels of captive care. For bone and product, the condition and appearance of the lion are not important, and the NSPCA saw a dramatic decrease in welfare standards and increased cruelty.

There are no regulations for the slaughter of lions for bone. Compare this to formal farming processes, where there has been research, guidelines, regulations and controls. As an NSPCA inspector, you are trained intensively and practically in all of these aspects, including what is considered 'humane' slaughter. So an inspector knows what to look for. [In the regulated animal trade] we go into an abattoir and know exactly how long that animal has to stand before it comes off the truck; how long and exactly what the conditions are for it to be moved in the slaughter area. The inspector can tell you all the scientific reasons relating to where best to stun the animal; how to check it for consciousness; how long you've got between stun and slaughter; where you have to cut; what are the conditions. For infringements of that, there's legislation, committees, policies that inspectors can immediately address. You say, 'This happened at this abattoir' and the guys jump. With lion bone, there's nothing. With the slaughter of lion, there is nothing guiding or regulating it. The level of cruelty is unbelievable. In some cases, the lions are shot through the ear with a soft-nosed small-calibre weapon so it doesn't damage the skull. There is a higher value for undamaged skulls. Sometimes vets are called in to drug the animal and then it can be shot. But many vets do not want to be associated with this. Vet services are costly and lion breeders are unwilling to carry this additional cost. So from the NSPCA's point of view, we're saying there are incredible levels of cruelty and there's no conservation value to it. It's just trade. For us, there is no justifiable reason. It's not an essential product. It's not feeding people. As a welfare organisation, we can't accept this.

And its not just lions. Tigers are being bred and slaughtered for bone on these farms too. It's a very hidden industry, fiercely protected. There are areas where you can farm and slaughter lions and nobody will ever know. On some farms, the lions and cubs in the front or public area are in beautiful condition, but it's what goes on behind the scenes.

And there is no rationale behind it. Bones are not just exported as bone, they are processed locally to produce tiger cake or lion cake, which is easy to get out. It looks like a bar of soap. You can put it in your luggage or your pocket and nobody checks. It's very underground but we suspect that when they have these pop-up abattoirs it's not just the bones they're processing. This is a huge industry with what could be up to 11,000 lions being farmed in captivity. It's a dynamic population with new cubs coming in and lions constantly going out through hunting, bone production and some live exports. Some of the bones come from old carcasses that are being dug up and others from stores. With a skeleton export quota of 800 per year, the maths isn't adding up.

Another senior NSPCA inspector with a recent horror story involving the neglect of and cruelty towards lions is Doug Wolhuter. In May 2019, he was among a group of colleagues who found more than 100 lions and other animals in a diseased, overcrowded and, in some cases, near-death condition in a captive breeding facility in North West Province. As with Reinet Meyer at the Wag-'n-Bietjie farm, an anonymous tip sparked the inspection at Pienika Farm. There, Wolhuter and his colleagues counted twenty-seven lions suffering with chronic mange, a skin disease caused by parasitic mites, which was so severe the animals had lost almost all of their fur. They were held in filthy, overcrowded enclosures with more than thirty lions in spaces meant for two animals. At least three cubs were suffering from a neurological condition called meningoencephalitis, an inflammation of the brain, which left them unable to walk. One was subsequently euthanised by a vet at the facility.

In July 2019, the NSPCA undertook a follow-up inspection at the same farm. This time, the inspectors obtained a warrant and found minimal improvement of the conditions there. A dead lion cub was being stored in a cold room, and two more cubs were concealed in a crate in a warehouse showing similar symptoms of brain disease to the two cubs that were removed in April. They were euthanised by a vet. Then, on further examination, the NSPCA found a chest freezer with approximately twenty lion and tiger carcasses of varying ages. Inspectors removed a further five carcasses for post-mortem examinations to determine the cause of death. Animal welfare charges were brought.

Wolhuter says:

This was one of the most striking cases for me. But we're [often] seeing overcrowding, inadequate drainage, poor diet, poor shelter, no protection from the elements, lack of vet care. If you take any basic welfare concern, we're finding animal welfare contraventions at these farms. There may be the odd exception, but there's probably over 400 facilities across the country, so to get a unit to every one of them is a challenge. But we're pretty sure that what we're seeing is the application of the 80:20 rule: 80 per cent of them are going to have the same issues. You've got breeding facilities which are not open to the public and those are the ones where you can in all likelihood expect more concerns because nobody's there to report on it. So we have to rely on insiders or someone happening upon the farm. We get most of our information ourselves. We also rely on other NGOs. And we pick up stuff on our routine inspections. We send staff on a two-week trip and they visit whatever facility is on our database and they look for more on that same trail.

The predator industry is growing at such a rate. Like in North West Province, you saw 20 per cent growth of predator facilities in two years. Guys are getting into [lion breeding and trading] for money. It's two particular provinces that are really going full tilt at it, North West and Free State. You have to ask: why are these two provinces growing at such a rapid rate? The answer is lack of regulation. That's where our fight must continue with the provincial government.

We went out on a joint inspection with [inspectors from] the North West Province to a few facilities. All they're interested in is the length and breadth of the cage and then they check how many lions are on the farm. Our inspections are far deeper. We'll check on diet, welfare, health, treatment. Where they spend possibly half an hour on a facility inspection, we spend three or four hours at least. We've got fantastic checklists. The checklists have a scientific basis. If we point out a permit has expired, they might just say, 'Well it can be renewed.' If your permit has expired, there should be huge consequences. These are threatened or protected species. If you can't look after these animals, they should be removed from you.[83]

Wolhuter says that a particular problem for NSPCA inspectors is the perceived reluctance of the national Environment Department to cooperate. The NSPCA has access to a database of predator facilities but, crucially, it has no addresses or GPS coordinates, just the name of each farm. 'I don't know why they aren't giving us the addresses,' he says in obvious frustration.

You'll get a province and a region, but there's a lot of land here, a lot of farms aren't signposted, so you could drive straight past it. They know the address themselves because they go and inspect. It feels, to an insider, like active obstruction. What further aggravates us is when the local departments go

83   Interview with Doug Wolhuter, 9 August 2019

and do an inspection on the permits and do the lion count, they'll phone the farmer a day or two before and say, 'I'm coming tomorrow at 2 p.m.' Are you honestly going to find many issues if you give forewarning?

Our mandate stops at the welfare stage. We could broaden it and say it includes the permit, which I think it does because if you have too many lions on your farm you're still getting permits, but who's enabling the cruelty? The answer is the farmer and the provincial government, because they're allowing that to happen. If at the inspection you've got too many lions in the facility, why aren't they taking any action in terms of their mandate? We've already started to discuss this by pointing out they're enabling cruelty through not maintaining their standard in terms of their legislation. We do know of facilities with 500 lions. We also know of farmers splitting their facilities so they don't have masses of lions on one farm. So you've got two different farms registered to the same owner, but they split the camps. Divide and conquer. This makes it harder for the provincial government to monitor, as well. It's tough to monitor the movement of the lions. And the nature of the beast makes it an aggressive encounter almost every time. It's very confrontational out there. People don't want us on their farms for whatever reason. Before every encounter you've pretty much got your heart in your mouth. But it all changes because even when you are physically obstructed, you know you are going in. Your mindset changes. It doesn't matter how aggressive they are, but if they want to continue to farm or breed with captive predators, then they will need to ultimately work with us, not against us.

My passion is to stop this abhorrent cruelty in the wildlife industry. In the wildlife industry there are no moral standards, no welfare being considered. That's got to change. If you're going to farm wildlife, you've got to have the practices and standards in place for welfare. I doubt we'll ever persuade the government to close the industry, but they have to consider the welfare. They must make sure if you go on a farm with wildlife you have adequate welfare standards, and that's a part of our function – to make sure it happens. I've been threatened. People telling me they're going to sue me, and recently death threats. It comes with the territory. We're lucky at the NSPCA. They make sure we're protected. We also don't say things out of turn. We don't mention names.

In a further disturbing twist, some campaigners fear that increasing numbers of lions are being cross-bred with tigers to produce so-called ligers, the offspring of a male lion and a tigress; or, less usually, 'tigons', where the father is a tiger and the mother is a lioness. With their squashed faces and abnormally large bodies, ligers can grow to be far bigger than their progenitors. In 1995, what was at the time believed to be the world's last liger, Tokkelos, was put down at the municipal zoo in Bloemfontein after developing cancer. (Some might say that the animal was lucky to have survived so long given that a decade previously it mauled a zoo employee to death.) After it was destroyed, zoo curator Sarel van der Merwe said that the zoo had no plans to breed more ligers because they are 'freaks of nature'.[84]

---

84   'World's last lion-tiger cross put down', Agence France-Presse, 27 November 1995

Yet in 21st-century South Africa, these cross-breeds are back in favour among those involved in the bone industry, and it is easy to see why. According to the *Guinness Book of World Records*, the largest known example of a liger, called Hercules, was bred in America and in 2013 was recorded as being 11 feet long, 4 feet tall and 922 lbs (418 kg) in weight. A three-year-old liger can be the same size as a nine-year-old lion. Its accelerated growth means it produces more bone more quickly. Once it has been slaughtered, it generates greater profits. (By contrast, tigons are usually smaller than either lions or tigers.) Is this type of unnatural breeding the reason why, in August 2019, there were three tigers each to be found at Ukutula Lodge and Moreson Ranch, as noted in Chapter 2?

Aside from the highly contentious ethical questions surrounding hybrids, there are undoubted concerns about the general health of every big cat that is bred for South Africa's bone trade. For the fact is that their physical appearance is of no concern to breeders. Animals which are bred for the hunting trade must be aesthetically pleasing. The only purpose of creatures produced for the bone trade is to deliver bone. Bodily defects, the result of rampant inbreeding, are not unusual and do not matter. Neither, apparently, does the threat of potentially fatal diseases which could be passed from lions to human beings.

Dr Peter Caldwell, the wildlife veterinary surgeon who in Chapter 2 raised serious concerns about the poor diet of captive-bred lions, believes that a major health incident will occur in Asia as a result of its people's rampant consumption of lion bones. (Indeed, shortly after Dr Caldwell gave an interview for this book, reports surfaced that a new disease called Covid-19 had broken out in China, a catastrophe that is addressed in more detail in the conclusion.) Dr Caldwell says:

> I feel that in the next ten years we're going to have a huge health crisis in the East. Five years ago I speculated that if it's not tuberculosis it's going to be brucellosis or one of those diseases that can easily be transferred from animals to human beings. Bacterias like clostridium, which produce toxins like botulism. Botulism is common in captive lions because of poor hygiene, where nobody's clearing up meat and old bones that have been fed to the lions. Clostridium botulinum is a bacteria that produces spores and toxin and it can grow in that dead flesh and bone. The lions go and chew on those bones, they get the toxin, and that can paralyse them. If that lion dies from botulism, the people who bred it won't waste that animal by burying it or burning it. Instead, they will put it into the lion bone and lion skin trade. And the toxin remains in the body of that lion that died from botulism, so the people who utilise or exploit that lion can die a miserable, painful death. Botulism is a disease that's prevalent in captive lions, especially in the facilities where the hygiene is not good and they don't clean the old bones out regularly. And this is just one example of a disease these lions get that can be passed to human beings. There are others.[85]

Indeed there are. Infectious diseases, notably tuberculosis, both in lions during their lifetime and in their bones after they have

---

85   Interview with Dr Peter Caldwell, 10 December 2019

been killed, also pose a threat. The lack of publicised TB cases in the lion industry might be used as a defence by those who operate in it, but because TB testing in captive-bred lions is not routine, experts believe that this under-examined issue presents myriad potential problems for humans as well as animals. The point is that nobody can prove that there *isn't* TB in the lion business, meaning that the precautionary principle has to apply. Karen Trendler says:

> With the poor conditions in the captive facilities, and the lack of veterinary attention, we don't know what the incidence of TB and other diseases in captive lions is. TB can possibly be transmitted to humans. So there's a very big public health issue that hasn't been looked at. Tapeworm can also be a problem. When I started in rescue and rehab, we wouldn't handle a lion that we didn't know unless we were wearing gloves. The Echinococcus tapeworm eggs stick to the fur and can transfer to your hands, from where they migrate through the skin and into the body, going through their life cycle and finally encapsulating into hydatid cysts. These can lodge in the brain or lungs. This is not alarmist. It's a very real risk. The worse the conditions of those animals, the poorer their immunity, the greater the parasite load.

Professor Paul van Helden of the University of Stellenbosch is an authority on animal TB. He says:

> I think there is a possibility of risk but it's probably quite small. Almost any mammal can get bovine TB, certainly, and

there's evidence that even human TB can affect a variety of mammals. There are two main pathogenic organisms which will cause TB in humans and animals: bovine TB (M bovis) and the human form (M tuberculosis). Either of them can be found in most mammals and certainly they can get into the bones. I have personally seen degraded lion bones which show that TB has been into the bones of lions. Those are wild lions that come out of a known area where there's lots of TB. So there's no doubt that TB can get into the bones of lions. Whether that's likely to happen in a farm situation is hard to say because nobody is looking or checking.

Diagnosing TB in lions is not easy, even when you have the cooperation of the landowner. I generally only work in the conservation areas with wild lions. If TB should get into the lions, either via infected animal foodstuff or from humans close by, there is a possibility it could get into the bones of farmed lions. Whether that poses a risk to humans depends on how those bones are processed and how long it takes for the bone to get from the lion to the consumer. We have no idea how long the organism could survive in the bone under the different conditions of processing and travel. If those bones are boiled, for example, you can be almost 100 per cent guaranteed organisms will be dead and so there won't be a risk. If they are taken, let's say, fresh and wet and passed on to the consumer, then the risk is high if that animal has TB. But if they are dried or boiled or treated with some agent that might kill the organism, the risk will be small. So it all depends on the conditions under which the bone is harvested, processed and moved on and on the time that elapses. I can't say there's a 1 per cent risk or a 10 per cent risk. I would never say there's no risk, but I think the risk is fairly small.

One should also realise that these animals are not only infected with TB. They are infected with other organisms and parasites as well. For example, you should never touch a wild lion with your bare hands if, for example, it has been shot or darted. You can pick up very nasty parasites from lion fur, some of which can kill. One has to be very, very careful with any wild animal product just as a general matter of principle. The risk in the case of an animal born in a zoo or something like that is obviously going to be much lower, but it depends on the conditions. Also, there's always a risk that an animal that's in contact with humans will pick up human diseases, including TB. There are numerous examples of elephants in Thailand, through Africa and in the USA which have picked up TB from humans. And they aren't in contact with the public per se, they're just close enough to the public. A TB sufferer would come along, cough, and the elephant would breathe it in and get TB. You could argue that should that happen to an animal that's being petted, and should that animal exhale or cough, the possibility is there that humans could pick that up. It's small, but it cannot be ruled out.[86]

Given this known risk of TB in lions, it follows that workers at South Africa's lion slaughterhouses are being exposed to it and so, by extension, is anybody with whom they come into contact. This means that their fundamental rights to a stable working

---

86   Interview with Professor Paul van Helden, 12 November 2019

environment are being put in jeopardy. Yet the South African government has done little, if anything, to address this basic welfare issue. And of course there are two glaring ironies at the heart of this problem. Firstly, it is utterly perverse that a demand for 'medicine' in Asia might actually be responsible for creating a health crisis in the African country which provides these alleged tonics. Second, it is paradoxical that those Asians who buy lion bone products for the purpose of what they perceive to be health benefits might actually be exposing themselves to disease.

At this point, attention must turn to the Switzerland-based organisation which oversees regulation of the bone trade, CITES. Its secretariat consists of thirty-eight employees but it appears to be a poorly funded regulator, relying solely on contributions to its trust fund from its 183 members, which should total $6.2 million per year. In fact, some members do not bother making a payment at all, meaning that its financial firepower is even weaker than it ought to be.

According to CITES rules, applications to export bones from South Africa are supposed to be logged with its provincial authorities. The bones are then meant to be weighed, tagged and have DNA samples taken to confirm an animal's provenance. In principle, these measures ought to go some way towards guaranteeing that the system operates fairly and responsibly. Yet those who oppose the trade believe that substantially more than 800 lion skeletons leave South Africa each year. Often, this is achieved through fraud, simply by under-declaring the number or weight of bones which are to be shipped or freighted by air. One study carried out by the EMS Foundation and Ban Animal Trading suggests that this deception, possibly carried out in conjunction with corrupt officials, is widespread.[87] CITES does keep a publicly available trade database from which anybody with access to the internet can locate a spreadsheet showing import and export ratios of animal parts. The trouble is that this system appears to be inefficient to the point of being almost worthless.

The database was developed and is maintained and funded by UNEP-WCMC on behalf of the CITES secretariat. UNEP-WCMC is the UN Environment Programme World Conservation Monitoring Centre, based in Cambridge in the UK. This organisation claims to be a 'world leader in biodiversity knowledge' and works with scientists and policymakers globally 'to place biodiversity at the heart of environment and development decision-making to enable enlightened choices for people and the planet'. It is not difficult to identify several major structural problems within it, however, and it is widely regarded as being in urgent need of reform.

Firstly, CITES stipulates that all parties have to submit permit data only once a year. This is almost certainly a legacy of CITES having been established in the early 1970s, before the prevalence of computers. Surely, in the digital age, it could be logged more frequently.

Second, the quality of the data in the database is poor. Most permits are issued manually, on paper or on old computer systems that do not reflect CITES listings and rules. (Incidentally, these permits are cheap, costing as little as $2 each.) Data collection is often incomplete, and submissions can be years late. In addition, permit data only reflects the *intended* quantity

---

87 'The Extinction Business: South Africa's "Lion" Bone Trade', (EMS Foundation and Ban Animal Trading, July 2018), pp. 40–41

of bones for export, not the actual quantity. Customs officials should record the quantities of any product being imported or exported, but these numbers do not make it into the CITES trade database. This means that the number of bones or bone products which are logged as having been exported from South Africa often does not tally with the number of imports reported by the country to which they have been shipped or flown. This mismatch is partially explained by the antiquated operating system, but fundamentally this is a flaw in the convention rather than being the fault of the secretariat. This can be posited because parties are only 'encouraged' to collect import data for Appendix II species like lions, and only some countries, such as America, mandate import permits for Appendix II species. As most countries do not require import licences, there is no robust checking system in place.

A third major deficiency is that the CITES trade database classifies bones under at least five different categories: bone carvings, bone pieces, bone products, skulls and skeletons. It is not clear what, if any, training South African officials in charge of overseeing bone export permits have in determining the body parts of a lion, but this lack of uniformity has created a system which is undoubtedly convoluted and seems to rely on the idea that the exporter is being truthful about the volume of bone they are taking out of the country. Furthermore, it is possible to export bones by claiming they are being used for scientific purposes, even if this is false.

Dr Pieter Kat, a geneticist and wildlife campaigner who now runs the UK-based charity LionAid with his partner Christine Macsween, is damning about the CITES arrangements. He says:

This database is a complete mess. South Africa exports stuff without any export permit numbers. So if you go down the various import and export columns, you will find South Africa say they exported two lion skeletons, for example, but the country to which those skeletons are imported – let's say Vietnam – will say that six have been imported. And that is the complete nonsense that is CITES. It exists supposedly so that interested people can see all the information – that's what CITES is supposed to do. It should enable us to extract that information and say, 'This is too high or too low,' and get a reasonable understanding of the amount of anything – lion bones, elephant tusks or whatever – that are being traded internationally. But the CITES trade database is so horrendous and so bad that we cannot get this. All we're doing is guesswork. If the organisation that is supposed to monitor international trade in wildlife and animal parts can't even keep their records properly, what hope is there?[88]

Indeed, it is clear that governments and perhaps even many conservationists take false comfort from the mere existence of the CITES trade database. But how many of them have studied it to the same degree as Dr Kat? He says:

People who have tried to make sense of this just don't know what to say, because you can't make sense of it. The minimum requirement is that any country exporting any wildlife products of species that are listed on CITES has to fill out an export permit. That's how they get their CITES licences for all this kind of stuff. Once that lion bone arrives in France or Germany or the US, the customs there are supposed to check that the bone has an export permit and then send the forms accompanying that bone to the local CITES office, confirming that the particular item for which the licence was granted has now been imported. An import permit is only issued for very few species. An import permit is not usually required. An export permit is usually all that is required. So this is clearly a failing of South Africa as the export country.

Furthermore, Dr Kat says that he has in the past argued with European Union and CITES officials, having found that the database claimed that lots of 'wild' lion trophies were being exported from South Africa. He says:

> I explained they don't hunt wild lions in South Africa. Most wild lions are in parks and reserves and you can't hunt them. Yet well over 200 supposedly wild lions were exported to the EU one year. So the EU went back to South Africa, said this isn't possible, and South Africa apologised and just amended all the records to say that the lions were captive-bred. It is ridiculous.

It is also depressingly clear that there is no incentive for CITES to do any better. It has no rival and it is not held to account by an independent body. This means it faces no pressure or financial penalty if it is found to have logged bogus information. As Dr Kat says, 'There's no forfeit for South Africa as the exporter, or CITES as the record keeper, to pay for this slipshod state of affairs. No entity can remonstrate with them. Nobody's even looking at it. As long as there's a piece of paper, nobody cares what it says.'

Dr Kat is not alone in finding fault in the CITES trade database. Representatives from two Australia-based animal rights organisations, Nature Needs More and For the Love of Wildlife, say:

We have been assured by world-leading experts in trade analytics that the CITES trade database is the worst-designed and most impenetrable data source they have ever come across. They explicitly stated that 'they would have given up trying to use the database within five minutes of looking at the CITES trade database without our help', it is so bad. They also stated that they agreed that as a first step to fixing the issues an electronic permit system would need to be adopted by all parties.[89]

It is worth remembering that this haphazard system applies to the legal bone trade. The illegal trade, which appears to be flourishing, is being given an even easier time. The fear must surely be that the appetite for lion bones will lead to them being poached in the wild increasingly, just as rhinos have been hunted intensively in recent years.

Before the aforementioned August 2018 colloquium began, its chairman Mohlopi Mapulane insisted that the conclusions it reached would be 'followed up ... with the sheer tenacity of a hungry lion chasing its prey'. Regrettably, however, these inspiring words soon lost their power. In October 2019, the Environment Minister, Barbara Creecy, *did* appoint a 25-strong

---

89   Interview with Nature Needs More and For the Love of Wildlife, 10 December
     2019

committee, also known as a High-Level Panel, which was concerned with the welfare of lions. Yet it was also tasked with investigating issues relevant to three other species: elephants, leopards and rhinos. This meant that the badly needed exclusive focus on lions was jettisoned.

What's more, the panel's terms of reference were weaker than many had hoped. While Mr Mapulane had talked of 'putting an end' to lion hunting and the lion bone trade, the new inquiry guaranteed only to 'review policies, legislation and practices'. Added to this, there is a strong suspicion that the panel's composition appears to be skewed in favour of those who would like captive-lion breeding for the purposes of trophy hunting and the bone trade to continue. Certainly, the panel's chairman, Mavuso Msimang, is thought to be in favour of the sustainable utilisation policy which has been so badly abused and upon which the lion industry seems to rely. (More positively, it is worth adding that Mr Msimang does have a strong record as an anti-corruption campaigner, however.)

Yet given the parliamentary portfolio committee's robust conclusions, many will question why the South African government decided to convene this new panel and risk opening up what could be viewed as yet another talking shop. Why procrastinate instead of taking action? One group consisting of twenty-four environmental NGOs thought it knew the answer. In November 2019, it sent a letter to the director-general of the Environment Department, Nosipho Ngcaba, suggesting that many on the panel were unlikely to back the idea of ending the commercial exploitation of lions. Having scrutinised the track record and qualifications of each panel member, this group deduced that fourteen members appeared likely either to support hunting or trade in species or body parts or to be apathetic towards the South African constitution's emphasis on ecological sustainability. Six members were found to back non-consumptive use. Just eight members were deemed to have the required scientific qualifications, while thirteen were considered to have no skills in the matters on which they will pass judgement. The views of five members could not be ascertained, 'which is in itself cause for concern', said the NGOs.[90]

The twenty-five individuals who comprise the High Level Panel were nominated by the public and, once cleared at government level, subjected to assessments and security checks. At the time of writing, it seems distinctly possible that this panel will sit for many months. It will be fascinating to see how effectively it is able to tackle the 'sustainable use' question, which, through featuring in South Africa's constitution, is widely considered to be one of the biggest impediments to halting the truly wicked exploitation of lions. Whatever conclusions it reaches, and putting every argument to one side, I believe that the truth about this matter is in the final analysis simple: those who object to any element of South Africa's lion industry do so on moral, ethical and welfare grounds. Those who argue in favour of having a lion industry in South Africa do so exclusively for financial reasons.

---

90 Don Pinnock, 'New "expert" panel may be weighted to duck Parliament's call to shut down canned hunting', Daily Maverick, 25 November 2019

PART II

CHAPTER 6

OPERATION SIMBA

I cannot abide those who are cruel to animals, but the sad fact is that in the digital age my strong aversion is aroused all too often. I have lost count of the number of people who post on social media platforms such as Twitter so-called kill shots of themselves grinning at the camera (or, even worse, kissing their partner) alongside a beautiful animal which they have recently slaughtered. Revelling publicly in the death of a creature in this way is completely alien to me. Frankly, I find it alarming on many different levels, to say nothing of repulsive.

I know I am not alone in holding this opinion. For example, in October 2017, I myself put out a tweet of a photograph showing a middle-aged man – who is unknown to me – posing idiotically by a dead giraffe. This photograph, which was in the public domain, is a classic of the hateful 'kill-shot' genre. The man's left foot is raised triumphantly so that it sits on top of the giraffe's neck, presumably bolstering the notion that he has somehow 'conquered' this tragic beast. He holds a rifle in his left hand, and with his right hand makes a thumbs-up sign. Whoever this person is, he should be sorely ashamed of himself.

Posting his awful photograph in my own tweet, I wrote:

'Please retweet if you believe I'm right in despising people who have fun doing this…' I did not have to wait long to see some results. My message was retweeted 59,000 times and it secured 5.5 million impressions, meaning it was seen that number of times by people on Twitter. As I said, I know I am not the only one who finds 'kill-shots' abhorrent.

This background helps to explain how I became involved in campaigning to end South Africa's repellent lion industry. As outlined in the Introduction, I decided to use a visit I made to South Africa to make some enquiries about lion trophy hunting and canned lion hunting. Once I realised just how miserable the entire life cycle of a captive-bred lion is, I knew that I had to act. From birth to death, and beyond, they are sitting targets whether the individual pursuing them wishes to dote on them or destroy them. Many people, it seems, want a piece of a lion and they do not care how they get it.

After that visit, I found myself unable to forget the distressing things I had been told, and I resolved to do whatever I could to confront the scandal of lion farming. It was as a result of this personal pledge that I decided to set up an undercover operation in South Africa with the aim of revealing more of this sordid business to the world. Little did I realise when it began that it would end with me saving a lion from certain death. We called him Simba.

I first learned of Simba after an investigator working on my behalf posed as the representative of a wealthy American client who wanted to hunt and kill a lion. The investigator approached Mugaba Safaris, a firm owned and managed by a professional hunter called Patrick de Beer. At that time, he was described on his company's website as having grown up 'in a safari fraternity' and was presented as a man who 'boasts unmatchable African bow and rifle hunting experience'. Dreaded 'kill-shot' photographs on the site showed him holding up a huge dead leopard and straddling a dead male lion. Far from appearing macho, some people might call this type of display pathetic and vulgar. You will not be surprised to hear that I would be among them.

My investigator was emailed a brochure with photographs of sixteen male lions, each with its own price tag ranging from $13,000 to $26,000, depending on the quality of its mane. He settled on Simba, a male aged about nine with a superb thatch of coarse hair on the crest of his neck and a scar running beneath one of his piercing yellow eyes. It is likely that he came from a lion farm before entering a breeding programme to produce more cubs. De Beer, who is known as 'The Lion Man', described Simba in a WhatsApp message as a 'very good cat with a dense mane'. He added, 'I am sure the client will be very pleased with his cat.'

The pair agreed a price tag of $23,000 for the hunter to shoot Simba, with half of the money to be paid in advance as a deposit and the balance to be produced in cash on arrival in South Africa. My investigator repeatedly asked to see Simba before the hunt in a bid to view the conditions in which he was being kept. He was rebuffed by De Beer, however, who wrote of his reluctance to show visitors captive lions in their enclosures. 'You have to understand that due to the sensitive nature of lion hunting all over the world we are hesitant to take people around showing then [sic] lions behind fences,' he said in another WhatsApp message. 'It just takes the authenticity out of the hunt.' As an alternative, he offered to send my investigator 'as many pictures and videos as [he] wants of the lion'. He added, 'We will photograph specific scars identifiable on the cat from various parts of the body to eliminate doubt. We guarantee the cat that he'll shoot is the cat as per the pictures sent to you.'

De Beer did indeed then send a series of pictures of Simba, including close-ups of his face, to illustrate the creature's identifiable scars and markings. 'There are many distinctive features of which the spots on the nose is [*sic*] the lion's fingerprints … it works the same as a human's fingerprints,' he wrote. 'Each lion is unique. Other features are the scars on the face (note 2x black spots next to the left eye) and the tufts of belly hair. Also a scar next to [the] nose under right eye which goes horizontal.'

With the haggling over, the hunt was booked for a date in October 2018 at Kalahari Lion Safaris, an exclusive hunting ranch on the edge of the vast Kalahari Desert in North West Province close to South Africa's border with Botswana. This ranch is run by a hunter called Freddie Scheepers and his wife, Zerna. My team learned that Simba was to be supplied by a lion breeder in the Bloemfontein area, but, try as they might, they were unable to identify the name of the farm or the breeder.

In late August 2018, in a last-ditch attempt to establish Simba's exact location, my investigator met Scheepers at his hunting ranch on the pretext of wanting to look over the accommodation on behalf of his pseudo client. This meeting also provided a useful opportunity for my mole to carry out an in-depth recce of the area where the lion was to be released and hunted.

By this point, a larger team supporting this undercover operation had been assembled in South Africa for several weeks and a safe house had been established at Mahikeng, the capital city of North West Province. The group had carried out surveillance of Scheepers's farm boundaries – particularly the main entrance, where much intelligence had been secured – and had also explored the wider area, including all border crossings into Botswana which could be used as escape routes from South Africa should the need arise. The closest medical facility, Ganyesa Hospital, had also been located. Such precautions are standard for this type of potentially risky exercise.

My investigator met Scheepers at the entrance to his farm at about nine o'clock on the evening of 27 August. As he pulled into the gated entrance, Scheepers, waiting in his 4x4 on the other side of the gate, flicked on his full-beam headlights in an attempt to study him for a few tense moments before unlocking the high gate. Scheepers's build is similar to that of many Afrikaans-speaking farmers, being the size of a rugby forward. He has strong features and a leathery tan courtesy of his outdoor life under the harsh Kalahari sun and he dresses in standard-issue khaki shorts, short-sleeved safari shirts and ankle boots with half-gaiters. He is a hard man and, potentially, an aggressive one.

Any hopes my investigator had about this assignment being benign were dashed when Scheepers walked over to his car, stooped towards the open driver's side window and growled, 'You'd better be who the fuck you say you are!' This unpleasant greeting was almost certainly caused by the pressure that had been placed on De Beer and, in turn, Scheepers by my investigator's repeated requests to view Simba, a lion with a hefty price on his head.

In an effort to lighten the mood, my investigator laughed jo-vially and remarked that this was not the friendliest welcome he had ever received as a paying client, adding, 'I'm at least pleased to meet you – I think!' Scheepers, somewhat taken aback, paused for a moment before shaking his hand. He mumbled something in Afrikaans that sounded conciliatory and ordered, 'OK, follow me – it's a long drive to the farmstead and the going is kak.'

In order to log the route, my investigator switched on a tracker app on his phone, enabling him to record the latitude and longitude of each of the ranch's nine internal cattle gates as he drove behind Scheepers. Some 25 km (15 miles) later, having passed through many acres of cattle country, they arrived at the outer perimeter of the hunting area. The track ran parallel to a 12-foot electrified fence for a short while and then veered to the right into a heavily constructed gateway with a steel multi-barred gate on runners. A sign reading 'NO ENTRY DANGER-OUS GAME' seemed something of an understatement. A final short drive later, the two-vehicle convoy went through another large gate and finally arrived at the farmstead, which was en-closed within the hunting area.

Scheepers introduced my investigator to Zerna, who was waiting to serve a late dinner to a party of Canadian hunters who were staying at the ranch hunting lion and buffalo. The atmos-phere was initially strained, and whatever sceptical thoughts Scheepers harboured about my investigator even appeared to have filtered through to the Canadians. Slowly, however, as the beer flowed and stories were shared, everybody relaxed slightly. Eventually Scheepers took my investigator aside and showed him some videos of Simba on his phone, which had been sent to him by the breeder. Scheepers would go no further than this, though. Again, he decreed that no physical viewing of Simba prior to the hunt would be allowed.

Plans were put in place for Simba to be shot between 22 and 25 October, though of course my team had no intention of going through with this grotesque excuse of a lion hunt. Even though doing so would have secured incriminating information – specifically how De Beer would have sent an illegal canned lion trophy from South Africa to America – absolutely nothing could justify killing any animal. Instead, they had a simple but effective scheme which would allow them to pull out of this arrangement at the last moment. It was intended to run as follows. On the day of the supposed hunt, my investigator, accompanying his American 'client', who was in reality a former US Special Forces veteran called Billy, would send a coded WhatsApp message to his support group as soon as Simba was sighted. Then, an emergency call would be made to the satellite phone carried by Billy conveying an invented story that his wife and family had been involved in a serious car accident. The hunt would be postponed on compassionate grounds and my investigator and Billy would be able to leave the area immediately. Subsequently, a strategy could be worked out to rescue Simba.

My investigator left Scheepers's farm on 28 August, having successfully hidden a tracker on his vehicle and returned to the safe house to brief the support team before flying back to Britain. Much valuable information had been obtained, not least the security arrangements at Scheepers's farmstead and its hunting area. It was now clear that he and Billy would be in a very tightly controlled environment. Indeed, if they became compromised for some reason, it would be difficult for the support team to rescue them. Not only that, but during his visit my investigator had noted that there were a number of potentially hostile individuals among Scheepers's ten-strong workforce, three of whom were excellent trackers. There were also numerous firearms on the property for hunting purposes. Plus, of course, Scheepers, who often carries a pistol, and another Boer professional hunter would be present. Added to these obstacles, the soft Kalahari sand in the area ruled out any covert close surveillance, as anti-tracking techniques would be totally ineffective.

The team's intelligence suggested that Scheepers would release Simba on the day of the hunt. This would break the law, which states that the minimum release period for a lion in a hunt of this nature in North West Province is ninety-six hours. Having surreptitiously installed flashback cameras – which photograph anything which goes past them and sends the image remotely to a mobile phone – at the main entrance to Scheepers's farm, the team planned to continue monitoring Scheepers right up until the hunt was to be held. They wanted to record the lion's arrival and to better understand Scheepers's patterns of behaviour. They might also be able to confirm the name of the lion breeder who would supply Simba for the hunt.

By late October, when the hunt was scheduled to take place, two members of the three-man main team went to Scheepers's farm in advance of Billy's arrival. Billy, the third member of the main team who would conduct the operation at Scheepers's farm, was due to arrive there in a helicopter flown by De Beer, who happens to be a commercial pilot. Unfortunately, however, a freak downpour the night before Billy's arrival put the flashback cameras out of action, the first tech failure to frustrate the operation.

Despite this setback, my investigator did not have a difficult decision to make. Weeks of planning and long hours of surveillance would be wasted if the hunt went ahead without any evidence being secured. Furthermore, the team would be put at risk to no real end. Acting quickly, he got a message to Billy, who was just arriving at O. R. Tambo Airport in Johannesburg, to activate the excuse about his wife and family's 'car crash' in the US, then and there. It was reckoned that if the hunt could be ditched convincingly and then rearranged for a later date, it would give the team time to reset and have another crack at Scheepers.

Billy was duly met at O. R. Tambo Airport by De Beer. As soon as he went through the Arrivals gate, he claimed he had just received a message from America asking him to fly home immediately because of the 'accident' involving his wife and children. One member of the support team who was present and who covertly observed the meeting said that Billy's performance was exceptional. De Beer was taken in entirely and a loose arrangement was made that Billy would return to carry out the hunt another time.

This left De Beer and Scheepers with a problem. They had released a captive lion into a hunting area, but they had no immediate client to kill it. As a result, they hatched their own plan to make even more money out of Simba before he would be killed. They decided to offer a different client the chance to shoot the creature with a tranquilliser dart. A British hunting enthusiast called Miles Wakefield, a 48-year-old insurance loss adjustor who lived in Essex and worked in London, was the man to be given this opportunity. At the time, Wakefield was enjoying a six-night stay at Scheepers's ranch, where he was hunting impala and other plains game. Evidently, the lure of shooting a lion with tranquilliser darts for the 'bargain' price of $4,000 proved irresistible; Wakefield jumped at the chance.

De Beer left Billy at O. R. Tambo Airport and, accompanied by his companion, a young Mozambican, flew his helicopter to Scheepers's ranch in North West Province. There, my investigator plus one of his colleagues who had joined the operation were informed by De Beer of Billy's 'news' about the car crash. They said they would like to remain at the ranch for a day or two as planned. They were allowed to do so, and this two-man team made good use of the time available to them.

When De Beer and Scheepers retired to organise Wakefield's dart hunt (or 'green hunt', as these events are known in hunting parlance) and to rearrange Billy's postponed canned hunt, my investigators set to work. Firstly, unobserved, they photographed the guest book listing all of the hunting clients who had killed lions on Scheepers's ranch during the past four years. Next, they managed to slip into Scheepers's slaughterhouse, situated away from the farmstead, through an unlocked window.

The approach to the slaughterhouse was extremely difficult to negotiate due to the soft sand on the property, which left obvious footprints that were immediately visible to the naked eye. Thankfully, they noticed that a track used by the farm workers' families ran close by. Removing their socks and boots, my investigators went barefoot, disguising their spoor among the footprints of the locals. Behind the slaughterhouse is a sawmill which had spewed out a substantial pile of bark debris. They climbed onto it, using it as a platform from which to get in through the window. Inside, they found several sets of salted lion bones – fully intact fleshed skeletons – plus two freshly fleshed lion skeletons. They took photographs and made a video before leaving.

On the morning of the day he was to shoot Simba, Wakefield went antelope hunting. Then he joined Scheepers and De Beer in the afternoon to search for Simba in what my investigator was told is a 445-hectare (1,100-acre) hunting area, even though in his opinion it seemed much smaller. They found the lion close to a perimeter fence where a 'bait' of offal had been left out and began their cruel pursuit of him in an open 4x4 vehicle. Wakefield took a shot from the vehicle from a distance of about 12 yards but missed. A terrified Simba bounded off into the bush and, with darkness approaching, the men returned to the comfort of the lodge to enjoy the swimming pool and open bar. Around the campfire that evening, De Beer related a sickening story of a lioness hunt he had conducted on Scheepers's farm a couple of years previously during which a client had shot an unfortunate lioness a number of times, wounding it severely but failing to kill it. Initially, the client apparently hit both of the animal's front paws before misfiring into its rear legs. De Beer then had to put the unfortunate cat out of its misery. He seemed to derive much pleasure from this story, though nobody else present found it remotely amusing.

The hunt resumed the next day, with the party again finding Simba near a perimeter fence. Once more he was chased in the pick-up truck, bouncing off the electrified fence on two occasions until he was so exhausted that he slumped to the ground, hot and distraught. Having failed to hit Simba the previous day, Wakefield took careful aim under the direction of Scheepers, who advised him to shoot a dart into the muscle of his right hind leg. Distressed, Simba leapt in shock after being struck and attempted to flee. Increasingly weakened by the drugged dart, however, his rear legs faltered and failed as Wakefield and Scheepers stalked him on foot. Disorientated, Simba staggered into a tree and wheeled away from his pursuers, apparently confused about which way to turn. Finally, he buckled, collapsing in the shade of an acacia thorn. At this point, Wakefield – turning back to grin at the rest of the party – fired a second dart into his right leg, in Scheepers's words 'to finish the job'.

Minutes later, when the drugs had finally brought down the proud beast, Wakefield posed for his 'trophy shot' next to the semi-conscious Simba, whose tongue was lolling from his mouth. Wakefield appeared barely able to contain his delight as the dazed lion tried to move his huge head. In video footage of the encounter, Wakefield can be seen exclaiming, 'He is turning his head and there's no fighting it!' A group picture was also taken showing Wakefield, Scheepers, De Beer and Danie Pretorius, another professional hunter backing up Scheepers on the hunt, lined up behind Simba proprietorially.

Under South African law, it is illegal to fire a tranquilliser dart at a lion for anything other than 'veterinary, scientific, conservation or management purposes'. Any dart must be fired by a vet or a vet has to be present. As previously stated, it is also illegal to hunt a lion in a vehicle unless it is being tracked over a long distance or the hunter is physically disabled or elderly. Furthermore, it is illegal to feed or bait a released lion. The fact that Scheepers violated these laws did not seem to occur to him when it came to poor Simba.

Simba was loaded into a secure trailer by De Beer and Scheepers's farm workers. Once again taking full advantage of a distraction, one of my investigators placed a magnetic tracker on its chassis. After Simba had been secured, Scheepers declared to all present that 'no photos of the hunt should be shared outside of this group as [what he was doing] was technically illegal' and he 'didn't want anyone getting into trouble'. Wakefield and the other guests, including my undercover investigators, departed the following morning, but not before De Beer and Scheepers insisted that Billy's return hunt should take place in February.

Six months later, when I exposed this so-called entertainment publicly, Wakefield told the *Mail on Sunday* he had been misled by Scheepers and De Beer. He claimed he thought he had taken part in a 'legal operation to relocate a lion in the interests of the health of the animal'. He maintained he was only told that there should have been a vet present after the event and that, if he had known beforehand, 'I would have immediately withdrawn from the operation'. He added, 'I was led to believe, by the two South Africans, Freddie Scheepers and Patrick de Beer, who are both professional hunters, that it was for conservation. By relocating the lion to another more controlled location the animal's life would be preserved.'

For his part, De Beer insisted that the stalking and tracking of Simba was not a hunt. He also asserted that Wakefield had paid for the upkeep of the lion in return for the chance to shoot it with a dart. Scheepers confirmed that there was no vet present but he, too, denied that any hunt had taken place, insisting that Simba had been darted merely in order to move him to another enclosed area after the original hunter had pulled out. 'That wasn't a hunt. We just darted it,' he said. 'What happened was the guy that was supposed to hunt the lion, when he landed in South Africa, his wife and his daughters were in a terrible accident so he had to go back. We decided to take the lion back to the enclosed area.' He also said Simba would not have survived where he was, a suggestion that is probably true given his status as a captive-bred lion with no experience of hunting his own food. Scheepers claimed that this was the 'first and only time' a client had paid to dart a lion and he insisted it was too dangerous to fire a tranquilliser dart at a lion while on foot. Others will have to judge for themselves whether they accept Scheepers's explanation.

The fact is that Simba was loaded into the back of a trailer after the time that had elapsed had been carefully monitored to ensure that the tranquilliser drug would not wear off and the huge beast was not about to come around and turn on his tormentors. This was not, however, the kind of conventional relocation operation that conservationists undertake across Africa. Simba was simply being shifted crudely to a holding pen where he would await the American hunter – in reality my investigator, Billy – who had claimed the right to kill him at a later date.

In the interim, my South Africa-based undercover team kept tabs on Scheepers's farm and other identified illegal lion breeding

After visiting South Africa, I was unable to forget how miserable life is for captive-bred lions, and I launched Operation Simba to confront the lion farming scandal. From left to right: Patrick de Beer, Danie Pretorius, Freddie Scheepers and Miles Wakefield pose with Simba after he was shot with a tranquiliser dart in February 2019. Private collection

In March 2019, I toured the Free State and North West Province in a helicopter and viewed six areas where lions are bred to be killed in a canned hunt or slaughtered for the bone trade. Lion farming's links to serious organised crime meant I had to wear a bulletproof vest in case the aircraft was shot at. From the air, you can see that what was once open land has now been carved up by tall wire fences into pens and enclosures in which lions live with scant shelter from the elements. There are thought to be at least 300 such operations in the country. Private collection

The safe house near Johannesburg used by my team for Operation Chastise in 2019. It was out of the way but within striking distance of the city's two airports, Lanseria and O. R. Tambo International, and served as the base, including its main operations room. Private collection

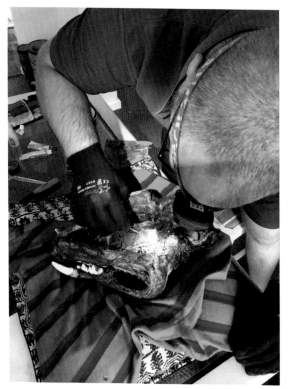

As part of Operation Chastise, the team cleverly adapted two vehicle trackers, discarded their magnets, and lodged them discreetly inside the cranium of a lion's skull and within a cavity in a neck bone so the bones' ultimate destination in Asia could be traced. Private collection

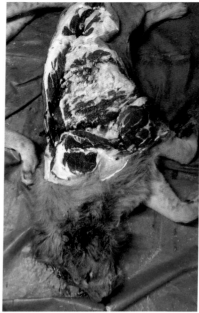

During Operation Chastise, a lion dealer who was given the codename 'Lister' worked undercover for my operatives. In his day job, he used his garage as a makeshift abattoir.

ABOVE LEFT Lion bones ready for collection from 'Lister' by the mysterious Asian bone dealer known only as 'Michael'. Private collection

ABOVE RIGHT A skinned lion partway through being processed by 'Lister'. Private collection

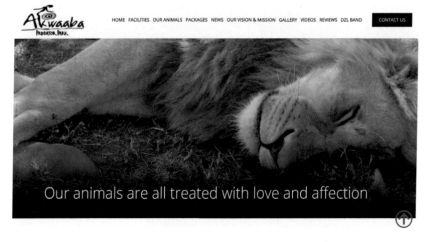

An image from the website of Akwaaba Lodge & Predator Park. This tourist facility claims to treat all of its animals 'with love and affection', yet 'Lister' regularly bought lions from there which were later shot in canned hunts or killed for their bones. Private collection

My team found that Akwaaba Lodge was also a breeding ground for ligers, the freakish lion-tiger cross-breeds. This liger cub was photographed in an enclosure at Akwaaba that is not routinely open to the public. Private collection

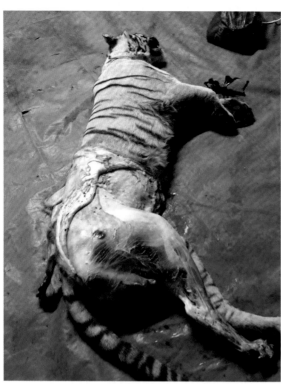

'Lister' also bought this tiger from Akwaaba Lodge which he processed on his property. Tiger bones command huge prices in Asia's 'traditional' medicine market, but after decades of rampant demand they have become harder to source. South African lion bones are now passed off as tiger bones to plug the gap. At least one real tiger is usually included in each cache of fake tiger bones to hoodwink buyers.

Private collection

In October 2019, I returned to South Africa to observe Simba, six months after his rescue. Part of the reason I had to wait so long was that he had to be hidden in a secret location. Even now, I cannot name it, such is the danger that certain figures in the lion industry are thought to pose to captive-bred lions. Private collection

October 2019: Simba in his new, permanent home. It is a 2.5-acre fenced enclosure where he will live alone in peace for the rest of his days. I have made a substantial donation to ensure he will be well looked after. Despite enduring years of abuse, he is, according to his keepers, 'a real gentleman'.

Private collection

operations in North West Province. Shortly before this operation ended, there was a dramatic moment when it was almost blown. The support team, which included British ex-Special Forces servicemen, used drones periodically to gather evidence covertly. During one mission, disaster struck when a drone developed a technical problem. It was forced to land inside an enclosure containing eighteen adult lions. Discovering it could have alerted the ranch to my team's presence and possibly allowed for the recovery of compromising metadata. Despite the terrifying risk of being mauled by the animals, the team decided on a plan to rescue it. One investigator, a former member of the Parachute Regiment's elite patrols platoon, volunteered to enter the enclosure in the dead of night in order to rescue the device, which was about 200 yards from the perimeter.

At 1 a.m., when lions are at their most active and most people are in a deep slumber, the team quietly placed blankets over the top of the 12-foot electric fence. The ex-Para then used a ladder to scale it, crept in and, with the aid of a GPS tracker, followed the coordinates to the crash site. 'It was a full moon, which wasn't ideal as lions hunt at this time and conditions were perfect for them,' he recalls. 'I was checking my back at regular intervals to make sure a lion hadn't picked up my scent. The drone was actually located some distance from the coordinates – I caught a glint of its airframe in the moonlight.' Astonishingly, the ex-Para managed to infiltrate the enclosure and dash back to safety without rousing the predators. With some understatement, he later described his mission as 'exciting' adding, 'I've got the best job in the world.'

In February 2019, Billy, again masquerading as the American

hunter, arrived at Scheepers's hunting ranch. De Beer wasn't able to be there on this occasion as he was away on business in the US. This meant there was no helicopter transit. Instead, Billy and another member of the team who would accompany him on the hunt hired a 4x4 jeep. As with the previous plan, the hunt was to be shelved at the last safe moment. It was decided to use another 'compassionate grounds' excuse before launching the scheme the team had devised to save Simba.

The set-up for this sting began on the farm's shooting range. Billy was asked to check zero on the .375-calibre rifle in preparation for killing Simba. He proceeded to fire rounds all over the target paper and pretended to be nervous about the hunt. Just as it had been months previously at O. R. Tambo Airport, his performance at Scheepers's shooting range that day was convincing.

After Scheepers had had enough of Billy's poor marksmanship – at one stage even complaining about the cost of bullets – he said, 'That's enough. Let's go and hunt your lion.' Following the same procedure as the dart hunt had done, Scheepers drove around the enclosure looking for Simba's spoor. Once found, he asked Billy to load his rifle and apply the safety catch. When this was done, they followed the tracks into the bush, swerving around the acacia thorns until they eventually roused Simba. This time the unfortunate lion roared his displeasure and fled onto the sand track at a speed that defied his considerable size. Scheepers drove after the terrified creature, which ran straight into the electrified fence. He was, quite literally, shocked, but he recovered quickly and turned back into the bush, melting away into a thicket of thorns.

Scheepers pulled up and took a moment to discuss the situation with his colleague, Danie. He told Billy and my other undercover investigator that Danie would drive slowly into the thicket until they found the lion, 'who would be tired now and getting hot'. Scheepers then re-joined the hunters on the back of the 4x4 and loaded his own rifle, explaining, 'Only for back-up, you understand, should the lion come or [if] you wound him.' It was strongly suspected by my team that Scheepers was going to shoot Simba himself at the first opportunity, defend his actions, but still demand full payment.

By now, the team had already made the decision to end this miserable excuse for entertainment, removing any further stress to Simba. The brutality of the chase had disgusted them. They told Scheepers that they wanted to return to the ranch to escape the intense heat and to eat lunch. Reluctantly, he ordered the vehicle driver, Danie, to drive back to the farmstead. On arrival, the team had a few minutes to go over the plan they had concocted. Then, at lunch, Billy pulled the trigger, so to speak, by declaring that he was not happy to continue with the hunt. To Scheepers's bafflement and evident dismay, he was told by this 'hunter' that he actually wanted to rescue Simba and relocate him in a sanctuary. Billy explained that his children, who had narrowly survived the previous year's 'car crash', had pressed him not to shoot the lion but to save it instead. He said that his conscience compelled him to do as they had asked.

The colour in Scheepers's face changed from purple to crimson red. He looked ready to explode. In an effort to diffuse the situation, Billy raised his hand and said, 'Everyone is a winner here. I will pay you the full price of the lion and his keep until a suitable sanctuary is found. Now, let's eat.' Post-lunch, the balance payment for Simba was handed over and a monthly cost agreed that was sufficient to ensure Scheepers kept him alive and well. Once the finances were agreed, my team packed and headed back to the safe house.

In March 2019, as we awaited news of Simba's fate, I took the opportunity to scour South Africa by air in order to gain a fuller understanding of how far the tentacles of the lion industry have spread. Having been given a briefing by my team in which we discussed the intelligence gathered from their on-the-ground recces, I took to the sky in a Bell 407 helicopter flown by a South African pilot. The co-pilot, an ex-Special Forces flight captain and one of Britain's most experienced military surveillance fliers, explained the route we would follow to cover the six separate areas I wanted to view. Each was a facility where lions are bred and reared either to be shot in a canned hunt or to be slaughtered solely so that their bones can be sold to dealers in Asia. A camera operator came with me to record what we saw.

Having been warned that some of the properties over which we would fly were owned and run by people with links to serious organised crime, and that there was therefore a possibility some of their staff may even fire at the aircraft as it hovered over areas of interest, I took the precaution of wearing body armour in the form of a bulletproof vest. It was also agreed that, as a ruse, the helicopter would follow existing power lines where possible, so that any air traffic controller monitoring the aircraft's transponder would assume we were surveying them. I am in no doubt that these measures were necessary.

During the course of the day, we flew clockwise in a loop

north from Bloemfontein in the Free State towards Klerksdorp in North West Province, and then headed south-east to Kroonstad in the Free State again before the final leg took us southwest via Winburg and back to the landing area. Below me were huge areas of what was once open land which has been carved up by tall wire fences into pens and enclosures in which scores of lions of all ages are forced to live with scant shelter from the elements. Many of the animals I saw paced up and down the perimeters of these inadequately sized cells in obvious desperation at their imprisonment, a classic sign of stress and unhappiness. The flight, including a scheduled refuel and lunch break, went to plan and we returned to the departure point with damning, sometimes distressing footage which proves how widespread and, dare I say it, sophisticated South Africa's lion trade has become. I found the scale of the handful of captive operations that I observed astonishing, to say nothing of disgusting. It is chilling to reflect on the fact that there are now believed to be in excess of 300 such operations in the country.

A few weeks later, in April 2019, came wonderful news. Getting on for a year since first being emailed Simba's picture, we finally managed to secure his rescue. By then, Scheepers was losing patience, and credible intelligence confirmed that he had found another buyer for Simba – a professional lion dealer who was going to arrange for him to be shot on another canned hunt. Simba's life had hung in the balance and his future went right down to the wire. A temporary new home was found for him, the paperwork required to relocate him was completed, and a professional team was engaged to carry out this move. Because Scheepers had also seemingly sold Simba to the lion dealer, who was preparing to pick him up at the very time our travel permits were approved and the team arrived at Simba's place of internment, it is no exaggeration to say that he was only hours from death. Mercifully, Scheepers had no choice but to release Simba to my team, and he was taken to a place of safety at a secret location.

CHAPTER 7

AFTER SIMBA

Operation Simba was an undoubted success in its own right. To have saved just one out of a possible 12,000 captive-bred lions from certain death felt like a small but crucial victory in the war to end what must surely rank as one of South Africa's darkest industries. Equally pleasing was that the case sparked an enormous amount of media coverage in Britain and further afield. Having completed the project, I contacted Ted Verity, the editor of the *Mail on Sunday*, to ask if he would be interested in publishing its results. We reached a gentleman's agreement that I would offer the project to him on the basis that he would give it 'at least four pages'. It was immediately apparent that he also recognises the importance of exposing the abuse and cruelty involved in breeding and keeping captive lions in South Africa, and the fact that unscrupulous individuals profit from their killing and their body parts. For he decided that an unprecedented eleven pages in a single edition of the newspaper should be reserved to tell the story of Operation Simba and much else to do with this sickening trade besides. And so, on 28 April 2019, starting with the all-important front page splash, I was able to disclose the truth.

It is highly unusual for a national newspaper in Britain to devote more than a few pages to one specific issue on any given day. For a weekly newspaper to take such a close interest in a controversy of this nature, thousands of miles away from the UK, and to give it sufficient space so that the topic could be examined in such depth through a series of revelatory articles and an opinion piece, was extraordinary. Spread over two pages there was also a sequence of sixteen frame-by-frame photographs depicting Miles Wakefield's grotesque parody of a hunt which felled Simba. As a result of the prominence which the *Mail on Sunday* and its website gave to Operation Simba, many other media outlets in Britain and around the world picked up the story, gaining the scandal of breeding and slaughtering lions the prominence which I believe it warrants.

Under the headline 'Exposed: Horror of Lion Farms', I was able to inform readers who would not otherwise have been aware of the captive-bred lion industry how it has quickly morphed into such a slick, though deeply unpleasant, business. I explained that I had commissioned a year-long undercover investigation involving former Special Forces and security operatives and that the result was a profoundly disturbing insight into the full horrors and illegal practices linked to lion farming and the gruesome bone trade.

I told how wealthy clients are sent brochures with photographs of captive male lions via WhatsApp so that they can choose which one to kill in exchange for high five-figure sums of money, depending on the size and quality of the animal's mane. Having exposed Miles Wakefield's experiences of shooting Simba with tranquilliser darts on an illegal so-called green hunt, I am given to understand that there were consequences for him personally. His employer in the City of London is said to have taken a very dim view of his having been party to chasing a defenceless animal in a 4x4 vehicle around a fenced hunting enclosure before shooting it from a range of just a few yards. Not long after my report appeared, he left his job.

Other disclosures in the *Mail on Sunday* included one about the tricks of smuggling. The UK representative of a South African safari company had advised one of my investigators in a taped telephone call how a US citizen could bypass the American ban on importing captive-bred lion trophies. Adrian Sailor, the UK representative for Settlers Safaris in South Africa, was contacted by one of my team to arrange a hunt for his 'boss', who he claimed wanted to shoot a lion. Sailor, the general manager of a car parts firm in the West Midlands, offered a choice of three male lions and sent photographs of all of them, along with suggestions of where to hunt them. It was then explained to Sailor that an American client wanted to kill a lion and have his 'trophy' returned to the US. As Sailor knew, however, since 2016 American law has banned the import of captive-bred lion trophies. Sailor, an amateur taxidermist, then volunteered a method of dodging the restrictions, suggesting that the client might want to initially export the lion to the UK, which is legal, and then send it on to the US by arranging for the lion's skin to be put inside the skin of a dead red deer. If salted and rolled, he advised, the stag skin sets hard, making it almost impossible for customs officials to detect the lion skin inside. 'You stick the lion, stick the lion skin, inside the bloody stag... It's all salted and rock hard,' Sailor said. 'It's a bit dodgy, but you know.' In messages to the *Mail on Sunday*, Sailor did not deny suggesting a deer skin could be lined with a lion skin, but he did stress that he was not involved in the lion hunt to which the conversation referred and said that 'no crime has been committed', adding, 'How will a lion fit inside a deer skin? Major size difference. I have no idea about any recordings.' Others must judge for themselves what they think of Sailor's explanation.

Alongside this, I was able to tell readers for the first time of the full horrors of Wag-'n-Bietjie Farm, where fifty-four lions were killed in just two days. I explained that the animals were first stunned with tranquilliser darts before being shot dead with a .22-calibre rifle. I told how the bullets were fired through the ear and directly into the brain of each animal because overseas buyers will not pay for damaged skulls. Photographs which we obtained showed a scene of utter gore. Although many of these pictures were considered too horrific to be shown in a family newspaper, the words of Reinet Meyer, the senior inspector at South Africa's National Society for the Prevention of Cruelty to Animals who had been tipped off about this abuse in the first place, stood in as a powerful substitute. Ms Meyer explained how she found lions housed in steel transport crates that were too small for them to stand up or turn around in. She told how they had been left in the crates without food or water for three days. She initially thought that one of them was dead because it was not moving. 'The lion was so depressed that it did not move at all,' she said. 'It was totally disgusting that they were kept like this. A lion is a wild animal, it wants its freedom, but now it's kept in a small cage for three days. It's absolutely deplorable.' She added:

We couldn't believe what was happening. You could smell the blood. The lions got shot in the camp and then were all brought into this one room. The flies were terrible. For me, a lion is a stately animal, a kingly animal. Here he is butchered for people just to make money, it's absolutely disgusting.

Elsewhere, I noted some South African breeders' renewed interest in playing with nature by cross-breeding lions and tigers to produce freakish 'ligers'. My investigators learned that, in their lust for profits, these immoral farmers were creating the bizarre overgrown animals because they are even more valuable when they are slaughtered and their skeletons are sold to south-east Asia and China, in turn satisfying the huge demand for traditional 'medicines'. I explained how some operators have imported tigers, which are not native to Africa, to breed with lions and produce ligers or tigons. My dispatch made clear that, due to the absence of a growth-inhibiting gene inherited by a cub with two lion parents, a three-year-old liger can be the same size as a nine-year-old lion, thereby producing more bone weight – and greater profits – once slaughtered. A fully grown liger has the greatest financial value, weighing an average of 71 stone and standing nearly 12 feet tall on its hind legs. I revealed the concerns of experts, who say this abusive breeding process often results in birth defects and the early death of cubs, as well as complications for mothers because they have to give birth to super-sized cubs.

A report published in 2015 estimated that there were 280 tigers in South Africa at forty-four sites. My investigation, however, suggested this was a dramatic underestimate, with around fifty tigers believed to be at just one location. At another wildlife facility in the Free State, my investigators found in a fenced enclosure a group of three tigers and five lions laying down together in the shade. In the same enclosure, another lion and tiger were found together near the perimeter fence. This was nothing short of unsettling. Why else would breeders put two different species together unless they were hopeful some of them might mate?

The *Mail on Sunday*'s coverage was not confined to an exposé, however. As well as informing people about the lion trade, I knew that the platform provided by the newspaper represented a valuable opportunity to apply some political pressure on two countries in particular. First, I called on the South African government to halt what I described as the 'horrific and abusive' activity of lion farming by making it illegal. I made clear that South Africa is the only country in the world that allows large-scale, captive-lion farming, and that it has an annual quota for the legal export of lion bones. I said that the South African government must ban captive-bred lion farming as it has no conservation value: 'The captive-bred lion industry shames South Africa – indeed it shames us all. By allowing such a barbaric practice, the South African government is harming the reputation of a country that treasures its position on the international stage in the aftermath of apartheid. Captive-bred lion farming is abusive and horrific.'

I also urged the British government to join its counterparts in Australia, France, America and the Netherlands in bringing in new import laws in order to discourage the practice of taking trophies into the UK. I wrote: 'I also call on the UK government to follow the lead of other nations, notably the US, in banning the importation of captive-lion trophies. We must do our bit to stamp out lion farming and show that we are not in any way complicit with it.' I knew that there would be much more to do if any of this was to be achieved, however.

On that basis, to coincide with this coverage, I decided to launch a website, www.LordAshcroftWildlife.com, which is dedicated to the plight of South Africa's lions and other creatures such as whales and rhinos. The site was activated at the same time as the *Mail on Sunday* published its special 'Operation Simba' edition. By having a permanent record of my work on lions in one place, and using a digital platform to publicise it, I was confident that others with an interest in the matter could learn from it and be inspired to do their bit as well.

In conjunction with the newspaper report and the website, I also made a documentary film on location in South Africa to draw attention to the wider issue of lion farming. It explains that the captive-bred lion industry is a relatively new phenomenon which has sprung up out of nothing more than a desire on the part of a small number of people to make money through exploitation and cruelty. Some of South Africa's most respected conservationists, including Dr Andrew Muir and Colin Bell, were kind enough to contribute to this part of the project. Their message was stark: not only could the remaining wild lions in South Africa all be poached within ten years thanks to the explosion of the captive-bred lion industry, but the reputation of South Africa, which as a country is so heavily dependent on tourism, could be damaged irreparably by the abuse of all lions as well. This film, available to view on my website and on

YouTube, has been watched some 70,000 times in a matter of months.

And there was more. The day after the *Mail on Sunday* published the story, I wrote to Her Excellency Ms Nomatemba Tambo, South Africa's High Commissioner in London, drawing attention to this troubling issue. In view of the reaction of this representative of South Africa's government in Britain, it is worth repeating my letter in full.

I wrote to Ms Tambo:

For the past year I have been investigating the farmed lion industry in South Africa, commissioning a substantial undercover operation that went into breeding farms, penetrated a slaughterhouse and took part in captive-bred lion hunts just up to the point before the kill. I started out by looking at what is known as canned lion hunting but soon realised that the farming of this endangered species for their bones is now a major industry. There are just over 3,000 lions in the wild in your country and at the same time some 12,000 captive-bred lions are in the system, some of which are used for 'trophy hunting', which is usually a charade, but with the majority slaughtered for their bones for the Asian market.

The South African government permits this and awards a number of licences for it, but the volume is far greater than admitted and the relatively lenient regulations governing this industry mostly ignored. This has little benefit to the economy as there are few people involved and it is a cash business. It has absolutely no value to conservation; these captive-bred lions suffer genetic disorders, cannot feed themselves and cannot be re-wilded. In addition, tigers are being bred in significant numbers in facilities across South Africa, some to be cross-bred with lions to become ligers, whose bone mass at three years old equates to that of a nine-year-old lion.

I exposed all of this in the UK's *Mail on Sunday* newspaper yesterday (copy enclosed) and, should you wish, I can provide you with evidence of the illegality we witnessed. On my website, www.LordAshcroftWildlife.com, there is more information, including photographs that were too distressing to publish in a newspaper, and I produced a short film. And if you choose to act on this information, those involved in collecting it and who were witness to the law-breaking are prepared to testify in court under conditions of anonymity.

I feel that it is my moral duty to expose this cruel and unnecessary industry as it shames us all. I urge you to consider supporting a call to ban this large-scale farming in South Africa, which is doing huge damage to your country's international reputation.

For my part, I will be pressing the UK government to ban the importation of the body parts of any endangered species; at least we can play our part in minimising this cruelty.

I had hoped that my reasonable approach to the High Commissioner would prompt some kind of acknowledgement from her office and, perhaps, a meeting. I am sorry to report, however, that, to date, I have received no response whatsoever. Under the circumstances, I find this lack of interest on the part of South Africa's authorities utterly perplexing. My having given a range of interviews on the subject over the ensuing days to the BBC,

Sky News, LBC Radio and talkRADIO, I am not prepared to accept the possibility that the High Commissioner's office was unaware of how much attention was paid to it in Britain, no matter how awkward Ms Tambo might have found this personally. Ultimately, it is sad that my offer to furnish her office with information has, for now, been ignored. That offer still stands, of course.

Moving on to the domestic political stage, on 29 April 2019 I also wrote to the then Secretary of State for the Environment, Michael Gove, seeking a meeting at which banning the import of captive-bred lion trophies into the UK could be discussed. I am pleased to say that this meeting went ahead just a few days later.

After it, on 9 May, I wrote a follow-up letter to Mr Gove in which I emphasised my horror of lion farming, sham trophy hunting and the bone trade. I also underlined the fact that the South African state not only allows mass lion breeding but also overlooks those who breach its own quotas. This allows cruelty and corruption to flourish. I pointed out that the UK could be more determined to bring this to an end through our influence and diplomacy and argued that everything possible should be done to discourage this industry. I suggested that banning the import of lion body parts to the UK, which is used as a conduit to other nations, would have a significant impact.

I also aired the possibility of tackling the bone trade by implementing something similar to the very effective UK Bribery Act. In pursuing this path, I said, the British would lead the world, leapfrogging the weakness of CITES and initiatives by other nations. My idea was to make it illegal for UK companies to be involved in the shipping, trading or the movement of money associated with bones and that their directors would be liable unless they had taken steps to ensure their firms were not involved. I believe this would encourage companies to take measures to protect themselves.

By happy coincidence, in mid-May, within just a couple of weeks of the *Mail on Sunday* scoop appearing, a round-table event took place in Westminster chaired by Mr Gove in order to discuss trophy hunting and conservation which was attended by several prominent animal rights activists, including Will Travers of the Born Free Foundation and Dr Pieter Kat of the charity LionAid. A representative from my office was also invited. It is clear that Mr Gove was – and is – sympathetic to the idea of a ban on captive-bred trophy imports and that he took the matter seriously. The impression formed was that he wished to outlaw imports of trophies of lions shot under canned conditions first, before considering the evidence for banning imports of trophies of all endangered animals.

By late May 2019, the incumbent Prime Minister, Theresa May, announced her resignation. This led to a Conservative Party leadership contest in which Mr Gove stood as a candidate. Naturally, this political battle consumed most of his time over the following weeks. In late July 2019, when the victor of that contest, Boris Johnson, was installed in Downing Street, he soon appointed Mr Gove to a new job in the Cabinet, as Chancellor of the Duchy of Lancaster. Mr Gove's successor as Environment Secretary was Theresa Villiers. In February 2020, she was replaced by George Eustice. Zac Goldsmith, a politician whose commitment to the environment and to animal rights has never been in doubt, was Parliamentary Under-Secretary of State in the same department between July 2019 and September 2019, when he was elevated to Minister of State. Lord Goldsmith, as he has been since January 2020, continues to press for a ban on all trophy hunt imports to the UK.

While Britain's political scene underwent these various changes, I maintained my public opposition to the abuse of lions in South Africa in other ways. As a result of *The Times* reporting on the issue of canned hunting in July 2019, I wrote to the paper outlining my knowledge of the problem. My letter, published on 3 July, ran as follows:

Sir, The fact that South African tour operators are deliberately targeting the UK to promote 'canned' lion hunts makes it all the more imperative that the British Government take a stand against this barbaric activity. Earlier this year I flew in a helicopter over many of the captive lion breeding centres (there are more than 200 in South Africa); the vast scale of this problem is hard to comprehend. Well-informed sources told me that there are now an estimated 12,000 captive-bred lions in South Africa – far more than previously thought and approaching four times the number of wild lions in the country. Almost all of these captive-bred lions are destined either for the lion-bone trade or for trophy hunting. As your leading article notes, there is little or nothing that the British Government can do to prevent canned hunting in South Africa. But we can 'do our bit' by joining other countries, notably the US, in banning the importation of lion parts from canned hunts.

In October 2019, I finally had a chance to go and see Simba in his new home. I had always wanted to meet him, and I decided to go to South Africa especially to do so. Part of the reason I had to wait six months for this encounter – his having been rescued in April 2019 – was that he had spent most of that time being hidden in a secret location whose name I cannot reveal even now, such is the danger that certain figures in the lion industry are thought to pose to captive-bred lions. When it was considered safe to do so, Simba was moved to a second secret location, where he remains very happily.

This new, permanent home is a 1-hectare (2.5-acre) fenced enclosure where he will live alone in peace for the rest of his days. He has a raised area where he can lie in the sun, but he also has shade from a group of nearby trees. I have made a substantial donation to ensure that he will be well looked after.

After years of malnourishment and abuse, Simba has been given a clean bill of health by a vet, but, unsurprisingly, he was described as 'deeply traumatised' immediately after his rescue. Indeed, the day before my arrival, he refused to come out of his shelter at all. Fortunately, for me, the next day he emerged quite happily and I was able to spend about an hour watching him. One of his new carers, who asked not to be identified, told me shortly after his move to safety:

He is a real gentleman. Even in the few weeks he has been with us, there has been a massive difference in his behaviour. When he arrived, he was hiding and growling. Now, little by little, he is more confident and allows us to be within 30 feet of him. The great thing is that lions forgive and dare to trust again, and to love unconditionally. This is where humans can learn from animals. Lion farming, on the other hand, touches the darkest side of humanity: it is pure ego, pure money, pure greed.

In November 2019, shortly after the Department of the Environment in London launched a public consultation on the scale and impact of the import and export of hunting trophies, I wrote an opinion piece for the *Daily Telegraph* in which I was able to share my understanding of lion farming and canned lion hunting. The piece concluded by saying:

> I support a total ban on trophy imports with the exception of a licensing regime for research purposes. I urge the Government to consider introducing penalties for breaching this ban that are of the same order as those that exist for the illegal importation of Class A drugs or weapons to Britain.

It was gratifying that the *Sunday Times* of South Africa reproduced the article word for word in its 1 December 2019 edition.

Since the conclusion of Operation Simba in April 2019, however, these were not the only things I did in my commitment to this burning issue. Indeed, as shall be seen in the remaining chapters of this book, in April 2019 another plan was put into action by me concerning South Africa's lion industry. This has generated still more important insights into this twisted business which I sincerely hope will contribute to its demise.

CHAPTER 8

OPERATION CHASTISE

Despite the feeling of euphoria at having saved Simba in the nick of time, and although this fact had in turn helped to shine a powerful light on the lion trade, it was clearer to me than ever that those who profit by abusing lions can operate with great ease in South Africa. Exposing the reprehensible nature of the industry was very important to me, but I knew that having taken my interest in the matter this far, I had a duty to go further. In large part, I was motivated by anger and incredulity at the idea that living creatures have been reduced to the status of mere commodities. I wanted to channel that sense of outrage into positive action. In short, I knew that I could make an even greater contribution to taking this brutal business down for good.

I decided that the best way to make progress would be to drill deeper into the problem and then to inform as many people as possible around the world about it, using more of my own exclusively obtained evidence. The more people talked about it, I reasoned, the greater the chance of a consequential resolution. Ultimately, I hoped, my findings could be presented to the South African authorities so that pressure could be brought to bear on the perpetrators. Why, after all, would the government and police of South Africa condone the serial cruelty and slaughter of arguably their country's most recognisable symbol – unless Karen Trendler's allegation of widespread corruption and indifference at an official level was accurate?

By the spring of 2019, as Operation Simba drew to a close, my thoughts had crystallised. I knew that for this industry's culture and practices to be further exposed, and for it to face the maximum amount of scrutiny, an enhanced investigative effort would be required. This would mean launching a second fully funded covert operation in South Africa, but one wider in scope than Operation Simba. Like any worthwhile investigation, I knew that such an enterprise would take time as well as costing money.

As with Operation Simba, this follow-up mission would be run in conjunction with a not-for-profit wildlife agency. It, in turn, would work with undercover operatives and former members of Britain's Special Forces who would be based in South Africa collecting the relevant information and evidence. It was decided that this new project would be known as Operation Chastise, the same name used by Wing Commander Guy Gibson VC for the Dam Busters raid of May 1943. The 'Chastise' moniker was considered appropriate because the concluding aim of the exercise was to blow apart the corrupt captive-bred lion industry and to break up the associated illegal lion bone trade, just as the daring effort overseen by Wing Commander Gibson's squadron had breached two dams in Germany. On a practical level, adopting 'Chastise' would also save time when it came to giving each operative a codename. For example, the day-to-day head of the operation chose as his own alias 'Gibby'. For security reasons, I shall only refer to Gibby and his core group of associates by their pseudonyms.

First, a team had to be assembled. A deputy – known as Hopgood, naturally – was recruited. He was a former senior non-commissioned officer with the Parachute Regiment. Hopgood's army background, experience on operational tours and specialist training since leaving the military meant that he could double up as an agent handler and team leader when necessary. His past involvement in intelligence-gathering through both interpersonal and technical means would also prove essential.

Next, a series of interviews with potential recruits was held over several days at the Frontline Club in London, which, appropriately, styles itself a meeting place for journalists, photographers, war correspondents and those interested in international affairs and conflict. Through this sifting process, the group required to assist with Operation Chastise was put together.

A safe house then had to be found on the outskirts of Johannesburg. The perfect property was soon secured. Tucked away in a compound with a swimming pool and its own pleasant garden, it would serve as Chastise's base, including its main operations room. The house's situation was remote enough that it could be used without generating suspicion but also convenient enough to be within striking distance of the city's two airports, Lanseria and O. R. Tambo International. As it was in an almost rural setting, there was only one neighbouring residence nearby. It was lived in by a former Rhodesian national called Pam, who also happened to be the owner of the safe house. As a result of her presence on the scene, it was considered judicious to befriend Pam in order to give credence to the cover story the team would use for the ensuing nine months. Creating a 'legend' is essential to any unit working secretly if they are to conduct their activities confidently and without drawing attention to themselves – or rousing the suspicion of others who may decide to raise their concerns with the authorities. The story the team used was one that had been plotted some weeks previously.

They claimed to work for a high-end property company which employed consultants who were based in offices in London, Luxembourg and Geneva. It was explained to Pam that the London office had been retained by a high-net-worth individual based in Monaco who wished to purchase several farms in South Africa with a view to creating a vast nature reserve. This job would take time and would require manpower, which accounted for the long lease on the house. The story had the added bonus of dampening any suspicions which Pam might have developed herself by forewarning her that different colleagues linked to this 'property-finding' job would be coming and going at regular intervals. A website for the front company was constructed using a domain name which was first registered in 1999. As an extra insurance policy, office telephone lines were set up in London, Luxembourg and Geneva complete with answering services. In time, individual business cards were also printed with a fictional professional title for each member of the team – land agent, surveyor and so on. Added to these precautions, an extensive portfolio of farms for sale in each area of operation would also be issued to team members, who were instructed to carry this list at all times in case they should ever be stopped and questioned by police. And the security of the cover story was bolstered to a yet greater extent by every team member taking a crash course in ornithology, with particular reference to birds in southern Africa. Every vehicle used by the team had to carry bird reference books, which would be left on open display on dashboards and back seats. This meant that if a vehicle was ever searched by police, the books would go some way to justifying a team member's possession of binoculars and telescopes. In reality, of course, these devices were key tools which were used throughout Operation Chastise.

A section of the safe house's living room was turned into a working office space. Before long, it contained several large computer screens which were used to support the overall effort. It was decided that everybody on the ground would carry a personal location device (PLD) which functioned via the TrackServer app. Everybody who needed to do so – regardless of their own location globally – would therefore be able to track in real-time those individuals who were out working in the field in South Africa. Hire vehicles, which were changed on a weekly basis for security purposes, would also have a magnetic tracker attached to them which could be monitored from any-where. The 'office' in the safe house was to be used to process the information collected by agents in order to generate active intelligence. Evidence would also be collated against identified targets in the illegal wildlife trade.

It was also decided that the safe house's dining room area should be reserved as a workroom for Ginger, the electronics specialist and drone pilot who would function as the team's equivalent of the James Bond character 'Q'. Ginger had to maintain and service all covert kit, such as flashback cameras, camera traps, button cams, audio recording devices, GPS trackers and any other electronic wizardry needed for the task. Upon realising that the safe house lacked a high-bandwidth internet connection – essential for uploading and downloading the video, audio and photographic files that would be collected – Ginger was also pressed into service so that he could install the broadband. This involved drilling new wiring through the walls, a modification which for a time caused the landlady, Pam, mild concern. A camp bed was also installed in the dining room because Ginger liked to sleep next to his equipment.

The open-plan sitting room was easily big enough to accommodate the key team. It contained a large glass table that worked well as a platform for an overhead projector, allowing detailed operational briefs to be beamed onto the wall. The bedrooms were spacious, comfortable and all had en-suite bathrooms, with French windows that opened onto the gardens and pool. The team had been careful to check the boundary integrity of the gardens before committing to leasing the house. They were surrounded by a steel-construct electrified fence which was hidden by cleverly designed landscaping, allowing my investigators to work from a secure and well-serviced base. This was, of course, vital given the anticipated length of the operation.

It is important to emphasise from the outset that everybody who worked on Operation Chastise was screened carefully before they were accepted. It cannot be said too many times that anybody who is considered to have interfered in South Africa's highly lucrative lion trade places themself in danger. Its practitioners can be aggressive and ruthless and it is certainly true to say that, as with any enterprise linked to criminality or corruption, the creeping possibility of murder is never far away. Not only that, but Operation Chastise was itself always going to be a very sensitive project. Had any authority in South Africa come to find out about it, they may well have taken a very dim view of foreign nationals running an undercover exercise in their country. I had no doubt that public interest arguments easily justified the team's modus operandi, but this was going to be a long and difficult job which would require patience and skill from everybody involved.

The ultimate objective of the assignment was to hand over every relevant piece of evidence we collected to the South African Police Service (SAPS). Legitimate security concerns, however, meant the task had to be run on a need-to-know basis until the majority of the team had exited South Africa and the facts could be given to a senior SAPS commander. For these reasons, every team member would be in a constant state of high alert for the duration, maintaining regular contact with the safe house to avoid any pitfalls.

Having selected the best operators available, my team gathered in Johannesburg in April 2019 to carry out the first stage of its clandestine undertaking. Everybody had been issued with their own dossier before leaving the UK. It included business cards, a property portfolio, a 'burner' phone (a pre-paid mobile phone which can be used and then discarded, thereby allowing the user to remain anonymous) and a personal location device. All communications would be made via a secure messaging app which automatically deletes conversations and files. Every team member's phone also contained the number of the British Consulate in Pretoria, but it was made explicit that the Consulate was to be regarded only as a lifeline of last resort in case a team member became compromised so seriously that leaving South Africa ceased to be an option for some reason.

The team discussed the best conditions in which the operation should unfold and conclude successfully. Every eventuality was covered, including what to do if the safe house was compromised, or a vehicle broke down, or a team member was subjected to a hostile encounter. It was agreed that everybody would work without any 'top cover', that is to say any support agency or other third party.

Once the objectives were defined, and the concept and execution of the operation was settled, a crucial piece of the jigsaw had to be found. In order to gain a meaningful insight into how each aspect of the lion trade operates, it was clear that we would need to gain contemporary information from an insider – somebody who was himself an active player in this ugly business. Under the circumstances, there seemed only one way of ensuring that this arrangement could work as well as it had to in order to bring about the best results and to guarantee everybody's safety: this insider would need to be paid to be my team's agent. Using our network of contacts in South Africa, we were soon able to identify the perfect man for the job.

CHAPTER 9

THE WORM TURNS

A source whose identity must remain secret advised us that they knew of a person who fitted the bill as our would-be spy: a former police officer turned livestock farmer and lion dealer whom we decided to call Lister. Our source said Lister was a devotee of anything to do with Special Forces military units and a gun enthusiast to boot. We were also informed that in the recent past Lister was known to have approached a television producer who worked on the South African investigative series *Carte Blanche*, offering to go undercover in the captive-bred lion industry in return for money. This proposal had come to naught, but it certainly gave us confidence that he might be a willing candidate for our purposes. Given his own involvement in the lion trade it was unfortunate that Lister might have to be paid, but, under the circumstances, a financial transaction of some sort seemed unavoidable.

When we first encountered him, Lister rented a farmstead deep in canned hunting territory itself, North West Province. As well as farming sheep and cattle, we learned that he acted as a middleman within the lion trade. It is not known how many lions he kept personally, but he facilitated deals between lion breeders, those who run lion hunting outfits, and lion bone traders, often moving the animals or their bones around on behalf of one of these parties or selling them himself. Our source suggested to us that Lister's interest in earning extra cash was sufficiently strong that, if the price was right, he would think little of betraying anybody with whom he did business.

Having been given Lister's name and contact details, a cold call was made to him requesting a meeting under a false pretext. Posing as the employee of a Swiss non-governmental organisation which specialised in conservation and human trafficking matters, a member of my team claimed to Lister that he was researching the well-known human trafficking route which runs from the tiny landlocked kingdom of Lesotho into South Africa and wondered if he could pick his brains in person. This story was chosen because we had been advised that Lister was familiar with many of the trafficking routes used and would probably take the bait if he was offered payment. Not a word about the lion trade was mentioned to Lister during that initial phone call in case he took fright.

The plan had the desired effect. Lister agreed to meet one of my operatives in the Protea Hotel in Bloemfontein at 11 a.m. on 18 April 2019. While the precise details of the meeting were being worked out over the phone, Lister showed himself to be hungry for cash by insisting that he must be paid a fee at the start of the meeting to cover his expenses and his time. Otherwise, he said, the meeting could not go ahead at all. Once a sum was agreed, the appointment was set. Owing to his experience at handling agents, Hopgood, the team deputy, was chosen as the person who would attend. As was the team's habit, they

conducted a thorough recce of the Protea Hotel and its surrounding area before the event in case things went awry for any
reason. Proving that one should always expect the unexpected,
however, their efforts were wasted: Lister changed the terms
of the rendezvous shortly before it was due to begin, thereby
beginning a game of cat and mouse that would keep everybody
on their toes for the best part of three hours.

At 8.30 a.m. on the day of the meeting, Lister sent a text message to the team insisting that it would be cancelled unless the
sum which had been agreed by phone was paid in person into
his account at the ABSA Bank in Bloemfontein straight away.
By disrupting the original arrangement, he was clearly trying to
assert some control over proceedings and showing that he has
a suspicious mind in the process. Considering that he had been
approached out of the blue, it was perhaps no surprise that he
was being careful, but his behaviour did prompt concerns. As a
former policeman, it was not out of the question that he might
lead my team into some sort of trap. It was imperative to stay
one step ahead of him in order to keep the team safe.

The bank was in fact very close to the Protea Hotel, opposite
a shopping mall where other members of the team were already
discreetly present to watch Lister from afar and to act as Hopgood's back-up if need be. Money was deposited into Lister's
bank account while the rest of the team took up their planned
positions.

Within minutes, another text message from him confirmed
that the funds had shown up in his account, but he then said
that he was changing the planned meeting location to the
Avanti restaurant just outside the fashionable Woodland Hills

housing estate, about 4 km (2.5 miles) away. The team there-fore had to regroup at the new site, which is just next door to a gated residential village, at top speed in order to get there before Lister. The Avanti restaurant is something of a congestion point, meaning the team could very easily be cornered there if events turned sour. In light of this, it appeared that Lister had chosen this new meeting place carefully, generating more suspicion that he was not acting alone. Nonetheless, my men were in situ just before Lister showed up, and they melted into the background, with the exception of Hopgood, who sat down at a table.

Lister knew Hopgood by sight, having been sent a photo in advance to aid identification and to put Lister's mind at rest. He spotted Hopgood sitting alone and approached. Offering his hand, he said, 'Howzit.' After spending much of the morning jumping through hoops, Hopgood finally had a decent chance to assess the man sitting opposite him who was, unwittingly, himself being stalked by our team like a lion in preparation for exploitation. For what Lister did not realise was that once he had signed up to be our mole, he would have a dual function. As well as using whatever information he was able to provide to us for the purposes of Operation Chastise, at the same time we would monitor him. Our spy was to be spied upon by us.

Lister is in his late forties and can be described as a typical alpha male Boer farmer. He has a large frame, rough-hewn features and he tends to dress in the same uniform every day: a short-sleeved shirt, shorts and safari boots. Physically, he is imposing enough to have an air of mild intimidation about him. Yet, as we were to discover, once a layer of his personality has been peeled back, he is a man of many contradictions. He swings from forcefulness to a state of near-nervousness when placed under pressure, and is seemingly riddled with doubt about his capabilities. Though he appears to be confident, he never quite managed to convince us that he was always entirely self-possessed during our dealings with him.

As Lister took his place, Hopgood noticed that he had a holstered pistol on his hip. It was partially concealed by his open fleece jacket. Although it is not unusual for people in South Africa to carry a weapon, this fact proved that the man we were dealing with considered his line of work to be dangerous enough to necessitate being armed in public. This was just one further reminder of the type of unsavoury individual with whom we were, for the greater good, forming ties.

Lister began to feed Hopgood information about young women being trafficked across the Lesotho border into South Africa. Hopgood raised his hand and, stamping his own authority on the situation, politely asked him to listen. He explained that he was contracted to work as an investigator for a Swiss NGO which he was not prepared to name but which was heavily involved in countering the illegal wildlife trade. His brief, he went on, was to gather information about the cruelties involved in the captive-bred lion industry as well as the illegal lion bone trade to the Far East. 'I know that we haven't been entirely honest,' Hopgood said. 'But I needed a face-to-face meeting with you to work out your suitability as a source to infiltrate the lion trade and to secure the evidence we need to prosecute the perpetrators.' Choosing his words carefully, he then told Lister that he knew Lister was involved in trading lions himself and added that he also knew of Lister's approach to *Carte Blanche*.

Lister admitted that he had indeed tried to sell his services to this television programme, but he explained that he had not received a penny for his expenses or time. He was clearly bitter about the experience. Almost as an afterthought, at the end of his rant he demanded, 'Who gave you my name and contact details?' Hopgood replied, 'You don't need to know that, but what you do need to know is we will pay you for your time and expenses. You're clearly connected and obviously an operator.' This gave Lister something to think about. As they carried on talking, Lister mentioned the recently wound-down Operation Simba. Although nothing about it had been made public at this point, our unusual decision to save Simba must have been the subject of gossip in the industry. 'I hope you're not working for them!' he said. Keen not to sail this close to the wind for long, Hopgood answered, 'No, we're not. In fact, they got in our way, so if you do know anything about that operation, please tell me. We're trying to work out exactly who's involved in it.'

Lister confirmed that he knew quite a lot about the illegal lion trade and might be able to provide information in return for money and a suitable vehicle. Hopgood promised nothing during that first meeting, only agreeing to pass on to his boss Lister's various stipulations. He was careful to be firm but friendly in order to gain Lister's trust. He also allowed Lister to believe that he had been personally selected for this assignment, leaving him with the positive impression that he was well thought of and that they would soon be working together.

Lister maintained that he was in the lion business for the right reasons, saying that underneath it all he was a conservationist who loved these creatures. Indeed, he said, he had previously even kept one as a pet at his farmstead. Hopgood was aware of this but feigned ignorance. What Lister didn't realise was that Hopgood was also aware that this pet lion had been sold into the canned hunting industry and executed as a trophy once he had outgrown his usefulness. In light of all this, Lister's righteous parting declaration that he wanted to 'purge the captive-lion industry of its rogue operators' was scarcely credible. As their ninety minutes together came to an end, Lister promised that he would give this new opportunity some thought and would be back in touch soon.

We didn't have to wait long. The following day, he sent the team a distressing photograph of a lioness being shot in a tree with a 9mm pistol. He indicated that he could get hold of filmed footage of this kill which, according to him, was so gruesome it would 'close down the whole industry if it was released', explaining that the lioness was shot multiple times with an inferior-calibre weapon. He asked for the eye-watering sum of $60,000 for this footage. It was easy to turn down such a ludicrously high price. More constructively, however, Hopgood was able to say that his budget would allow him to pay Lister a small monthly retainer if he was prepared to share everything he knew about the lion trade and provide information that would secure prosecutions.

Lister signalled a definite interest in helping my team, prompting them to act quickly to hold his attention while also getting themselves ready for the next phase. A four-person agent-handling unit, including Hopgood, would be active on my team. They would be introduced to Lister over the ensuing few weeks in order to build a relationship with him. Using four people allowed two pairs of two to take on a 'good cop/bad cop' approach. It also meant that the operation could carry on running at full speed even if a team member was busy with another part of the investigation.

At the same time, due consideration was given to Lister's request for a vehicle. This would be a significant expense and would take a sizeable chunk out of the operation's budget. On the other hand, it would win his confidence and present an excellent opportunity to install covert video and tracking technology over which we could retain control. After weighing the cost against the potential reward, the purchase was authorised provided we were convinced of Lister's intentions after the next meeting.

This was set up as soon as practicably possible. As well as the picture of the lioness being shot out of the tree, Lister also mentioned that he had an image of a lion that had been shot in the spine and told Hopgood he had footage and photography depicting other horrors which he was prepared to release in return for cash. Hopgood was relaxed and non-committal, simply asking to meet so that they could discuss the eventual outcome of any partnership. Lister agreed and returned to Bloemfontein for a second encounter at the Avanti restaurant on 29 May. On this occasion, he played it straight, not bothering with a late change of location or the sudden demand that money be put into his bank account upfront. The team took no chances, though. Harbouring an instinctive mistrust of Lister, they were deployed around the mall and car park just as they had been before, observing the meeting and ready to assist Hopgood and one of my other investigators, who accompanied him, if required.

During that second meeting, Lister appeared nervous. Given

that he was also armed, this made him potentially unpredictable. If he became aggressive, or a third party attempted to detain a member of the team, a plan was in place to deal with the situation. Hopgood plus a colleague approached Lister, who was sitting alone at a table. As had been the case previously, the meeting was surreptitiously recorded in case anything was said that the team needed to explore for themselves.

Lister launched straight into a list of concerns he had, namely that he would be putting himself at risk if he were to help the team expose the cruelties and malpractice inherent in the captive predator industry. Hopgood pacified him by making it clear that any necessary specialist or sensitive surveillance tasks would be done by him and his team. All Lister needed to do was reveal what he knew about the industry, and the team could act on whatever he provided.

Lister, however, had in mind a more involved role for himself. 'You must understand one thing,' he said. 'You will never get this kind of footage on your own, I am telling you now. You won't. The farmers, they won't trust you, they won't let you in.' Hopgood allowed Lister to continue. 'What you must also understand is that I have spent years infiltrating this industry. It takes a long time to gain their trust. You won't be able to get the kind of footage that I can get.'

There it was. From his position inside this despicable business, Lister had effectively offered to record the misdeeds to which he was privy and to provide the footage to the Operation Chastise team. His aim, he claimed, was to end the cruel practice of killing lions for their bones. Clearly aware that this was his moment to prove he was being genuine, Lister offered to show my operatives the complete footage of the lioness shot in the tree then and there. Both of them gathered around Lister's seat as he played the film on his phone.

In it, two men drive a pick-up vehicle into a fenced enclosure. Speaking in Afrikaans, they appear to be looking for something. The camera pans onto a lioness which has climbed into a tree and is perching precariously in the fork of the branches, looking forlorn and distressed. The men speak again before a gunshot is fired from the truck. A branch splinters and the lioness roars in pain. She falls from the fork in the branches and pulls herself around tentatively, putting as much of the tree trunk as possible between herself and her pursuers. Undeterred, the men in the vehicle shoot into her again and again. Eventually, having decided they are not getting the result they want from their current position, they move closer. The driver then brings the vehicle round to the other side of the tree, where the lioness lies panting in a pathetic state, one shoulder shattered and bullet holes already pockmarking her flank. The men change guns, as they have run out of ammunition for their rifles. This time using pistols, they try again. Several shots later, the poor beast – literally riddled with bullets – finally expires. In this shooting spree, stretched over seven and a half minutes, the lioness is seen being shot ten times while the men chat to each other casually. Readers of this book can view the film on my website, using the QR code on page 276 and on the inside front cover, though I must warn them that it makes for harrowing viewing. This, sadly, is the reality of the lion farming industry in South Africa.

Lister, who had made the recording himself, explained that their marksmanship had been deliberately poor that day. They had not wanted to damage the animal's skull because doing so reduces its value in the bone trade, he said. Hopgood, a man who cannot be described as squeamish and who has seen through two frontline tours of duty in Afghanistan, was visibly shocked. Blood and suffering were not new to him, but this display of deliberate cruelty turned his stomach. His colleague, who had also experienced some very testing conditions during his service in MI5, was similarly disgusted. As they returned to their seats, Lister filled the expectant silence. 'This is shocking,' he said. 'This is terrible. This is what we must stop.'

In Chapter 2 of this book, I wrote about a tourist facility, hunting lodge and wedding venue with its own chapel called Moreson Ranch, located about 200 km (125 miles) south of Johannesburg. It is co-owned by two professional hunters, Awie Marais and Tielman de Villiers. I can now reveal that the footage Lister had filmed and which he showed to my team that day was captured at Moreson Ranch – and that it was Marais and De Villiers who shot the lioness so callously. It is appalling to think that these men would encourage people to get married on the very property where they are happy to slowly butcher a defenceless creature over a period of almost ten minutes, as they had done on film. Similarly, it is chilling to think that young children might go and pet lion cubs at Moreson Ranch, as my team did, while behind the scenes Marais and De Villiers carry out truly warped killing expeditions nearby. There can be no justification for such barbarous behaviour, but this is the reality of the captive-bred lion trade in South Africa.

My team congratulated Lister on having obtained the footage, confirming it was exactly the sort of evidence they were hoping for and assuring him it had lived up to his initial promises. There seemed little doubt he was the right man for the job. Hopgood chose this as the moment to mention to Lister that he had provisional clearance to buy a second-hand vehicle for him if he could be trusted. With the prospect of a 4x4 on the horizon, Lister then reeled off the other kit and equipment he felt he would need. By his reckoning, he would require two years to secure sufficient evidence; he would also have to have recording facilities in the vehicle, and he asked for night-vision equipment. Not wanting to diminish his enthusiasm, but concerned at the potential level of risk involved in this overweight and unfit Boer man snooping around lion farms at night, Hopgood politely ignored this last request, saying his boss was only just about to accept the idea of buying the vehicle and they would have to work on that first. The meeting ended.

The team knew they had to get hold of the highly compromising footage they had just been shown so that it could be distributed to a wider audience, but they were also aware that they could never pay Lister the $60,000 he wanted for it. Craftily, Hopgood had used his own iPhone to covertly record parts of the footage over Lister's shoulder at the restaurant. This was some sort of consolation. But, the footage aside, the bigger prize had been won that afternoon: Lister was on board.

Just as the support team was about to collapse all surveillance at the rendezvous, a white Toyota was seen entering the car park. It was driven by a woman who fitted the description of Lister's wife. After watching Lister join her in the vehicle, where they sat for a few minutes, one of the team walked casually round to it and, stooping as he pretended to tie his shoelace, reached under the car and placed a magnetic tracking device on the chassis. He then walked away coolly. The team had rehearsed this move on various vehicle models hundreds of times before deploying to South Africa and had practised further once target vehicles had been identified, always careful to stick the tracker in a place that would be both difficult to find and hard to dislodge. The device was activated and it appeared immediately on the TrackServer master screen, in the south-east corner of Woodland Hills car park.

Once back at the safe house in Johannesburg, the team had to source a second-hand Toyota with the required specification. After scouring the length and breadth of South Africa for several days, one was found in the city of Port Elizabeth, about 1,600 km (1,000 miles) from the safe house. Two team members headed south to check it over and were delighted to find it was perfect: the right price and exactly the type Lister wanted. They had it registered in Lister's name and immediately drove it back through the night to the safe house. Attention then turned to fitting the vehicle's covert recording equipment. This would require flying in two specialists from London with the necessary technology.

With a tight turnaround on the cards and no access to the vehicle beforehand, they had to guess the length of the wiring they would need and the size of port they would have to play with in order to fit the cameras and switches. They caught a night flight, landed at O. R. Tambo International with kit bags containing tools and spare parts and were whisked straight to the safe house to get started. After two full days' work, the Land Cruiser was equipped with two cameras. One was forward-facing and covered the width of the cab. The other overlooked the rear load bay. Audio recording equipment and a GPS tracker were also fitted to the vehicle. The Land Cruiser was ready for the operation and just needed to be handed over to Lister.

Hopgood had been keeping Lister updated on the progress of the vehicle, pressing him for as much information as he could in return. He arranged a meeting not far from the city centre to hand over the Land Cruiser and to show Lister how to work the recording switches. He had a couple of other items of essential equipment to hand over, too: a small covert keyring camera that could be left on the dashboard and a personal location device, such as the team carried. Lister's vehicle, and Lister himself, if he carried his PLD, could now also be monitored on screen.

Lister seemed thrilled, saying the Toyota was 'like new for sure'. Now, the onus was on him to deliver a present to us. He duly obliged, electronically transferring to Hopgood the full video of the lioness being shot out of the tree, plus two other shorter clips of lions culled for their bones, both just as cruel. One showed a sedated lion being executed with a .22-calibre pistol shot to the head in the load bay of a 4x4, and the other showed another lioness being shot multiple times, including in the spine, in a particularly sadistic fashion. In total, nine lions were savagely killed in the footage Lister supplied from Moreson Ranch.

The videos were saved to a secure storage drive and my team turned their attention to the next stage of the plan: specifically, what evidence Lister would deliver using the kit that had been sourced for him and what else he could reveal about the corrupt captive-bred lion industry and the illegal bone trade. I was happy with Operation Chastise's progress and the successful recruitment of Lister. The worm had turned.

CHAPTER 10

CEMENTING THE STING

By late May 2019, Operation Chastise had its own man embedded within the captive-bred lion industry in the form of our ex-police officer, Lister. The intention was to exploit this asset for as long as he continued to produce information that could be developed and acted upon. The team knew that from the moment Lister had been recruited the mission was, in essence, a sting.

Although there were justified reservations about working with Lister, the importance of his status as an undercover agent could not be exaggerated: he was well-connected and actively involved in the trade of live lions and their bones. Indeed, he had claimed to one of my operatives that he was South Africa's biggest lion dealer. As long as he was kept on a tight rein and continued plying his trade as normal, he had the potential to produce important material which could be handed over to the authorities. The tracking devices secreted on his wife's vehicle and on the Land Cruiser he had been loaned would strengthen the effort because his whereabouts were being watched remotely at all times via the screens at the safe house. So too would the personal location device he had been given and a mobile phone he requested, which was uploaded with spyware. This meant that my team would be able to see every message Lister sent and received and could also access his voicemail as well as keeping track of his internet searches.

During the team's first meeting with Lister, he had claimed that his principal aim was to purge the industry of rogue operators – of whom we were always convinced he was one – but at no point did his adoption of this morally upright position ring true. The consensus was that his main goal in signing up to the project, aside from making some money for himself, was in fact to remove his business rivals. From Lister's perspective, exposing them would be like throwing a grenade into their camps, potentially giving him a greater share of the market. Since we were aware of this, we knew what warning signs to watch out for.

Technically, Lister was now embroiled in what could be called a 'false flag' operation – in other words, a covert operation that was designed to conceal whoever was truly responsible for it. He had been told that a Swiss NGO was paying Hopgood and the team to carry out the investigation. He also believed that the team comprised a group of specialist investigators with military and intelligence backgrounds headed by a former British intelligence colonel, known as the Chief. (In reality, the Chief would in time be played by my investigator Gibby, albeit wearing a disguise.) This meant that those team members who would interact with Lister had to remember their cover stories for being in South Africa – that they were property consultants – and their undercover sting roles.

The third meeting with Lister came on 14 June, two days after the Land Cruiser had been delivered. This time it was a home fixture for him, as he invited Hopgood and his 'good cop' colleague to his farmstead. Taken at face value, Lister's willingness to play the host indicated that he was comfortable with my investigators being on his turf, again suggesting that trust was being gained all the time. They left the safe house for the four-hour drive to Lister's rented farmstead in North West Province with plenty of food and water on board plus two jerry cans, ensuring they would be self-sufficient if they needed to cross the border to Botswana and 'bug out' should anything go wrong. As usual, they were to covertly record the meeting.

Lister lived in isolation at the end of a mile-long track. My men logged the position of every internal gate and every possible exit point before finally arriving at the compound protecting Lister's farmstead. It had an electrified fence topped with razor wire. He stood in the doorway of his bungalow, his German shepherd guard dog straining at the leash, as they parked. Lister was armed, but there was no sign of any lions. It transpired that those lions which he owned were kept on other people's land in different locations throughout North West Province. Paying rent to 'farmshare' in this way is relatively common and helps to keep overheads down.

He welcomed the two operatives and apologised for the dog's presence, saying he would shut it away in one of his rooms. By showing the snarling animal to his visitors, however, he had made his point: he had back-up if need be. Stepping into the bungalow, the operatives soon noticed a Glock 9mm pistol sitting on a bookcase lined with dozens of military history tomes. Lister reappeared and invited them into the living room. They then realised that the holster securing the pistol to his hip was unclipped. Lister followed them in, accompanied by a young girl aged four or five. Placing her in a play area in a corner of the room, he asked my investigators to sit. Having clocked a second pistol on a sideboard, this time a CZ 9mm, plus what looked like a moderated Vektor CR-21 bullpup assault rifle, they remained standing as they assessed the situation.

Showing off this mini arsenal appeared to be another attempt by Lister to intimidate his guests. Seizing the initiative, Hopgood made light of the number of weapons dotted around the place and picked up the rifle, making it safe. My other investigator made the pistol safe when it, too, proved to be loaded. Whatever Lister had anticipated, my men were not remotely fazed by the guns. They were alarmed, however, to find loaded weapons had been left lying around so casually in a house also lived in by a young child.

They put Lister at ease by giving him a Samsung Galaxy S10 phone, as requested, explaining its features and capability. He had wanted a device on which he could record conversations – 'to record evidence, you understand', he told them. He was clearly pleased to be issued with this new toy, though obviously had no idea my team had downloaded and hidden the FlexiSPY app on the handset. This technology records phone calls, penetrates email and text messages and tracks location without the user knowing. Having thanked them, Lister produced a bottle of brandy and suggested they have a drink. Hopgood declined, but his colleague accepted. Then, the discussion changed to one about figures in South Africa's illegal lion trade.

It was impossible for Lister to talk about these rogue elements without discussing the South African Predator Association. This body presents itself as the responsible voice and regulator of the trade, but in the privacy of his home Lister said many of its members do not care about lions' welfare and seemed concerned only with pursuing their own interests. He was also scathing about the current president of SAPA, Kirsten Nematandani, who appeared to have the misfortune of having been cynically appointed within SAPA's upper echelons in 2016 to make it appear that SAPA was committed to black economic empowerment. What kind of self-respecting organisation operating in a controversial sector would choose as its head a man whom FIFA (which is not known for its robustness) has banned for five years on ethical grounds?

Lister said he believed that if certain negative influences could be removed from SAPA, it could become a force for good for lions. He claimed to be in regular contact with Pieter Potgieter, a former head of SAPA, and stated that he and several others were pushing for Potgieter to regain his position as head of SAPA's council so that its alleged credibility could be restored. He also told the team that SAPA had a policy decreeing that none of its members should do business in any environment in which he, Lister, is involved. He then claimed that some SAPA members were so desperate to sell lions, the recent American ban on the import of captive-bred lion trophies having effectively cut off a large portion of their market, that many were still selling to Lister discreetly.

Confirming that they were interested in learning more about SAPA, and agreeing that ridding the industry of its illegal operators was the best way to safeguard the African lion's future, my men took their leave after almost two and a half hours with a promise from Lister that he would tell them more about the dark side of the industry in regular reports.

Over the following weeks, Lister began to drip-feed the team information: names, places and events. It was a start, albeit a slow one. Each time Lister made contact, he would hint that there was more to come, promising that he could film illegal activity or obtain images of it. His material could be frustratingly slow to arrive. Nevertheless, each nugget that he did offer was examined by the team in the hope that they could make something of it or could use information already in the public domain to filter what was worth pursuing.

After the discovery of the Wag-'n-Bietjie slaughterhouse in April 2018, there was a particular desire to find similar examples in order to prove the thesis that this had not been an isolated case and that lions were being killed routinely in South Africa's unregulated death factories. Lister provided the location of two more slaughterhouses in the Free State. One was in the vicinity of Welkom, the second largest city in the province, and the other was in Reddersburg, a small cattle farming town 50 km (30 miles) south of Bloemfontein. He also supplied images of freshly stripped lion skeletons from the Welkom facility, run by the Wessels brothers, Sarel and Tiaan, who were said to have fallen out and were apparently feuding. Lister told us he had delivered lions to both facilities before and would do so again, and he undertook to get more footage of what he found there. He maintained that some 300 lions had been processed at the site in the previous year and that business was brisk. But he emphasised to the team on several occasions what he claimed was the highly volatile nature of the Wessels brothers.

Our research confirmed that Sarel and Tiaan Wessels did indeed appear to have links to some unprepossessing individuals. As was reported in the Afrikaans press in October 2017, Sarel Wessels was allegedly involved in a 'barbaric' attack on a lawyer, Kobus Senekal, said to have been carried out by a businessman called André Knipe, which ended in Senekal's hospitalisation.[91] Wessels reportedly 'held [Senekal] down' during the assault.

Another name provided by Lister was that of Marnus Steyl, a game farmer whom the team had come across during the course of Operation Simba. While Steyl had been careful to maintain an even smaller online footprint than the Wessels brothers, he could not bury the news that he was once accused of being implicated in a conspiracy which centred around the illegal hunting of rhinos so that their horns could be exported to Asia. The syndicate that spearheaded this nefarious activity was run by a Thai national called Chumlong Lemtongthai. In July 2011, Lemtongthai was arrested on suspicion of hiring prostitutes to smuggle the poached rhino horns, which were disguised as legal hunting trophies. Having been exposed by a whistle-blower, the case went to trial. After Lemtongthai entered into a plea bargain agreement, the five people who were co-accused in the case, including Steyl, walked free from court in November 2012.[92] Subsequently, Steyl has allegedly carried on making money in the lion bone business.

Clayton Fletcher was also suggested by Lister as a big player in SAPA who was linked to questionable dealings when it came to lions. Fletcher's name was familiar to the team, too. Firstly, he

91   'Attorney from Bloem brutally assaulted at court', *Beeld*, 12 October 2017
92   'Deal's a Deal, Says Judge', *The Mercury*, 10 June 2015

207

had given an interview to London's *Mail on Sunday* newspaper in 2017 in which it was stated he was 'proud' that his father, Douglas, was apparently the first person to hunt a captive-bred lion in South Africa back in 1985.[93] This is an unverifiable claim, but it is hardly one to boast about in any case. Second, he had also been linked to a network of alleged rhino poachers and was himself due to stand trial (under his full name of George Clayton Fletcher) in October 2010 before the case collapsed.[94] Furthermore, he was a neighbour of the ranch owner and professional hunter Freddie Scheepers, whose name had figured so prominently during Operation Simba. The team had inadvertently crossed paths with Fletcher on his way to set up the hunt for Simba.

Walter Slippers was also put on the team's radar by Lister. In 2016, some distressing photographs were published depicting some of the 250 lions living at Ingogo Safaris, a breeding and hunting farm owned by Slippers in Limpopo Province. The photos, taken by a neighbour, showed captive-bred lions which were so emaciated their bones protruded. It is not clear how old the pictures were, but the NSPCA, which investigated, claimed they were contemporary. After an inspection, which found that not all the lions on the property were as malnourished as the ones in the photos, Slippers was let off with an official warning.[95]

---

93 Barbara Jones, 'Revealed: sick trade of lions taken from their mothers, reared by humans and shot by "hunters"', *Mail on Sunday*, 25 November 2017

94 Susie Watts, 'Failure to Prosecute and Mixed Messages: How South Africa can Single-Handedly Lose the Second Rhino War', Conservation Action Trust, May 2017

95 Zainab Akande, 'Photos Show Lions Starving at Nightmare Breeding Farm', The Dodo, 13 July 2016

Unbeknown to Lister, the team was also collecting information about him – specifically, the locations he visited as he
traversed North West Province and the Free State in the newly
kitted-out Land Cruiser. It soon became clear that he was not
being open about certain locations he visited, instead passing off
old knowledge that he had about the lion trade in order to keep
the team occupied. Using mapping analysis tools, the team identified a handful of farms that were part of Lister's pattern of work
and placed whatever they could find in a dossier alongside the
information he had supplied about the operators he had named.

By the start of July, a decent number of relevant locations
and persons of interest had been identified thanks to the team's
compilation of the open-source material available. It was decided to build on this work by conducting reconnaissance
probes at every site, either at close range or at long distance
as was feasible, and then reporting back. Identifying buildings
and persons of interest from the target list proved challenging
at every turn. High electrified game fencing, on-site security
and long access roads – many with CCTV – frustrated attempts
to secure information or confirm intelligence already received.
My operatives were not the type to be put off easily, however.

The Welkom slaughterhouse – run by the Wessels brothers
and their business partner Joubre Knoesen, and for which
Lister had already supplied some images – was the prime target.
There was no doubt that animals were being slaughtered there.
Even from the outer perimeter the nauseating stench of rotting
flesh was unmistakable. My men homed in on the property
from a distance and tried a close-quarter covert approach to
film what was going on inside, to no avail. It was as tight as a

drum. Forced to rethink their plan, they covered their tracks and returned to their vehicle, which they had concealed nearby.

Then they moved their attention to another property owned by the Wessels brothers, Lechwe Lodge, a hunting lodge and conference centre which also doubles up as a wedding venue. It lies south of the city of Kroonstad, also in the Free State. In 2004, the NSPCA discovered that six lions were brought all the way from Spain to this seemingly respectable establishment in conditions which were completely unacceptable. The animals' appalling journey began with a 3,000 km (1,800-mile) journey by road from Spain to Luxembourg. After this, they were flown to Johannesburg in cramped crates which reportedly did not conform to International Air Transport Association standards. From the airport, they were driven a further 180 km (110 miles) by road to Lechwe Lodge. The NSPCA said it was not clear if the lions had been sedated at any time on the journey, increasing their stress levels.[96] Who can say why the lions were forced to endure this misery? It seems highly unlikely any of them was moved to South Africa for benign purposes, however. It was further reported in July 2015 that the wildlife conservation unit of the National Animal Protection Association (NDBV in Afrikaans) and Free State Nature Conservation found two dead lions at Lechwe Lodge. Another seventeen lions were also discovered on the property, two of which were described in the press as being 'severely underweight' and the other fifteen of which were said to be in a poor condition. At the time, Lechwe Lodge was embroiled in a liquidation lawsuit. When

---

96   'NSPCA Outraged by Lions' Traumatic Journey', South African Press Association, 9 March 2004

the liquidators heard about the precarious state of the lions, they reportedly bought meat at their own expense in order to feed the animals.[97]

My team drove down some single-track access roads around the back of Lechwe Lodge into an area marked 'OFF LIMITS' and soon passed a further sign marked 'DANGER: WILD ANIMALS FOR 3KM'. They made a 360-degree loop of the venue, conducting a full survey and recording a significant number of lions in two separate clusters of sectioned holding pens within the property perimeter. These were situated away from the public area at the main lodge house. It is anybody's guess why these lions were not on public display. What is worth remembering is that it is standard practice in South Africa that lions which are ready to be hunted, or are simply held at a facility for tourism purposes, are kept looking fit and healthy in order to bring money in. Lions whose primary purpose is breeding, on the other hand, are often neglected and remain behind the scenes where no one can see them.

The team completed similar surveys on several other properties of interest before returning to the safe house ten days later with an extensive set of reports and imagery detailing the farms' approaches, fencing, access, security, buildings of interest which were visible, plus the type and number of pens visible and whether livestock or game species were there. Concerns such as the presence of CCTV cameras or vehicles patrolling the inner fencing were logged and recommendations of how each target could be further exploited if required were also made. Being

---

97   Dirk Lotriet, 'Two lions die at liquidated lodge', News24, 21 July 2015

familiar with as many different sites as possible was important in case Lister's information led the team to any of them at short notice. In the meantime, with penetration efforts on the ground mostly thwarted by the farms' security, pressure on Lister had to be maintained.

On 29 June, Hopgood met Lister at the Butcher Shop & Grill in Johannesburg – a busy restaurant and, therefore, a safe place to talk. This time, Lister was accompanied by his wife. He was clearly excited and had much to tell. He said that he was going to visit two bone traders he knew of who wanted to show him some fresh lion bones which were for sale. The meeting was scheduled for 1 July. Crucially, it appeared that the bones originated from wild lions which had been poached in Botswana. This would be an ideal opportunity to test the covert camera kit that had been fitted to the Land Cruiser, as well as Lister's personal covert camera kit. He was reminded to take his personal location device so they could see where he was. Unbeknown to him, the team would be monitoring his vehicle and phone as usual, so this would be a useful test of Lister's honesty in reporting his location. Even if he left the PLD at home by accident or on purpose, his whereabouts would be known.

In the event, Lister did well. Footage from the cameras confirms that he drove to a location close to Christiana, an agricultural town in North West Province, and pulled up outside some wooden fencing. A small enclosed trailer, the sort that might be used to carry kit on a camping excursion, was parked outside the gate. The footage then shows that he got out and spoke to two white middle-aged men. Lion bone sets were lifted from the trailer and taken inside the fencing to be weighed. Lister surreptitiously photographed this process, capturing several shots of the weights of the bone sets. He declined to purchase any, saying they were too small for his purposes, and he retreated safely from the meeting with his integrity intact. The two would-be vendors were, of course, disappointed not to have made a sale.

Lister told the team of his certainty that the bones were those of wild lions that had been poached in Botswana. He said that the two men, whom he named as 'Tewie' Viljoen and Karel Van Heerden, were involved in the poaching and smuggling of rhino horn and hid the illicit parts inside the spare tyre of a 4x4. He had also recorded their vehicle registration numbers. This was all good-quality evidence which represented a step forward. The vehicle tech fit had also proved itself. (Incidentally, in October, Tewie Viljoen would be arrested on suspicion of trafficking rhino horn. He appeared in court under his full name, Matheus Willem Johannes Viljoen.)

Lister had shown that he had access not just to lion farms in South Africa but to the flow of illegal endangered wildlife from its northern neighbour Botswana. The team were on the right track and were close to confirming a direct link between wild lions and the captive-bred lion trade. Needless to say, this blew a hole in the oft-repeated argument mounted by SAPA and others that the captive trade is beneficial to wild lion conservation.

Hopgood arranged to meet Lister again at the Butcher Shop & Grill in Johannesburg to receive the footage. The time they spent together also provided an opportunity to service the cameras in Lister's 4x4. While they talked, Hopgood made sure to acknowledge Lister's efforts, stating that the Chief would be very happy with this development, giving him confidence that he had invested in the right man, but it was also made clear that he needed to secure further intelligence in this area. Removing these people from the game, lock, stock and barrel, was essential, he said, and not enough progress was being made.

While they talked, another of my investigators entered the same Sandton City car park where Lister had left the Land Cruiser. Wearing sunglasses and a baseball cap, he walked a circuitous route to the vehicle and, using the spare key the team had retained, proceeded to service the camera and tracking technology. Lister had also left in the Land Cruiser a blue plastic carrier bag containing a salted lion's head and a neck section of the skeleton, which were destined ultimately for the bone trade in Asia. Both were encased in bubble wrap and were sitting in the passenger footwell. These animal parts were meant for the team, who would have to conceal a tracker within the bones so that their onward journey from South Africa could be recorded. To perform this delicate operation, the carrier bag and its contents had to be transported back to the safe house, where some precision tools were stored. This course of action would be essential to confirming the trafficking routes.

Working on the basis that Lister might have set them up, or that the police might have been monitoring them, the team planned what is known as a 'brush pass'. When my operative had finished looking over the camera equipment in the Land Cruiser, he sent one of his colleagues waiting nearby a message simply reading 'Move'. Both the investigator who had just been in Lister's Land Cruiser and his colleague were carrying matching blue plastic carrier bags. While the first bag held the bones that Lister had left in the Land Cruiser, the second bag was a dummy. It contained an old jacket and a jumper roughly taped up into a ball shape. The operative carrying the dummy bag was waiting on an upper level waiting to take delivery of the bag containing the bones when the lift doors opened. They timed it perfectly. The dummy bag was handed to the operative getting out of the lift, while the bag with the bones in it was left on the lift floor, directly under its CCTV camera and therefore out of view. It was picked up immediately by the operative who got into the lift and taken back to the safe house without detection.

In the meantime, Lister had given Hopgood some further promising new information about his own contacts, referring to them as 'serious players in the trade'. He revealed that he bought lions and tigers from a man of Asian origin called Nazeer Cajee, based at a tourist facility in North West Province called Akwaaba Lodge & Predator Park. 'It's a big predator park,' he reported. 'I sell them to Jason Whitehead of Sans Souci Safaris in the Kalahari.' Then he added, 'Nazeer also breeds ligers for bones and sells live ligers to Arabs.'

At last, Lister was proving his worth.

CHAPTER 11

AKWAABA LODGE & PREDATOR PARK AND SANS SOUCI SAFARIS

By early August, my team had worked its way through the information Lister had provided and developed a decent intelligence picture of the operation. A network diagram of Lister's known associates was drawn up, providing leads which could be checked on social media platforms and other open-source tools. Transcribing the covert audio recordings of meetings held with Lister also helped to guarantee that no other lines of enquiry were missed. Occasionally, this would elicit a comment that had slipped through the net. One such overlooked nugget was an allegation made by Lister that a nature conservation official had been present at Moreson Ranch when the shocking slaughter he had recorded had taken place. Lister said the footage dated from January 2018.

The team also arranged for this shocking video to be translated from Afrikaans to English. This confirmed that Lister was the cruel profiteer whom everybody had suspected. Far from showing any animal welfare instincts, he had in fact directed the gunmen, Awie Marais and Tielman de Villiers, to shoot the cats in particular areas of their bodies. This meant they avoided damaging the lions' skulls and big bones, thus protecting Lister's own profit as a lion dealer. A seemingly contradictory second video showed Lister trying to emphasise the cruelty involved in the killing at Moreson and attempting to distance himself from it. Yet on closer inspection it could be argued that he was merely playing to the camera, portraying himself as a good man who was disgusted at what was going on. He nearly came unstuck when one of his accomplices heard him say, 'This is a sin.' When they asked him in apparent disbelief to repeat what he had just said, Lister can be heard brushing off this request and changing the subject, presumably to save his own skin.

Elsewhere, the tracker technology we had employed showed that Lister had been going to one particular location semi-regularly and then heading directly on to another location in the Kalahari, close to the Botswana border. Occasionally he would drive from the first location to his home address, stay at home for the evening and then carry on to the second location early the following morning. The tracker technology also identified movement during the night when his vehicle was stationary, suggesting that a live lion was boxed up on board. (A lion's sometimes abrupt motions would cause enough movement to 'wake up' the tracker.) Based on what Lister had told Hopgood at their previous meeting, these locations were soon realised to be Akwaaba Lodge & Predator Park in Rustenburg in North West Province, which presents itself as a family-friendly tourist facility, and Sans Souci Safaris, a lion hunting farm also in North West Province.

Akwaaba Lodge had cropped up a few months earlier during Operation Simba, when it had been suggested as a front for a captive predator breeding facility. Five lions had been poisoned there by poachers in October 2018, one of which had its paws removed and part of its face cut off.[98] A news report of the incident claimed that the park's security detail had interrupted the poachers who did this, causing them to flee with the parts of just one animal. It was suspected that the damage to the face of the lion came from an attempt to remove its teeth, which are used as trinkets, jewellery and amulets in Asia, as well as in traditional 'medicine'.

Progress was being made in other areas as well. The lion skull and the neck section of the skeleton Lister had provided, which the team had collected from his vehicle in a Johannesburg car park, had each had a tracking device fitted within them. Great resourcefulness was shown in achieving this. The team adapted two vehicle trackers, discarded their magnets and found a way of lodging them discreetly inside the cranium of the lion's skull and within a cavity in the neck bone. This was considerably cheaper than using a bespoke iridium alternative and yet it produced the same capability and, arguably, an enhanced one. Both trackers were added to the screen at the safe house and were ready to be monitored. All that remained was for Lister to identify the right opportunity to push these bones, fitted with the tracking technology, into the trade.

The next meeting with Lister was scheduled for 13 August, but he had been jumpy, trying to rearrange the date several

---

98   Zamira Rahim, 'Lion has face and paws cut off as four other big cats die of poisoning at South African wildlife reserve', *The Independent*, 5 October 2018

times. Pressure was therefore applied to focus his attention. He was quick to respond, ringing soon afterwards and suggesting a meeting at his farm a few days ahead of the agreed rendezvous so that the lion skull and neck bone, complete with the tracking devices, could be handed back to him. The only time that the team could meet him did not suit Lister, who claimed he was occupied with 'farm business', so he offered to send a trusted colleague to collect the package from an agreed site, the Monte-casino leisure complex in Johannesburg, instead.

Because our side did not want to risk being compromised by this unknown colleague of Lister's, a simple 'dead-drop' was executed, in which an item is left in a concealed place, remov-ing the need for human contact. In this case, the package was put in a dustbin on the level 3 car park of the Montecasino mall. Crumpled KFC cartons were placed on top of the bag for cam-ouflage, along with an empty bottle of Castle beer. When Lister rang to confirm that his man was on site, he was told of the dead-drop plan. This took him by surprise, as he had expected a face-to-face meeting, but his representative, whom my team observed remotely, found the package and drove it to Lister's farmstead. Back at the safe house, the activated trackers were visible on our screen and could soon be seen moving along the N12 highway at 80 km/h (50 mph).

On the morning of 12 August, the team created a WhatsApp group called 'Farm Group' and included Lister in it in order to make him feel more involved. This tactic worked. He immedi-ately sent some still images of what looked to be a freshly killed tiger, together with four short videos of the animal being carried into his vehicle. It had a nasty flesh wound on its flank, though it was not clear what might have caused this. The footage, which he said had been captured at Akwaaba Lodge & Predator Park, also featured an Asian man in a white saloon car. Lister then forwarded to the team some voicemails from this Asian man, identifying him only as 'Michael'. Lister said Michael was a big player in the bone trade. In the messages, Michael could be heard making arrangements for Lister to collect some alcohol which a cache of bone sets could be dipped in ahead of being air-freighted out of the country. It was clear that Lister was already in possession of these bone sets.

Two members of the team made the journey by road from the safe house up to Lister's farmstead during the early evening of 13 August, as arranged. On arrival, they told him that the covert cameras in the Land Cruiser had to be serviced before they could begin the debrief. Lister agreed and showed them to his outhouse, where he had parked the vehicle. Once inside, he pointed to the skull containing the tracker, which his colleague had only recently fished out of the Montecasino car park dustbin in Johannesburg, and complained that it had a broken tooth. This imperfection made it worthless in his opinion. He grumbled that he would have to give it to Michael, the mysterious Asian bone dealer, free of charge. Protecting the interests of Operation Chastise, Lister was pressed to confirm that the skull and the neck section containing the trackers would still be secreted in the shipment regardless of their perceived condition. He said this would go ahead as planned.

Next, he pointed to a significant cache of lion bones and a fleshed-out tiger skeleton. These were the remains of the tiger that had been killed at Akwaaba Lodge which he had sent pictures of via WhatsApp. My team took photographs of the gruesome scene inside Lister's makeshift abattoir as he complained that he and his labourers had had to work through the night to dip the dried bones in alcohol. The lion bones, he revealed, had come from Sans Souci Safaris. All of the animals had been skinned, deboned and boiled. The sick task of processing these bones was evidently the 'farm business' that had prevented Lister from going to the Montecasino mall himself a couple of days previously.

He walked over to the fleshed-out tiger. Half of its face mask was still stuck to its skull in order to prove to both the buyer and the end user that it really was a tiger as opposed to an 'inferior' creature. He bragged that he had been offered another five tigers, before pointing out the difference between the salted bone sets – fully fleshed whole skeletons which had been rolled and left in salt – and the alcohol-dipped sets that are cooked and left to soak in alcohol. Many buyers, he said, now preferred the alcohol-dipped sets, apparently because the calcium paste produced from the salt-dried sets is considered too piquant. For him to stand there and school my team in the changing tastes of Asia's animal bone market while surrounded by carcasses certainly showed where his true priorities lay.

The team counted fifteen sets of lion bones at Lister's property that evening, plus the tiger set, the presence of which is likely to have been intended to give the false impression to the end buyer at the final destination in Asia that all of the bones were tiger bones. Lister volunteered that this shipment was to be taken out of the country illegally, underlining the fact that he was involved at the very dirtiest end of this dirty business.

Associating with this man was becoming increasingly undesirable, but it was a tactical necessity.

The conversation turned to Michael, the elusive Asian bone buyer. Lister again claimed that nobody in the trade in South Africa knows exactly who he is, but he did warn my men that he is not a person to cross. 'He's got his route and it goes right through O. R. Tambo Airport,' was all he would say. The plan regarding the delivery of the bone sets – including those bones in which our tracking devices were secreted – was then explained. Lister would box them up, put them on his 4x4 and drop them off at an address in Johannesburg, whereupon the vehicle would be driven by one of Michael's henchmen to an unknown location. The 4x4 would be returned to Lister – minus the bones – about an hour later. Although my team pushed Lister to be more specific about where in Johannesburg he would take the bones, he would not or could not elaborate, maintaining that the drop-off point was always different and he was only ever told it shortly beforehand.

Lister then repeated that the tiger had been killed at the Akwaaba Lodge & Predator Park. This wildlife park claims on its website to treat all of its animals 'with love and affection', but Lister said that it had died after being given an overdose of tranquilliser. He emphasised that Akwaaba's owner, Nazeer Cajee, had darted it personally using a tranquilliser prepared by the facility's foreman. Discussing how the tiger was killed, Lister said, 'It was killed by overdosage.' He said there was no vet present, adding, 'I've got the footage of it where the guys of the lodge were preparing the darts and everything … The guy that darted the tiger was Nazeer Cajee himself.' Lister also said

Cajee knew it was being sold for its bones because he, Lister, told him as much. Cajee was apparently unconcerned. 'Nah,' said Lister, 'the thing is it was killed for the bones and he knew it, I told him straight. I said, "Listen, this tiger is going to go for the bones," and he said, "[Oh well,] if that's the market, that's the market." And he was paid 100,000 rand [$5,500] for that tiger.'

Lister then revealed that he himself had bought in the region of $65,000 worth of lions from Cajee over the previous two months. He also said that Cajee had many ligers at Akwaaba Lodge & Predator Park that he sold for about $6,400 each, or $16,000 if they were exported to Arabs. 'No, the thing is, it's got an exhibition centre, and at the back – if you go and google his place you will see exactly what I mean – he's got his exhibition cages, and at the back he's got cages where his ligers are kept, there are many ligers, a lot, ya.'

At this point it is worth going over a 2010 interview that Nazeer Cajee gave to the *Asian Age*. In it, he was described as 'the only non-white predator breeder in South Africa.' He claimed to give tiger and lion cubs born at his farm the best care, describing them as being 'like my children'. He said, 'The newborns spend two or three months at my home in Rustenburg. They sleep on my bed. I bottle feed them until they start drinking and eating on their own.' Speaking of his expertise in hunting, he explained: 'I did a course in hunting. The syllabus was exhaustive, with lessons in animal psychology, geography, skinning, reading of the pugmark, zoology, botany, shooting and ballistics, besides other subjects. I also learned many critical lessons through experience.' When asked if claiming to love animals while at the same time being happy to kill them represented a clash of interests, he responded: 'There is a difference between hunting and poaching. Hunting is conservation through utilisation. If I don't allow hunters in my park, the number of animals will reach unmanageable levels. For instance, the area of my park will remain the same after fifteen years but the animals would have multiplied exponentially. How will I be able to take care of them without any revenue? And why would anyone bother to rear an animal if it doesn't have any value?'[99]

It is also worth remembering the public image of Akwaaba Lodge & Predator Park. On its website, under the heading 'Our Vision and Mission', it asserts:

Almost all of the cubs we house in the park belong to other predator breeders who are also not involved in hunting, from time to time we do hand rear cubs that were neglected by their mothers either because the mum does not have milk to feed them or the litter is too big for the mum to handle [sic]. Our animals are all treated with love and affection. All visitors will see that our park is well maintained and the animals display no stress in their behaviour and are happy and relaxed. We aim to inform and educate. The animals are known by name worldwide and treated like royalty. We have tremendous respect for each one.

There was more. During the 13 August meeting, Lister also provided robust evidence of lions from Akwaaba Lodge & Predator Park being collected and delivered to a hunting farm in

---

99   T. N. Raghu, 'A caring foster father to his kids', *Asian Age*, 23 June 2010

North West Province, the aforementioned Sans Souci Safaris. According to Lister, a particularly grisly-sounding hunt had taken place a few days before, and he had managed to capture elements of it using the recording equipment we had given him.

Lister said that Sans Souci Safaris had agreed at late notice to find a lion for a Russian client to kill with the aid of a pack of dogs. One of the men behind Sans Souci Safaris, Jason White-head, had rung Lister eager to source an animal for this Eastern European tourist. Lister had been willing to oblige. He had driven to Akwaaba Lodge & Predator Park to collect the lion in question. He then went directly on to Whitehead's estate in the Kalahari.

Shortly after his arrival at Sans Souci Safaris, the lion was released. Hunting hounds from Namibia were waiting nearby on a trailer and less than six minutes later were themselves released and giving chase. The dogs wore GPS collars so that they could be followed easily. After a further ten minutes they had cornered the lion. 'The Russian client comes nearer with his professional hunter but I couldn't film, because my [4x4] had the lion crate in the back so we [Lister and the owner] had to go and hide that away,' Lister told my team. He concluded his account by saying it was 'quite interesting to watch, I can assure you those dogs are excellent. Ya. The lion didn't have a chance.'

The wretched lion having been drugged and then couriered by road in a small crate for many hours before being let loose into a confined area and pursued by a pack of hounds, it is hardly surprising that its prospects were so hopeless. Despite his relaxed attitude to this killing, Lister continued to claim that his involvement in the trade and, indeed, his being attached to

Operation Chastise, was solely due to his desire to shut down lion farming. After everything the team had witnessed and heard that evening, however, this compassionate façade was impossible to take seriously.

After they had finished looking over the bones, my two operatives plus Lister went into his house, where he soon produced a vodka bottle full of brown liquid. This, he explained, was tiger bone wine and should be considered a present. (Needless to say, although the team took this miserable mixture back to the safe house, nobody ever drank it.) He then moved on to explaining another potential deal in which he was involved. This scheme would see wild lions in Botswana poisoned so that their cubs could be trafficked into South Africa. 'You must remember that in this business you plan and plan and you try and come in … for example this Botswana deal. I was, I'm still active, but I can't press it [or] these people just disappear,' he said. 'I'm now waiting for these people to contact me. I must be there within hours.'

The team asked for more details of how this plan would be enacted given the short amount of notice he suggested he would have. He said that in Botswana wild lions are considered a pest by farmers due to their habit of hunting cattle and other valuable livestock. As a result, it is not unusual for them to be poisoned and shot. The bones are sold into the trade in South Africa and their cubs, if there are any, are brought into South Africa's tourist market. A useful bonus of this is that the cubs can widen the gene pool of the captive population. Lister gave us the name of 'one of the big guys doing this stuff'. For legal reasons I shall refer to him as 'Joel Archer', although his real name was familiar to my team via Operation Simba. Lister went on, 'Yes, and he [Archer] sells them at a big profit. So … what I was going to do there, I can't just storm into Botswana asking for bones, I'm gonna compromise myself. So I'm gonna play this slowly.' He added:

And now I'm waiting for this guy to call me. I'm gonna meet up with him and they're gonna show me the cubs in cages. Obviously I'm not gonna buy anything. I'm gonna tell them, 'Listen, I'm not interested in the cubs, I want a certain lion.' I'm going to tell, explain to them about lion genetics and everything. I'm very into genetics when it comes to lion in any case. I want to see where these lions come from, I want to show you the lion I want, and then you poison it for me. Obviously I'm going to film the whole thing. And then, un-fortunately a lion is going to die, that is, that's true. And it's a wild one, and that is a hell of a big issue for me.

Arriving back at the safe house, the team downloaded all images and video immediately, ready to compare them with the vehi-cle tracking log. It was soon apparent that Lister had delivered some new and compelling evidence. The technology confirmed that he had collected a lion from Akwaaba Lodge on 30 July and had then driven overnight to Sans Souci Safaris. Video from his 4x4 showed that another lion was picked up by him from Akwaaba Lodge on 8 August and, after another overnight drive, was released from a box on the back of his 4x4 on the morning of 9 August. It was unloaded in front of another vehicle with a meshed frame which contained the pack of hunting hounds.

The footage shows the lion was set loose at the same time as the hounds began howling and barking excitedly. Although Lister had parked his vehicle, and the camera was static, it had clearly picked up audio of the dogs being released ten minutes later, seemingly confirming Lister's account to my two operatives.

This would have been a direct contravention of the law. In North West Province, a lion must be delivered into a hunting enclosure a minimum of ninety-six hours, that is to say four days, before the hunt takes place. The law further stipulates that it is illegal to hunt big cats with hounds – with good reason. For the fact is that this medieval practice cannot be classed as hunting as any reasonable person would understand it. Instead, it is nothing more than the brutal slaying of a semi-tame, drowsy lion in a controlled environment which is dressed up as a hunt. In reality, this is just another form of canned hunting, albeit a particularly debased one. I am told by those with knowledge of the niche activity of hunting lions with hounds that, once cornered, some of the dogs are injured and possibly killed by the frightened lion as it swipes at them in defence. Before too many dogs succumb to being maimed or worse, the client must therefore be taken very rapidly to the area where the lion is pinned back so that it can be shot as soon as possible. Rushing to this 'dead cert' kill apparently adds to the fever of excitement that grips the 'hunter'. Yet this disturbing form of so-called entertainment surely throws up many animal welfare questions, which must be addressed urgently by the South African state if its reputation for responsibility is to be upheld.

The footage retrieved from the memory cards supported the idea of serious malpractice at Akwaaba Lodge & Predator

Park and complemented the short videos and images Lister had sent by WhatsApp two days earlier. It showed the pathetic end to which the tiger was subjected after being darted by Nazeer Cajee, Akwaaba Lodge's owner. Cajee's identity as the perpetrator was confirmed by comparing the footage with open-source intelligence and images. Having somehow suffered a major flank wound during the darting process, which was visible when it was carried unconscious out of its enclosure, it was finally killed by a tranquilliser overdose. Once dead, it was loaded onto Lister's vehicle and taken to his home address for processing by him.

The footage also shows Michael, the Asian bone buyer, giving Lister money with which to pay for the tiger. Michael would also purchase the fifteen lion bone sets stored at Lister's home address. All of this gives the impression that Akwaaba Lodge & Predator Park's private conduct is completely at odds with the profile it projects publicly. The evidence Lister provided proves that, far from being a place where young children and their parents can go and spend time with creatures that are treated like 'royalty', this facility is an active supplier of big cats to the canned hunting industry and to the illegal lion and tiger bone trade.

Having secured irrefutable evidence that Cajee regularly supplies live lions to a hunting farm in North West Province, and kills lions and tigers for the bone trade, it is worth remembering that the Akwaaba website offers visitors the chance to see Siberian tigers, cheetahs, black leopards, lions, white lions, spotted hyenas, jaguar, lynx, servals and ocelots. Tourists can also bottle-feed cubs and pet cheetahs, or enjoy a 'walking with lions' experience. The dark reality of this supposedly benign leisure spot could not be more different. Akwaaba Lodge's ruthless buyers and sellers of lions seemingly have nothing but the exploitation of animals and money in mind.

The video and audio footage, coupled with the tracker log, had revealed vital intelligence. It would help to build the case that would be presented to the South African authorities. However, Lister had revealed that yet more information could be collected concerning Akwaaba Lodge's liger breeding programme. Securing this was considered essential. And, separately, Lister had also revealed that he was on the brink of gaining us access to wild lions being brought into South Africa from Botswana. This, too, represented a breakthrough in the investigation.

It was decided that in order to have some control over how and when these important pieces of the jigsaw would be secured, one of the team would have to work alongside Lister. This was a high-risk strategy, because the operative could easily find himself in mortal danger if he was ever compromised. The upside, however, was that Lister could be directed and steered. In the end, a Kenyan member of the team, called Munro, was chosen for this delicate task. He could speak several indigenous African languages, including Tswana, the language mostly used in North West Province. This would allow Lister to pretend that Munro was one of his farm workers. Furthermore, with considerable military experience under his belt, Munro was certainly able to handle himself in a tight corner. In fact, his only drawback was that he had a gold tooth. This decorative touch undermined his claim to be an impoverished manual labourer who lived a hand-to-mouth existence. For this reason, he would have to go to a dentist and have it extracted. Munro duly agreed, soon showing a plain white false tooth instead.

Not long afterwards, Munro accompanied Lister on a trip to Akwaaba Lodge & Predator Park, posing as a farmhand. Arriving at the main reception, they were met by Nazeer Cajee. While Lister and Cajee exchanged pleasantries, Munro stood nearby recording them covertly. The trio then climbed into Lister's 4x4 and drove to the back end of the lodge, out of view from the public areas. They stopped at one of the storage sheds to unload a lion cage which belonged to Cajee and had been used by Lister on his previous visit to transport the tiger. Once the cage was unloaded, they drove towards some enclosures. It was immediately clear to Munro that these were being used to keep cross-bred predators that Cajee did *not* want the public to see. In one breeding enclosure, Munro observed a male and a female liger which in his estimation were aged about eighteen months. In another enclosure he saw at least six liger cubs mixed with approximately twelve lion cubs. Other predators were also spotted, including six fully grown white lions, four ash-brown lions, four white tigers and three orange Bengal tigers. Cajee then mentioned to his guests that two ligers were being sold abroad the following week, but he did not name the buyer or the day of the sale. Having successfully photographed some of these hybrids, there is no question that to Nazeer Cajee's already extensive charge sheet must be added his grim obsession with encouraging lions and tigers to mate in order, presumably, to swell his income. Indeed, it is quite possible that he is the biggest player of all within this appalling underground activity in South Africa.

Having proved himself a capable farmhand, it was immediately decided that Munro must maintain this identity so that he could accompany Lister to Botswana to gather the available evidence of wild lion cubs being brought into South Africa. This could, in time, also be presented to South Africa's authorities.

CHAPTER 12

'MICHAEL' AND THE MUTHI MARKET

August 2019 was a productive month for the Operation Chastise team. Not only did the tracking technology installed on the phone and vehicle of Agent Lister pay dividends, but he himself was able to deliver incriminating evidence of some of the major players in South Africa's damnable lion industry. After reviewing the footage he had captured, my team believed that both Nazeer Cajee, the owner of the allegedly reputable wildlife facility Akwaaba Lodge & Predator Park, and Jason Whitehead, of Sans Souci Safaris, had serious questions to answer. Yet while some footage of the mysterious bone dealer 'Michael', of whom Lister always seemed so wary, was also secured, his true identity remained unknown.

Frustratingly, the team discovered via some independent research that the car Michael had been seen driving at Akwaaba Lodge & Predator Park had a false number plate. The two telephone numbers that he used around that time were also considered to be dead ends, being linked to 'burner' phones. So, who was 'Michael'? Lister thought he was of Taiwanese origin, but the team believed he was more likely to be a Vietnamese national. It was during the middle of the month that they managed to get one step closer to establishing his real name. On 14 August, he turned up at Lister's rented farmstead in North West Province to inspect the illegal bone sets that my investigators had seen the evening before. This time, Michael drove a different car, a BMW. Lister noted down its number plate and, after the meeting, passed these details to the team, along with a breakdown of what he had ascertained during the meeting.

The BMW Michael drove offered some positive intelligence on this occasion. Through further independent research it transpired that it was registered to a female Russian national at an address in the Johannesburg suburb of Sundowner. This residence was immediately checked and found to be a self-contained property within a gated compound. The team then ran the Russian's details through every open-source network at its disposal. A positive match of a photograph of Michael was found on one of her social media accounts. While Michael's real name remained unknown, confirmation did at least exist of a link between the pair.

The visit that Michael paid to Lister's house on 14 August was a stressful one for our agent. Worryingly, Michael dropped into the conversation that he had heard a rumour that Lister was trying to expose the lion bone industry. He then apparently told Lister he had already made enquiries about this allegation and found it to be false, and was therefore happy to continue doing business with him. If nothing else, this faintly menacing exchange further underlines the risk that anybody who involves themself in any aspect of the illegal lion trade faces, let alone a lion dealer who is trying to serve two masters at once. It is a business whose practitioners guard their interests jealously, rather like those who operate in the drugs trade. This leaves them open to threats, intimidation, violence and possibly death. Lister was certainly unnerved, and later told the team of his sense that Michael had made a half-hidden threat. Why, after all, would he have mentioned Lister's rumoured duplicity if he had no serious concerns about it?

During their 14 August meeting, Michael also revealed to Lister that ten boxes of lion bones had been confiscated by the authorities at O. R. Tambo Airport the previous week. He then maintained that the media in South Africa would not come to hear of this through any official channel because those in charge do not even regard such a 'small' seizure as a serious offence, and the perpetrators would face no penalty. How did Michael know all of this? He went on to disclose to Lister his own modus operandi for moving bones illegally through O. R. Tambo Airport – an insight which Lister was also able to pass on to my team. Michael said that he bribed corrupt airport staff to wave his contraband boxes through without them being searched. He said this is the quickest route to get the bones to Asia. When Lister asked Michael why fewer people send bones via sea freight than was the case previously, he replied, 'You have to buy space, you have to buy the whole crate, and to send twenty or thirty sets like that is not worth it, so you need at least 100 sets to do it to be financially viable. That is why they don't do that any more. That's why they use the nearest airport. They buy the officials there and they send the stuff.' If this is even remotely accurate, it is a devastating indictment of South Africa's so-called customs patrols at its international airports, which raises major questions about the robustness of the country's approach to tackling the bone trade, among other illegality.

Lister was convinced that the illegal bone sets that he had just produced, including those containing my team's trackers, would be sent overseas via O. R. Tambo Airport, but he was alarmed still further when Michael divulged that this cargo would be delayed because of the previous week's confiscations. 'Everybody's become a bit hyped and on the alert, so the whole chain is going to wait,' Michael told him. This meant that Lister would have to keep the bone sets on his property for longer than he had expected. Michael also challenged him over the weight of some of the sets, saying that those he considered too light needed to be replaced. To ensure the shipment went ahead, Lister agreed to give the lighter sets to Michael free of charge, reducing his own profit share. This idea may have been accepted by Michael at the time, but in fact not a single bone left Lister's garage during the month of August. Indeed, it would be almost four more weeks before they were moved elsewhere. This was a worry for the team, because the batteries in the trackers that had been fitted so carefully had a three-month life span and the clock was ticking.

At the end of August, two of my operatives offered to take Lister and his wife and child out for dinner at his favourite restaurant in Johannesburg. This goodwill gesture was considered an easy way to keep him onside and to encourage his confidence, given how shaky Michael had made him feel. Another reason for issuing this invitation was that the battery of the tracker which had been fitted to Lister's wife's vehicle a few months previously was running low and needed to be replaced with a new one.

The Listers arrived at the city's Radisson Blu hotel, having been booked into a family room for the night. Lister himself was then asked to meet my team in a conference room downstairs to run through a few questions relating to the bone shipment that was supposed to have been picked up by Michael but which, to everyone's consternation, so far remained in Lister's outbuildings. Once Lister was safely occupied with two members of my team, a third operative slipped away to comb the car park for his wife's vehicle.

Lister began by explaining that Michael had, since their meeting on 14 August, demanded three further new bone sets, claiming that some of the weights of the existing cache were still too low. (An average of 20 kilograms (44 lbs) per set is now said to be considered necessary to make the cost of exporting them worthwhile.) He also repeated his observation that there was a growing preference for bone sets that had been soaked in alcohol rather than salted. On an operational level, he claimed that each bone buyer in South Africa runs his or her own team and has someone on their payroll at O. R. Tambo Airport. Formerly, bones were smuggled by boat to a bigger ship, but the sea route was considered to take too long, as well as being financially unviable for smaller quantities.

Despite Lister's obvious lack of ease, the team continued to keep Michael as the focus of their questions. He, after all, was a principal player who set prices and dates and negotiated the passage of bones through the airport. It was essential to use this opportunity to establish as much as possible about him. They established that Michael has a white driver and is considered to be a mysterious figure even within the bone trade, insofar as none of the other bone buyers appear to know him.

Lister added that, to the best of his knowledge, bones that leave the country legally and illegally go to the same 'big boss', who apparently pays about $900 per kilo. Lister also spoke in indefinite terms of a prospective deal on the horizon involving a Taiwanese national.

He was then asked about a game farm near Hartbeesfontein in North West Province which was then known as Voi Lodge, owned by some Vietnamese nationals. Allegedly, it was breeding tigers and was suspected of having links to an international wildlife trafficking network. Lister had confirmed previously that he had a friend who had supplied this place with bones. He had also alleged that big-cat bones are processed on the property, which is why it came under my team's scrutiny during Operation Simba – indeed, it was one of the targeted operations I surveyed by helicopter in March 2019. Since that flight, the team had conducted a drone survey and found that the enclosures at Voi Lodge which are believed to hold tigers appeared to have expanded by almost a third in area. Yet the site's impressive security meant that it was impossible for anybody to remain near its boundary fence during daylight hours without being seen, and ultimately the team's attempts to infiltrate it had to be abandoned. Lister said he could shed no further light on goings-on there, but it is worth noting that subsequent to this meeting, it was reported that in November 2019, two Vietnamese foreign nationals, Nguyen Huu Dong, aged twenty-three, and Chu Duc Thang, aged thirty-five, were arrested following a police raid on the property in which 100 rhino horns, several unlicensed and illegal firearms, hundreds of rounds of ammunition, four dead tiger carcasses and a significant amount of cash and foreign currency were discovered.¹⁰⁰ The NSPCA also opened a case of animal cruelty and neglect when inspectors visited the farm soon after their arrest, having found more than fifty captive tigers and about ten lions suffering from heat exhaustion which were confined to living in dirty and unhygienic conditions. To the bemusement of many animal rights activists, however, both men were released on bail in February 2020, prompting new questions about how seriously the authorities in South Africa take evidence of alleged wrongdoing and criminality.

After the team had finished talking to Lister about Voi Lodge, they adjourned to eat dinner with his wife and child. It had been a short meeting, but as much information as possible had been gleaned without pushing Lister too hard. The aim had been to leave him at the end of the evening feeling incentivised and motivated to continue delivering corroboration of the law-breaking inherent within this despicable trade. Furthermore, while they had been talking, his wife's vehicle had been located and the tracking device on it successfully replaced. Over dinner, Lister told several grisly stories about recent farm murders of which he was aware, and he appeared to relish the shocked reactions of my two operatives. As noted already, he was not a man towards whom it was easy to feel a great deal of affection.

By the start of September, the bone shipment with the trackers in it remained on Lister's property, with no inkling of when it might be moved. While the team waited, they decided to explore downtown Johannesburg's muthi market (meaning

---

100 Ntwaagae Seleka, 'Cops recover 100 rhino horns, four tiger carcasses, guns and ammunition during raids', News24, 27 November 2019

traditional 'medicine' market) to try to establish whether any lion parts from captive-bred operations ended up there. The market, which is run mainly by Zulu-speaking people, is based at Faraday in Marshalltown and caters to those who wish to use the vast range of lotions and potions which are made up on site using a variety of plants and animal parts. A source had suggested to the team that because lion skins have little value to farmers or bone buyers, a small number of them have been seen at the market, and this might generate a possible lead.

On entering the market, it was immediately obvious that it is not policed in any serious way and neither, on the strength of the team's visit there, is the law enforced regularly, such is the breadth of dead specimens being traded openly. Leopard and lion skins abounded, as did pangolin skins, big-cat skulls and even rare vulture heads. One of my operatives began taking pictures with an iPhone while his colleague bought time by handing 50-rand notes (worth just over $3) to any stallholder who raised questions about this 'intrusion'. The pair moved reasonably fast, but word soon spread around the market that a couple of Europeans were photographing cat skins. After several minutes, a small but growing crowd of curious locals started to follow them around the maze of market stalls. As my operatives moved towards the exit, they saw a huge male lion skin hanging from one of the supporting pillars which holds up the market's tin roof. All questions about this skin were batted away by the stallholder. When one of the operatives asked the seller if he could please stand in front of the skin while a photo was taken in order to achieve a sense of scale, he refused, threatening instead to put a fatal Zulu curse on him. They soon left by the nearest exit, pleased to have obtained solid confirmation of the illegal wildlife trade being conducted openly in a public place in South Africa's biggest city without hindrance from the authorities.

In the meantime, further checks were being run on the Russian national and associate of Michael. She was found to be in her thirties and well-travelled. Other addresses to which she was thought to have any link were also checked and the team spent many hours studying social media accounts. Through this, they discovered the existence of a network of Russian nationals in South Africa, each of whom had links to several South African nationals who themselves had connections to the operation's targets and various professional hunting outfits that had form for unethical practices. A larger picture was beginning to take shape.

By early September, Lister began to share the team's concerns about whether the batteries in the bone tracker would last until the bones reached their final destination, almost certain to be a processing plant in Asia. Then, days later, a new opportunity presented itself. Another bone buyer, a man called Martin Le Roux, ordered a further twenty sets of bones from Lister. He duly sourced them from his contact, Jason Whitehead of Sans Souci Safaris, meaning that by the middle of the month Lister had two substantial hauls of illegal lion bone sets, and one tiger bone set, sitting in his outbuildings. The first was intended for Michael; the second for Le Roux. Around this time, Michael had told Lister that his bones were going to be moved imminently and Le Roux apparently wanted to move quickly as well.

Seizing this chance, two members of the team left the safe house early on 16 September and headed to Lister's house with the intention of fitting another tracker into a lion skull. This would mean that a second shipment – Le Roux's – could be tracked. By arrangement, Lister left the Land Cruiser he had been loaned at the gate of his property so that one of my operatives could service its cameras. Having checked this equipment and swapped the camera memory cards for a fresh set, my man then took the lion skull that had been left for him in the passenger footwell and drove a short distance away to a secluded layby while his colleague waited as a lookout further up the road. Once parked, my operative took out his tool bag and began to cut away the palate bone in a lion skull. Then he inserted a configured tracker into the cranium and resealed the bone by gluing and masking the saw cuts. When this delicate operation had been completed, he returned to Lister's vehicle, put the skull back and, having collected his colleague, headed to the safe house near Johannesburg.

En route, they received a phone call from Lister with news that Michael had decided to collect his bone sets in Johannesburg that afternoon. The handover was to take place at the Caltex Kingfisher petrol station just outside the Fourways district. They headed there immediately and reached a decent stakeout position ahead of the pick-up time. A photographer with a long-range lens was also contacted and primed to cover the illicit meeting.

Several hours later, as he approached, Lister sent the team a message alerting them to his arrival. They watched as he pulled into the petrol station, drove past the fuel pumps and slotted the Land Cruiser into a parking space in front of the shop. He went inside and was briefly out of view of my operatives. A few minutes later, a white Jeep Cherokee with a distinctive star motif on the driver's door pulled up two spaces to the left of Lister's vehicle. A thin white man wearing dark sunglasses got out. He met Lister and handed over a brown bag, in exchange taking the keys to the Land Cruiser. Lister then got into the Jeep Cherokee with another man – later confirmed to be Michael – while the man in sunglasses drove the Land Cruiser out of the car park. All of this was captured in a series of photographs.

Back at the safe house, the trackers on the Land Cruiser and inside the lion skeleton were being watched in the control room. Images on screen confirmed that the Land Cruiser entered a gated residential community, went static for a short time (presumably while the contraband was being unloaded) and then returned to the Kingfisher service station, whereupon the covert team watched Lister exit the Jeep and return to the Land Cruiser, swapping places with the man in sunglasses. The drop-off address was soon identified as a compound in the Fourways district, north of Johannesburg.

At the safe house, the analysts immediately started working on the images and intelligence that had been acquired. A photo posted on Instagram of the Russian national with her dogs lazing by a swimming pool was confirmed as an accurate match for the Fourways compound's garden. Then, two days later, the alarm of the tracker fitted to the bones meant for Michael was activated, indicating movement. The team traced the bones to the Apple Storage unit, which was subsequently established to be a dedicated storage area serving O. R. Tambo Airport. An accurate fix was made on the standard-sized shipping container in which the tracker had been left and, using their contacts, the team was able to gain sight of the storage records. These were registered in the name of an individual called Timothy Comyn. Open-source searches confirmed that the man in sunglasses who had collected the bones at the petrol station matched Comyn's description. Footage from the internal cab camera of the Land Cruiser, which had been used to transport the bones, showed they had first gone to the Fourways compound. The same footage revealed Comyn unloading the bags of bone sets into a garage. All of this counted as more important evidence of players operating in the illegal bone trade which could be handed over to South Africa's authorities in due course.

If Lister seemed to have been unsettled by his various dealings with Michael over the previous weeks, his temperament remained steadier in relation to wild lions – specifically, his confidence that he could obtain proof of wild lion poaching in Botswana. He insisted that their bones would be trafficked into the South African bone trade and any cubs that were found with them or near them would also be trafficked into South Africa and then sold at a premium into the captive-bred lion hunting industry to improve its shrinking gene pool. Somewhat grandly, he even informed the team that he was willing to commission some poachers in Botswana himself to poison a pride of lions and through this would then trace the trafficking route into South Africa. This suggestion was met with horror and it was made clear to him that infiltrating an existing Botswana bone pipeline would be more than adequate to illustrate that wild lions were being brought over the border. If these nefarious activities could be shown to have occurred even once, a very significant hole would be blown in the story repeated ad infinitum by South Africa's lion breeders and canned hunters that lion farming and canned hunting actively protect Africa's wild lion population.

Yet despite Lister promising repeatedly to help the team in this regard, he had failed to do any such thing by mid-September. He told the team that he had organised a meeting with several of his contacts on the Botswana side of the border, but for his own reasons he had cancelled this plan twice. On a third occasion, he had been unable to attend the meeting because the clutch on the Land Cruiser had malfunctioned – something the team knew to be true. Nevertheless, frustration was growing at his lack of progress. Further pressure was applied during a meeting at his house on 29 September, during which it was made clear to him that every decent attempt had to be made to prove that Botswana's wild lions were being traded illegally and then fed into South Africa's lion market. Again, Lister promised he would act, and again he said he would be willing to take a member of my team, Munro, with him so that he could pose as a farmhand and gather evidence independently.

The 29 September meeting also provided an opportunity to service the camera in Lister's Land Cruiser and to survey the second cache of lion bone sets – those destined for the bone buyer Martin Le Roux. The team observed that all of the skulls in this cache had a suspiciously neat .22-calibre hole through the cranium, almost certainly demonstrating that the lions had either been drugged and then killed with a bullet to the head, or simply shot while in a cage. The precision with which each bullet seemed to have been delivered rubbished Lister's claim that he dealt only in 'ethically' hunted lion bones. More importantly, however, was that Lister also spoke of Le Roux as a big buyer of bones, adding another name to the list that the team intended to hand in to the South African authorities.

Two weeks after this meeting, in October 2019, a study was published by Panthera, the organisation dedicated to the conservation of all forty of the world's wild cat species and their habitats. It concluded that there is a growing threat to Africa's wild lion populations that is directly attributable to the targeted poaching of body parts, specifically teeth and claws. The study reported that lion populations had declined across Africa by an estimated 43 per cent over the previous twenty-one years, and that their range had declined by 75 per cent over the previous half-century. Loss of prey and habitat were offered as the main reasons for this downturn. Persecution from livestock farmers was also cited as a key factor. Lister had told the team already that livestock farmers in Botswana often regard wild lions as a pest which they will destroy if need be. Panthera's report made for sickening reading, but it strengthened my resolve and the team's determination to end this appalling trade, which has now seemingly infected most of southern Africa.

CHAPTER 13

ENDGAME

In early October, as promised, Lister began applying some pressure on his Botswana poaching contacts. When they confirmed that they would soon be going on a poaching trip in the Kgalagadi Transfrontier Park, he seemed positively gleeful. Lister told the team that these men were serious criminal operators who knew how to kill wild lions specifically for the bone trade. This meant that they would either poison the animals or shoot them in their stomachs in order to avoid damaging a single piece of their highly valuable bone tissue, leave them for twenty-four hours, and then track them. Both methods guarantee that they would make as much money as possible after the lions had suffered a slow and painful death. Lister displayed no sensitivity at all to the predicament of these creatures. Indeed, he had suggested previously that he might supply the poison which could be used to assist the poachers in their appalling scheme. Although it was becoming increasingly difficult for my team to work with Lister owing to his callous attitude, nobody lost sight of the fact that this was a valuable opportunity to collect vital evidence which could be handed over to the South

African authorities. Munro, a member of my team, was ready to accompany Lister, posing as his farmhand.

The team established that the poachers were hunting lions to order ultimately on behalf of a South African national who was known to them only as 'Tiaan'. The hunters' immediate boss, who was called 'Big Bimbo', looked after the business side of the transaction; they were merely the trigger men. It then transpired that Tiaan had bought bones and cubs from Big Bimbo before but information about him was pretty limited. He was known to drive a white Ford twin-cab pick-up vehicle, and a phone number for him had also been unearthed, which could be checked. There were strong suspicions that this might be Tiaan Wessels, the co-head of the Welkom slaughterhouse who was mentioned in Chapter 10. In order to secure the best possible evidence about him and the poaching enterprise in general, it was essential that Lister should engage with Bimbo directly rather than with his foot soldiers. After this point was drilled into Lister, he promised to do so.

While waiting for news of exactly when his trip to Botswana might take place, Lister sent a message to the team on 10 October informing them that Martin Le Roux, the bone buyer mentioned in the previous chapter, would send a vehicle to his farmstead that evening to pick up his bone cache. Like the bone set collected by Michael, Le Roux's cache had also had tracker technology installed in it by my team, making this an important development. Lister was instructed to position the camera on his vehicle so that it captured footage of the cache being picked up by Le Roux's representative. Lister agreed to do so, but before he could return to his farmstead, he said, he had some other lion business to complete. Given that some of this 'other business' was captured on film, it is worth describing it briefly.

Lister had recently loaded a huge male lion onto the back of his vehicle at Akwaaba Lodge & Predator Park and driven it to Sans Souci Safaris in the Kalahari for release into a small holding pen in the centre of its hunting area. The client who was to shoot this poor beast had apparently been delayed, meaning that the lion would be kept for a few days in a smaller enclosure rather than – as the law decreed – released into a sizeable hunting block to be 're-wilded'. Lister covertly filmed it being unloaded and the results were truly pathetic to watch. Having been kept in a cage so cramped that it was unable to turn around properly, it bolted into the enclosure as soon as it could and hit a fence at full speed, bouncing off it. While it turned to run back, its captors, Lister and Whitehead, who were still standing on the back of the Land Cruiser, started shouting at the terrified animal, driving it into a deeper panic. It then sought sanctuary in the branches of an acacia tree nearby, where it defecated, almost certainly through fear. Here, in this short film, was a perfect encapsulation of the low status to which one of Africa's most recognisable species has been reduced. To see this quivering wreck seeking safety in a stunted thorn tree within an enclosure the size of a tennis court was shameful.

When he returned home, Lister reversed the Land Cruiser into his garage and moved Le Roux's bone cache into the area covered by one of the cab cameras. Two further cameras, one covering the inside of the garage and one trained on the drive up to the garage, were also filming. The cameras showed that the bone exchange itself was overseen by Lister's wife, making her an accessory to this criminal enterprise. Martin Le Roux's foreman, a Mr Hannes Martin, arrived at Lister's farm just after 8 p.m. in a white Toyota. Martin loaded the bones, camouflaged them with grass thatch and left. My team tracked their progress and noted three hours later that the tracker became stationary at a remote farmstead near Theunissen in the Free State, 95 km (60 miles) north-east of Bloemfontein. The team soon established that this was a farm owned by Martin Le Roux, a fact that Lister was able to confirm. Operation Chastise now had two active bone caches in play, each installed with tracking technology. The only concern anybody had related to their batteries. By this point, they already showed a 30 per cent loss of power due to the delay in handovers. My team hoped that the shipment would soon move, but ultimately they would be disappointed.

Three weeks into October, my team was organising its first trip to Botswana. They set up base in two houses, one in the capital, Gaborone, and another just over the border in the South African city of Mahikeng in North West Province. Having two safe houses was considered sensible so that all eventualities could be covered, and an evacuation plan was also drawn up should anybody become compromised. On the morning of 23 October, Lister crossed the border into Botswana at the village of Bray. Shortly before 9 a.m., my operatives dropped Munro, disguised as a farm worker, close by at an agreed pick-up point and continued to track him via the GPS signal on his personal location device. Lister collected Munro and they headed to the rendezvous with Lister's poaching contacts close to the village of Kokotsha. The two poachers were known as Little Bimbo and Lucky. Both men, who are in their twenties and of African descent, were small and scruffy. Big Bimbo, who is also African, was their boss, though as yet nobody in the team had met him.

Munro observed that Lister was very open and friendly with the poachers, but he was soon outraged to discover that Lister had ignored the pleas of the team and brought with him some poison to give to these two crooks. Munro stepped in before Lister had the opportunity to physically hand it over to the poachers, warning him in very direct terms that if he went through with his warped plan, he would be filmed doing so and would then be reported to the authorities. Lister stood down, but he was clearly disgruntled. It was Munro's opinion that Lister was so desperate for these wild lions to be poached because he was running short of cash and needed to get his hands on their eminently valuable bones. Even if this was true, it was completely unacceptable.

The group headed off towards the Makgolwane Pan to sight lions which the poachers had tracked previously. Lion spoor was soon detected, but tracking proved fruitless: Lister's considerable bulk meant that he was simply not fit enough for this kind of work. The group then moved on towards a second area known as Tsintlhane Pan, where Little Bimbo and Lucky had also tracked a small pride of lions not long before. This time, they struck gold. Little Bimbo wanted to follow the pride, but Munro called a halt to proceedings, using Lister's obvious lack of fitness as an excuse. He had confirmed that the poachers were prepared to commit wildlife crime and for the purposes of the operation that was sufficient for now. He wanted no more to do with this endeavour. Furthermore, he did not relish the prospect of being shot by the Botswana Defence Force for poaching lions in a protected area. Based on what they witnessed during this short expedition, neither Munro nor Lister had any doubt that Little Bimbo and Lucky were practised players who had killed wild lions before. The poachers headed off to continue their hunt alone. Munro was picked up by his colleagues shortly afterwards and the group headed back to the safe house to re-evaluate the plan.

Having got the necessary confirmation that these poachers were experienced and ruthless, it was decided that Lister should again be leant upon in order to drive home the point that he had to help the team achieve some tangible results before the end of the year. On 31 October, he was invited to another meeting in Johannesburg, this time held in a conference room at the InterContinental Hotel at O. R. Tambo Airport. Lister was told in advance that among those present would be the head of the Swiss non-governmental organisation who was funding Operation Chastise. In reality, this man, whom we called 'Herr Schmidt', was a work of fiction, simply a cover story along with his 'NGO'. The part of Schmidt was played by a member of my team whom Lister had not met before. To give proceedings the ring of authenticity, it was announced at the start of the meeting that everybody's mobile phone would be switched off and placed face up on the table to ensure that nobody recorded the conversation or relayed it to a third party. A video camera was secreted on a high bookshelf behind Lister's chair to monitor him.

First, Herr Schmidt demanded a full review of the operation. Having listened somewhat impatiently to Lister's explanation, Schmidt made it plain that he was not happy with its progress and warned that funding would cease altogether unless more was achieved. Lister clearly felt as though he was on the back foot and promised to obtain evidence of the Botswana wild lions being poached and trafficked into South Africa as soon as possible. He also suggested that he could film a canned tiger hunt. This was something he had spoken of previously in rather half-hearted terms, but he seemed entirely serious about it on this occasion. He claimed that 'Joel Archer' was involved in canned tiger hunting and said he was sure that Sans Souci Safaris would have a Russian client with an interest in shooting a tiger. This chimed with information that my operative, Gibby, had ascertained during Operation Simba. And Adrian Sailor, a British taxidermist and hunting outfitter who had come to the team's attention during Operation Simba when offering advice on how to smuggle a captive-lion skin into America by hiding it inside the skin of a red deer, had also told Gibby that Archer regularly hunted canned tigers. Sailor had even referred to a Russian client who took a tiger skin home in his suitcase from South Africa rolled up in a 'wet', or untreated, state. Herr Schmidt called a halt to this short but tense meeting, and Lister promised to do his best to get the results required.

As a result of this, Operation Chastise continued to gain momentum into November. On 3 November, Lister attended another meeting with the team to plan for his next trip to Botswana, where he would again link up with the lion poachers, and to discuss his ability to record the canned tiger hunt. He proved to be very talkative, announcing that he had purchased a lion the previous month in the farming town of Boshof in the Free State. He also accused the Lion and Safari Park near

Johannesburg of selling lions into the canned lion hunting industry. He maintained that Sans Souci Safaris was struggling financially because a lot of its lion permits had been cancelled, necessitating more under-the-table hunts. And he moaned that the bone caches belonging to Michael and to Martin Le Roux were still waiting to be exported from South Africa. He explained that a bust at O. R. Tambo Airport in early October was responsible for this inactivity. One person was arrested after the Environmental Management Inspectorate, known colloquially as the Green Scorpions, foiled an alleged lion-bone smuggling attempt. The bones, which were destined for Malaysia, were discovered when a crate arrived at the airport for shipment without proper documentation. According to the transportation document, the shipment had been wrongly declared. When the crate was inspected, twelve boxes of lion bones, wrapped in aluminium foil and weighing 342 kg (750 lbs), were discovered. Lister said that there was something of a panic on, and Le Roux wanted to wait until things quietened down. Michael had apparently rung Lister to report that his corrupt facilitators at the airport believed there was no chance to move the contraband. He then revealed that Michael processed bones at his property about eight times a year, usually between fifteen and twenty sets at a time. These insights were noted down carefully for the dossier that would be presented to the authorities in due course.

Lister also used this meeting to share with the team a short but disturbing video he had in his possession of a man who he said was a professional vet deliberately overdosing a lion with a syringe full of tranquilliser, injecting it directly into the sleeping lion's heart. He would not reveal the vet's identity or the location where this gruesome premeditated murder (for that is what it was) took place, but it was yet more evidence of the appalling abuse lions face.

While this footage was distressing to watch, over the next few days the team was shown in even plainer terms the levels of cruelty which are casually inflicted on lions by those involved in the trade. On Tuesday 5 November, Lister collected a lion at Cheetau Lodge in the Free State, which is owned by a SAPA member called Bok Van Zyl. The lion was destined to be killed at Sans Souci by one of Jason Whitehead's clients two days later, but the hunt had to be postponed by twenty-four hours due to unforeseen circumstances. Lister supplied footage to the team of the lion being loaded onto his 4x4 and money changing hands at Cheetau Lodge. It was assumed by everybody that he would put the lion into a holding pen, where it would be kept until Friday 8 November, the new date on which it would be hunted. What happened instead was that it was kept for forty-eight hours in a cramped crate on his farm, defying every welfare stipulation that one can think of. As a result of having to endure these dreadful conditions, the lion died. An unapologetic Lister claimed nonchalantly that its death was attributable to the lion reacting badly to the drug that had been used to sedate it. He then complained about the money he would lose, only becoming cheerful again when he told the team subsequently that he had found a replacement lion and would process the dead one for its bones. He then supplied footage of the replacement lion being released at Sans Souci and of the dreaded 'kill shot' once it had been slain.

Despite Lister's abysmal behaviour, the team pressed on, certain that he represented the surest way of securing the proof needed to contradict the notion that the mere existence of captive-bred lions somehow guarantees the safety of wild lions. By late November, the team was satisfied that Lister had indeed been retained by the aforementioned slaughterhouse owner Tiaan Wessels to bring some wild lion bones from Botswana into South Africa. Lister kept many of the details of this operation to himself, but, having confirmed that he would be happy for Munro to accompany him while working undercover, he revealed that his client was expecting him to bring several live cheetahs into the country. He also disclosed that this illegal haul of cheetahs and lion bones were to be flown, rather than driven, across the border.

By 2 December, Munro was back in Botswana with Lister, this time to meet Big Bimbo. The rendezvous took place on the Botswana side of the McCarthy's Rest border post. Tall and better turned out than his junior colleagues, Big Bimbo was ready and waiting for them. Munro was introduced as one of Lister's farm labourers and, fortunately, Big Bimbo seemed unperturbed by the presence of this stranger. The trio climbed into Lister's Land Cruiser and headed for Big Bimbo's house, leaving his car parked at the border. Upon arrival, he showed off to his visitors a wild cheetah which had been captured recently plus three wild cheetah cubs, all kept in separate rooms in an outhouse away from the main building. Munro also counted six sets of lion bones next door to where the adult cheetah was kept.

While Lister negotiated with Big Bimbo, three unknown men arrived in a 4x4 which held a further ten sets of lion bones. They were Big Bimbo's associates or hunting friends and, Munro decided, they had probably put in an appearance in order to show Lister how plentiful these bones were because he had not indicated how many in total he wanted to buy. After a further inspection of the bones, Lister told Big Bimbo that he was not happy with the quality of some of them, saying they were missing certain parts. He also said that he could only take a small number into South Africa at any one time. Just before they left, Munro saw Lister give Bimbo some drugs. It transpired that these were to be used to dart the cheetahs the following morning before they were flown into South Africa. Lister even showed Big Bimbo how to administer the injections.

Next, Lister, Munro and Big Bimbo drove back to where the car had been left near the border. Playing the role of his boss, Lister told Munro that he needed to keep an eye on the vehicle while he and Big Bimbo went off to conduct a recce of the various possible exchange points across the border. This was in fact a pre-arranged ploy. As soon as they were out of sight, Munro put a tracker on Big Bimbo's car, just as Lister knew he would. He was then collected by a member of the team and driven back to the safe house.

Lister and Big Bimbo stayed in South Africa scrutinising the border until the light began to fail. All the while, Munro and another member of the team were monitoring Big Bimbo's tracker on their screen, waiting for his car to move. It remained stationary until about 10 p.m., when it travelled from the border to what they realised was a police station in Tsabong in Botswana. This was a surprise, but the team decided to wait until morning to find out what had happened. At first light, they headed to the police station and there, sure enough, was Big Bimbo's car.

Immediately realising that he had likely been arrested for some reason, they returned to the safe house, closed it quickly, and went straight back to the remote airstrip near McCarthy's Rest on the South African side of the border, where the expected cheetah and lion bone transaction was due to take place.

My two operatives waited there for several hours, unable to contact Lister because of a poor signal and unclear about his precise whereabouts. At about midday, they left the area, hoping to be able to photograph the plane as it came in to land. Shortly afterwards, they spoke to Lister, now some distance away, who informed them that the plane had landed and had waited for thirty minutes before taking off without having collected the booty. He named the airline as Saaiman Aviation and said that one of Wessels's foremen had been on board. Wessels had apparently rung Lister and threatened him if he was being messed around or set up. Realising that the situation had gone spectacularly wrong, my men moved to a petrol station in Kuruman, a town in the Northern Cape province, where they met Lister. They agreed that Lister would go home and would inform them once he heard from Big Bimbo.

On Thursday 5 December, the tracker on Big Bimbo's car showed that the vehicle was moving. Lister was alerted and rang him. It transpired that Big Bimbo had been arrested after he and Lister had parted company on the South African side of the border a couple of nights previously. For reasons best known to himself, he had decided to cross the border back into Botswana by jumping a fence rather than by the conventional border crossing. The police had picked him up and apprehended him as soon as he got into his car because they had been watching it. Big Bimbo told Lister that the merchandise needed to be moved as soon as possible by exactly the same means. Lister had agreed to this and, having told the team, it was expected that the plan would be repeated. Then, however, Lister went cold. On 6 December, he told the team the transaction would have to wait until January 2020 as he had to go to Namibia. This was the last time the team had any contact with him.

That same day, the team received a tip that a middle-aged man had walked into Kimberley Police Station in the Northern Cape and told officers about an illegal wildlife trafficking operation that he knew of involving a Botswana national. He gave a number of details of the transaction. He had also apparently spoken about the two bone sets to which my team had fixed trackers, belonging to Michael and Martin Le Roux. The team's source confirmed what was by now obvious: this 'walk-in' was Lister. Big Bimbo was re-arrested that day. On 8 December, it was reported in the South African media that he was due to appear at Kuruman Magistrates' Court on Monday 9 December after allegedly attempting to sell a live cheetah and some lion bones, an illegal activity involving protected species. The botched deal was estimated to have been worth in the region of $25,000.[101] Lister had double-crossed everybody. The only course of action left to the team was to leave the safe house and wind up Operation Chastise. Handing over the known locations of illegal bone sets to the authorities, now that we would probably be unable to pursue the trail any further, would mean that the police would at least be able to open an investigation

---

101 Tammy Petersen, 'Botswana national in dock after allegedly trying to sell lion bones, live cheetah', News24, 8 December 2019

of their own. By now it was clear to me that we had the information we had set out to collect and that continuing with this project would bring diminishing returns. The longer the team spent in close proximity to the lion farmers, the greater the risk in view of Lister's duplicity. We now knew what we needed to know, and it was time to draw matters to a close.

Two important pieces of business therefore remained before my operatives left South Africa. First, taking advantage of a well-placed connection of the team's, a meeting was arranged with Colonel Johan Jooste of the South African Police Service, the commander in charge of the wildlife unit at Pretoria's police headquarters. Having cut off all contact with Lister, and because the batteries on the trackers in the two contraband caches were getting low, it was decided to pass all evidence over to Jooste straight away. This strategy was not without risk. The team knew it was just about conceivable that, depending on his general attitude, this senior policeman might decide to turn the tables on my team and perhaps even make an arrest. The idea of foreign nationals having run an undercover operation in his country over a period of months might unsettle or anger him.

As the man who ran Operation Chastise on a day-to-day basis, it fell to Gibby to take the lead during this meeting. He was accompanied by another member of the team. On Thursday 12 December, they went along to the meeting with Jooste as scheduled. A thorough security check was conducted before they were led into Jooste's office. They were introduced to a hard-looking man with a dark beard and a big frame called Colonel Smith. Jooste, who can be described as fair-haired and overweight, was also present. Both officers had a faintly menacing presence about them. Gibby was introduced, using his real name, and he then recounted the story of Operation Chastise, named Lister, and handed over a folder of A4 photos of the lion bone and tiger bone contraband. He also offered to give Jooste the dossier of evidence, the locations of two separate caches of illegal lion and tiger bones (and possibly rhino horn), plus the address of the bone dealer, 'Michael'.

Jooste's response was frosty from the word go. He asked under whose authority Gibby had run an investigation in his country and province. Gibby acknowledged that an investigation had taken place but for operational reasons, together with advice he had received, he had chosen to conduct it alone. He made it clear, however, that the intention had always been to hand the dossier of evidence over to the police. Jooste repeated himself, so Gibby apologised and asked if there was any way they could get past the impasse, saying it was obvious that they had a common interest in exposing wildlife crime.

Jooste then told Gibby that he and his colleague were lucky not to be spending Christmas in a Pretoria jail wearing orange overalls. Looking him up and down with something approaching disgust, he quipped, 'And orange isn't your colour.' At this point, Colonel Smith interrupted and asked Gibby if he was an American citizen. When they heard that he is in fact British, they seemed to like this even less. Gibby said that he was prepared to take all responsibility for the operation but again, calmly and patiently, he suggested that it was surely reasonable for everybody to focus on bringing these wildlife criminals to justice.

Gibby's colleague then asked if there was any possibility of continuing to work their source. Jooste said no and asked him what intelligence he had. Not having been privy to the entire operation, unlike Gibby, he stalled. At this, Jooste ended the meeting and passed the photos back to Gibby. He said he was not going to get the Christmas present he wanted; the bone caches would not be seized and, owing to a lack of proper evidence, Michael would not be receiving a visit from the police. He added that tracking people and property was illegal in itself and jeopardised any evidence the team might have secured. Wishing them a Merry Christmas at home in the UK, both of my men were dismissed. This ninety-minute meeting, which everybody had hoped would end positively, had in fact been a total waste of time. Jooste and Smith had been aggressive towards my men instead of actively engaging with the information they had tried to give them. For reasons which will never be entirely clear, they showed complete disregard for the obvious illegality they were told about. Was it simply that they had no desire to involve themselves in what might have led to a complicated and potentially exhausting case? Only they can know the answer to this question. Others must draw their own conclusions.

Clearly compromised, Gibby and his colleague had to leave South Africa straight away. En route, Gibby ordered the last remaining operative, Munro, to return to the bones meant for Michael which were being stored near O. R. Tambo Airport. His brief was to gain access to the shipping container and attach a new, fully charged tracker into the bags of lion bone. On 19 December, Munro accomplished this, adding the new tracker into one of the bags. He filmed the merchandise in it with an iPhone to satisfy everybody that it was the right bag. This was not the outcome that had been foreseen, but it did allow the team to continue to monitor the contraband remotely from Britain for at least a further three months. At the time of going to press, the cache had not moved but the tracker was still working.

As for Munro, he returned to the safe house in Johannesburg, sanitised it and then left it for the last time before returning to his native Kenya. Operation Chastise was over.

CONCLUSION

The idea that evil flourishes when good people sit by and watch but do not act is well known. When it comes to South Africa's lion industry, this sentiment is wholly appropriate. For this 'business' surely ranks as a prime example of how quickly profound wickedness can take root and wreak havoc on a thing of beauty in a civilised country.

I travel widely and it is well known that one of my ambitions is to visit everywhere in the world that is interesting. I consider myself fortunate to be able to do this. But one country has drawn me back time and time again: South Africa. I love its landscape, its wildlife, its food and wine – both of which elevate it to a top destination for many – and, in particular, its people. Everybody I have met there is pleasant and proud of their nation. This means that lion farming, and the cruelty and criminality that go with it, comes as a huge shock. How can it go on in the same country of which I am so fond?

The fact of the matter is that over a relatively short space of time, a small number of people in South Africa have been allowed to systematically abuse lions to such a degree that a separate species, the captive-bred lion, has in effect been created.

With an estimated 12,000 of these animals now being held in pens around the country, this species outnumbers the wild lion population by four to one. Having been born into hopelessly grim and abusive circumstances, these poor creatures are manipulated by tourists, later killed – often for 'pleasure' or 'sport' in canned hunts – and finally stripped for their parts, much as a thief might plunder a car. All of this is done in the name of profit. A lot of the money generated by these lions is the product of illegal activity, making these gains truly ill-gotten. In my opinion, this puts the beneficiaries of the captive-bred lion industry on a par with drug dealers.

In a world whose animal population is diminishing, and whose human population is growing, the problems associated with the lion industry, which is now a global entity, are complex. And yet, as both of my lengthy studies of this sick trade demonstrate, it really does seem that South Africa's authorities have no interest in tackling this hateful situation in earnest. As this exposé has shown, southern Africa's wild lions are now in peril. Arguably, the authorities have become the enablers of all of this, overseeing lion hunting regulations and awarding licences for the export of lion bones with what appear to be the lightest of touches and wilfully ignoring wrongdoing when they learn of it.

Consider my own experiences. In April 2019, when Operation Simba drew to a close, I wrote to Her Excellency Ms Nomatemba Tambo, South Africa's High Commissioner in London, drawing attention to this troubling issue, sending her a copy of the *Mail on Sunday* with the findings of my first, year-long investigation, and offering to furnish her office with further evidence of illegality. This was met with silence and, to the best of my knowledge, none of the individuals identified in Operation Simba has been so much as questioned about their actions, let alone arrested. Then, as described in the final chapter of this book, in December 2019, two members of my team went to the Johannesburg headquarters of the South African Police Service to meet the head of the endangered species protection unit, Colonel Johan Jooste, in order to present him with the results of the even more in-depth Operation Chastise. Far from being interested in accepting the dossier of evidence that had been gathered so carefully in an often-hostile environment, the colonel threatened to imprison my men instead.

Canned hunting and the captive-bred lion industry in South Africa have been exposed by others at intervals over the past thirty years. As the latest person to lay bare its twisted reality, I feel justified in adding my thoughts to the argument. I find it deeply distressing that those in a position of power and responsibility appear not to care about these issues at a time when they are worse than they have ever been. It is with a heavy heart that I must admit that the results of my investigations call into question South Africa's claim to be a nation with an enlightened outlook on the world. How can it be, when it allows one of its best-loved symbols to be born simply in order to suffer and then be slaughtered?

There are examples of politicians speaking out on this issue, but they are all too rare. In 2015, Derek Hanekom, South Africa's then Tourism Minister, said:

I think [canned hunting] has already damaged Brand South

Africa – how significantly, I'm not really able to tell. The practice of canned lion hunting or breeding in captivity comes with a lot of negativity and therefore it does and probably will do further reputational damage unless we take some decisive measures to discourage it.[102]

Five years later, the problem has intensified, and Mr Hanekom is therefore correct in his analysis. Further reputational damage has indeed been done to Brand South Africa. It is no exaggeration to say that its status as a responsible tourism destination is now under strain.

Colin Bell, one of Africa's most renowned conservationists and tourism experts, shares these worries, but his powerful thoughts on the issue carry a warning of even greater turmoil in conservation terms if nobody takes a grip of the situation soon. He says:

I am concerned about the fallout from canned lions and the effect that this will have on the tourism industry, as this is the only industry that will be able to sustainably fund the running of our national parks and game reserves in Africa and thus ensure their long-term survival. The presence of lions and the rest of the Big Five that attracts tourism to these parks and reserves is therefore vitally important to ensure their long-term sustainability and viability in a continent that has increasing population growths and pressures.

However, my main concern about the canned lion

102   Interview with Derek Hanekom for the 2015 documentary *Blood Lions*

industry is not that. It is that I am concerned that once the international criminal syndicates have worked out how to create demand for the body parts of lions, wild lions right around Africa will become increasingly heavily poached like rhinos and elephants. This stems from the proven principle that the prices paid in Asia will always be higher for wild produce than for farmed produce. Once we unleash demand for lions through legitimising canned lion farming in any form, criminals will seize and thoroughly exploit that opportunity, which will result in increased poaching of lions in the wild, and that will escalate to unsustainable levels. The criminal syndicates will no doubt, in time, start creating the demand in Asia for the body parts of lions way beyond the current tiger bone and tiger wine markets that exist right now. If that is allowed to prosper unchecked, wild lions throughout Africa will be targeted and poached to unsustainable levels and then the entire future of all our wild places in Africa will be under relentless and unsustainable threats. When that happens, I fear the worst.[103]

What, then, can be done to solve this problem? First, the South African government must ban captive-bred lion farming, which has no conservation value. The case for a uniform nationwide hunting law, as opposed to a series of provincial laws, should also be made. In January 2020, the South African environmental economist Ross Harvey concluded that switching the country's focus to nature tourism as opposed to trying to attract

---

103   Interview with Colin Bell, 4 August 2019

trophy hunters could create eleven times as many jobs. In view of South Africa's uncertain financial position, perhaps the time has also come for a national debate on the future of hunting in the country. It must be hoped that the 25-strong High Level Panel appointed by Environment Minister Barbara Creecy in October 2019 to examine the plight of lions and other animals leaves no stone unturned.

Yet in view of the relaxed attitude shown by South Africa's authorities to date, more immediate action outside of its legal system can and should be facilitated. Wildlife and conservation groups need to coordinate their campaigns and studies to bring an end to the captive-bred lion industry, for there is always greater strength in higher numbers. Airlines, shipping firms and freight companies across the world need to be lobbied even harder until they realise it is morally unacceptable for them to transport the trophies or bones of captive-bred lions. And the world's tourist industry needs to do more to inform and educate everybody who visits South Africa that 'voluntourism' holidays, cub petting and 'walking with lions' experiences are key parts of the cruel lion business. It should become socially unacceptable for any tourist to indulge in any of these activities. Furthermore, I call on the British government – and every other government that has not already done so – to introduce new import laws which discourage the practice of importing captive-bred trophies.

Workers' rights groups in South Africa must also take a stand. Lion farming is a cash-based industry that puts the money that hunters pay into the hands of a small number of people who rear the captive-bred lions and organise the canned hunts. This means the economic benefits to the state and to wider society are negligible. As Howard Jones, when he was the chief executive of the international wildlife charity the Born Free Foundation, told me, 'This is a brutal, careless industry that has to hide what it is doing. Why is [the South African government] tied up with a corrupt industry?'

Two further questions must be addressed. First, a debate has to be held on what to do with the estimated 12,000 captive-bred lions currently living in South Africa. Some members of the public might be appalled to hear that euthanising them might be one solution, but those who would be against such a programme have to remember that these animals were only born to die anyway. They have been bred solely to live short, sad lives and then killed. Furthermore, due to inbreeding, many of these lions are ill and lead miserable lives. They cannot be re-wilded. It seems unlikely that it will ever be practical to put every captive-bred lion in a sanctuary, because, as likely as not, new cruelty issues would become apparent. These problems would just manifest themselves in a different area. Added to this, the donor base willing to underwrite such an enterprise is limited. As I know personally, the cost of keeping a lion in the best possible conditions for the rest of its life is considerable, and I have only done this for one. Having had a hand in creating this monster, the South African state must deal with the consequences – however unpalatable – responsibly.

The second question that has to be confronted relates to public health. In December 2019, reports emerged of the potentially fatal coronavirus disease, Covid-19. By January 2020, the World Health Organization had designated it a 'public health emergency of international concern'; by mid-April, there were 2 million reported cases worldwide, with more than 120,000 dead. It is commonly accepted that this disease originated from a seafood market in the Chinese city of Wuhan where wild animals such as bats, birds, snakes and rabbits are traded illegally. As coronaviruses are known to jump from animals to humans, it is thought possible that the first people infected with the disease – a group primarily made up of stallholders from the seafood market – contracted it through their contact with animals. In this book, Dr Peter Caldwell, the South Africa-based wildlife veterinary surgeon, states his belief that a major health incident will occur in Asia as a result of its people's rampant consumption of South African lion bones. He cites a range of infectious diseases that could be released, including brucellosis and tuberculosis. The same risk applies, presumably, to those South Africans who handle these animals before they are killed. It is also worth emphasising that the tranquillisers and poisons used to slaughter lions may well be harmful to human health too. The unregulated way these chemical products are used mean that anybody who consumes lion bones takes a further risk. Foetuses may, for example, be born with congenital abnormalities. South Africa's authorities have shown that they are prepared to turn a blind eye to a trade that is designed to profit from the abuse and suffering of an endangered creature and which then profits again from these animals when they are dead. Having seen the chaos caused by coronavirus, however, is Dr Caldwell's health warning one that South Africa can afford to ignore?

On 24 February 2020, the Standing Committee of the National People's Congress – China's top legislature – decided to ban the illegal trading of wildlife with a view to 'eliminating the consumption of wild animals to safeguard people's lives and health'. This welcome move, designed to 'safeguard biological and ecological security and effectively prevent major public health risks, among other purposes', might just have an impact on South Africa's lion bone trade. Only time will tell. Of course, other parts of south-east Asia, notably Vietnam, may not take such a stringent approach, thereby allowing the trade to carry on as before, aided by South Africa's bone export quota system.

Shortly before this book was published, I spent a few days at a game reserve in South Africa quietly watching several of the big cats living there, each perfectly developed over millennia for their way of life, and soon to be extinct unless action is taken. I know that two major reasons for their decline are loss of habitat and poaching. Separate to this, however, is the lion industry. I do not understand how mankind can be deliberately abusive to any animal. People may be brutal through ignorance, or by taking shortcuts to save money, but what I have exposed in this book is conscious, intentional cruelty, sometimes carried out with or for pleasure. I cannot think about this without feeling a burning sense of shame. The question is: for how much longer will South Africa allow its captive-bred lion industry to prosper?

QR CODE FOR
WILDLIFE WEBSITE

Distressing photographic and video evidence of the cruelty inflicted on farmed lions was collected for this book by an undercover team. To view it, please scan the QR code below with the camera or QR code reader on your device or visit the website www.LordAshcroftWildlife.com/restricted.

This QR code is also located on the inside front cover of this book.

INDEX